Dangerous Language — Esperanto and the Decline of Stalinism

"This book gives a carefully supported account of a crucial aspect of the Esperanto movement's history, focusing on political repression by totalitarian regimes, especially those of Hitler and Stalin. It also sheds light on opposition elsewhere and is eye-opening for anyone interested in language policy and global communication."

—Ulrich Ammon, *Emeritus Professor of Germanic Linguistics at Duisburg-Essen University, Germany*

Ulrich Lins

Dangerous Language — Esperanto and the Decline of Stalinism

Ulrich Lins
Bonn, Germany

Translated by Humphrey Tonkin

ISBN 978-1-349-95801-6   ISBN 978-1-352-00020-7 (eBook)
DOI 10.1057/978-1-352-00020-7

© The Editor(s) (if applicable) and The Author(s) 2017
Softcover reprint of the hardcover 1st edition 2017
The author(s) has/have asserted their right(s) to be identified as the author(s) of this work in accordance with the Copyright, Designs and Patents Act 1988.
This work is subject to copyright. All rights are solely and exclusively licensed by the Publisher, whether the whole or part of the material is concerned, specifically the rights of translation, reprinting, reuse of illustrations, recitation, broadcasting, reproduction on microfilms or in any other physical way, and transmission or information storage and retrieval, electronic adaptation, computer software, or by similar or dissimilar methodology now known or hereafter developed.
The use of general descriptive names, registered names, trademarks, service marks, etc. in this publication does not imply, even in the absence of a specific statement, that such names are exempt from the relevant protective laws and regulations and therefore free for general use.
The publisher, the authors and the editors are safe to assume that the advice and information in this book are believed to be true and accurate at the date of publication. Neither the publisher nor the authors or the editors give a warranty, express or implied, with respect to the material contained herein or for any errors or omissions that may have been made.

Cover image © imageBROKER / Alamy Stock Photo
Cover design by Samantha Johnson

Printed on acid-free paper

This Palgrave Macmillan imprint is published by Springer Nature
The registered company is Macmillan Publishers Ltd.
The registered company address is: The Campus, 4 Crinan Street, London, N1 9XW, United Kingdom

Editorial Note

Transliteration from Russian and Ukrainian is based on the Library of Congress system. To make it easier on the reader, in Russian family names the ending 'ii' has been changed to 'y', and soft signs and diacritics have been omitted. In the footnotes and bibliography, however, I have followed standard Library of Congress transliteration. In references, in general, a translation is added only if the original is not in Roman script; names appear in the form used in the publication in question.

For individuals from East Asian countries the family name appears first, and the given name follows.

In the notes the full title of a book is indicated only in the first reference in the chapter in question; in subsequent notes it appears in abbreviated form. For frequently cited works (among them *EdE*, *EeP*, *PVZ*), see the list of abbreviations and, of course, the bibliography. Only in exceptional cases are electronic sources indicated (links were last checked on 28 September 2016) In the case of journal articles, the title of the periodical is normally followed by the volume number and year of publication. Where pagination extends over the entire volume, I have not indicated the specific issue in which the article appears.

U.L.

Preface

The present volume is a continuation of the history of the suppression and persecution of the Esperanto movement in the twentieth century whose account I began in my earlier volume *Dangerous Language—Esperanto Under Hitler and Stalin*. The two volumes form a complete whole. As I explained there, the earliest draft of this history was published in 1973 by the publisher l'omnibuso, in Kyoto, Japan. This version, little more than a pamphlet, had only a small print run, but in 1974 its contents appeared as a section in Lapenna's *Esperanto en perspektivo*. In 1975 the publisher Iwanami, in Tokyo, produced an expanded version, translated into Japanese by Kurisu Kei.

In 1988 a new, completely rewritten text appeared—the result of several years of research in a vast array of source material.[1] It was my desire to make an original contribution to research on the hundred-year history of Esperanto, devoting particular attention to a specific aspect of that history—an aspect long neglected, indeed regarded as something of a taboo, even among Esperantists. The topic was the opposition and persecution that Esperanto encountered for political and ideological reasons. I wanted to describe the fate of the adepts of a language that, over the

---

[1] It was published, in agreement with the Universal Esperanto Association, by the German publisher Bleicher, and reprinted in 1990 in Moscow by Progress Publishers. In 1988 a German-language version also appeared, and this was followed by translations into Italian (1990), Russian (1999), Lithuanian (2005) and Korean (2013).

decades, police, censors, nationalist ideologues and assorted dictators had denounced as 'dangerous'. Accordingly, I did not address the 'internal' history of the Esperanto movement—a story that has been told many times before—so much as the hostile reactions that Esperanto and its speakers had endured from political regimes and ideologies, particularly Nazism and Stalinism.

New information, particularly archival material, has come to light since the 1988 edition and the fall of the Berlin Wall in the following year. So the present version of the study is different again. For the English-language version, I expanded the story into two volumes, the first dealing with the persecution of Esperanto speakers and the suppression of the language in Hitler's Germany and Stalin's Russia and the second describing the underlying causes of the demise of the language in the Soviet Union and its revival, first in Eastern Europe and then in Russia itself, after the death of Stalin and the gradual decline of the ideas we associate with Stalinism. It is this second half of the account that is discussed in the present volume.

Thus, the revised Esperanto edition[2] on which this English translation is based takes into account a number of newly discovered documents, among them materials from the Soviet NKVD to which Russian researchers had access as of 1990 for a (limited) time. I have also tried to take into consideration relevant studies that have appeared in various countries and languages over the past 25 years. My research has benefited greatly from material preserved in the German Federal Archive in Berlin, including the papers newly acquired following German reunification. For several years my work has been assisted by consulting the Hector Hodler Library in Rotterdam, the Planned Language Collection and Esperanto Museum of the Austrian National Library in Vienna and the library of the Japanese Esperanto Institute in Tokyo. Also extremely helpful has been my easy access to the University Library and the Friedrich Ebert Foundation Library, both in Bonn. I remember with particular thanks the fact that Teo Jung, before his passing in 1986, presented me with collections of Esperanto periodicals from the 1920s and 1930s and that Kurisu Kei put at my disposal particularly valuable material on the Soviet

---

[2] *La danĝera lingvo*, Rotterdam: Universala Esperanto-Asocio, 2016.

and Japanese Esperanto movements. I am grateful to SAT and Eduard Borsboom who allowed me to consult unpublished letters to and from Eugène Lanti. In addition to those mentioned, I owe thanks to many people, among them former Soviet citizens, who provided me with information and clarifications that helped in the preparation of the present text. The names of many of these individuals are mentioned in the footnotes. Finally, I am grateful to all those who helped in the technical preparation of the two volumes.

As I pointed out in the first volume, I cannot begin to measure the constant support provided by my wife Akie and from which the present study has greatly benefited. And I am grateful to Professor Humphrey Tonkin, who has long taken an interest in publishing an English version of the book and who has devoted himself to the task of translating it with unmatchable care and enthusiasm. My thanks go also to Ulrich Becker, who has hunted down references to English-language translations of works cited.

April 2016   Ulrich Lins

Contents

Part I The Death of Esperanto in the Soviet Union   1

1 The Events of 1937–38   3

2 Esperantists in the Great Purge   17

3 The Emergence of Soviet Patriotism   29

4 International Correspondence   37

5 Silence Descends   53

Part II Esperanto Reborn   69

6 After the Second World War: The Great Silence
   in Eastern Europe   71

7 Stalin Against Marr   85

8	The Needs of the Present	97
9	Revival of the Movement	107
10	Eastern Europe: Progress and Problems	123
11	The Soviet Union: Between Hope and Doubt	135

Part III	Conclusion	163
12	Dangerous Language or Language of Hope?	165
Bibliography		177
Chronology		183
Author Index		189
Subject Index		195

Abbreviations

ASE	Asocio de Sovetiaj Esperantistoj (Association of Soviet Esperantists)
BEA	Bulgara Esperantista Asocio (Bulgarian Esperantist Association)
BIL	P.E. Stojan, *Bibliografio de internacia lingvo* (Geneva: UEA, 1929; reprint Hildesheim & New York: Georg Olms, 1973)
BLEA	Brita Laborista Esperanto-Asocio (British Workers' Esperanto Association)
CK	Centra Komitato (Central Committee)
CPSU	Communist Party of the Soviet Union
EAĈSR	Esperanto-Asocio en Ĉeĥoslovaka Respubliko (Esperanto Association in the Czechoslovakian Republic)
EdE	L. Kökény & V. Bleier (ed.), *Enciklopedio de Esperanto* (Budapest: Literatura Mondo, 1933–1934, reprints 1979 and 1986)
EeP	Ivo Lapenna and others, *Esperanto en perspektivo. Faktoj kaj analizoj pri la Internacia Lingvo* (London & Rotterdam: UEA, 1974)
EKRELO	Eldon-Kooperativo por Revolucia Esperanto-Literaturo (Publishing Cooperative for Revolutionary Esperanto Literature)
GDR	German Democratic Republic
GEA	Germana Esperanto-Asocio (German Esperanto Association)
GLEA	Laborista Esperanto-Asocio por la Germanlingvaj Regionoj; Germana Laborista Esperanto-Asocio (German Workers' Esperanto Association)
GPU	Gosudarstvennoe politicheskoe upravlenie (State Political Directorate, i.e. the Soviet secret police 1922–23)

IAREV	Internacia Asocio de Revoluciaj Esperanto-Verkistoj (International Association of Revolutionary Esperanto Writers)
ICK	Internacia Centra Komitato de la Esperanto-Movado (International Central Committee of the Esperanto Movement)
IEL	Internacia Esperanto-Ligo (International Esperanto League)
IPE	Internacio de Proleta Esperantistaro (Proletarian Esperantist International)
ISA	International Federation of the National Standardizing Associations
ISE	Internacio de Socialistaj Esperantistoj (Socialist Esperantist International)
IWA	International Workingmen's Association
JEI	Japana Esperanto-Instituto (Japanese Esperanto Institute)
JEL	Jugoslavia Esperanto-Ligo (Yugoslav Esperanto League)
KP	Komunista Partio (Communist Party)
LEA	Laborista Esperanto-Asocio (Workers' Esperanto Association)
LKK	Loka Kongresa Komitato (Local Congress Committee)
LPLP	*Language Problems and Language Planning* (periodical)
MEH	L.L. Zamenhof, *Mi estas homo*, ed. Aleksander Korĵenkov (Kaliningrad: Sezonoj, 2006)
MEM	Mondpaca Esperantista Movado (World Peace Esperantist Movement)
n.	note
NDEB	Neue Deutsche Esperanto-Bewegung (New German Esperanto Movement)
NKVD	Narodnyi komissariat vnutrennykh del (People's Commissariat for Internal Affairs)
n.s.	new series
NSDAP	Nationalsozialistische Deutsche Arbeiterpartei (National Socialist German Workers' Party)
OGPU	Ob'edinënnoe gosudarstvennoe politicheskoe upravlenie (Joint State Political Directorate, i.e. Soviet secret police 1923–1934)
Orig	*Iom reviziita plena verkaro de L.L. Zamenhof. Originalaro*, ed. Ludovikito (= Itō Kanzi), 3 volumes (Kyoto: Ludovikito, 1989–1991)
PEK	Proleta Esperanto-Korespondanto (Proletarian Esperanto Correspondent)
PIDE	Policia Internacional e de Defensa do Estado (International Police and State Defense, i.e. Portuguese secret police)
PIV	*Plena Ilustrita Vortaro de Esperanto* (Paris: SAT, 1970)

PVZ	Ludovikito (= Itō Kanzi, ed.), *Plena verkaro de L.L. Zamenhof*, 58 volumes (Kyoto: Ludovikito, 1973–2004)
REGo	*Rusia Esperanto-Gazeto* (Russian Esperanto Journal)
RSDLP	Russian Social-Democratic Labor Party
RSHA	Reichssicherheitshauptamt (Reich Security Main Office)
SA	Sturmabteilung (the paramilitary wing of the NSDAP)
SAT	Sennacieca Asocio Tutmonda (Worldwide Non-national Association)
SD	Sicherheitsdienst, the Security (Intelligence) Service of the SS
SEJM	Sovetia Esperantista Junulara Movado (Soviet Esperantist Youth Movement)
SEU	Sovetlanda Esperantista Unio (Soviet Esperantist Union), as of 1927 Sovetrespublikara Esperantista Unio (Esperantist Union of the Soviet Republics), the main organization of Soviet Esperantists; in Russian: Soiuz Ėsperantistov Sovetskikh Stran (Soiuz Ėsperantistov Sovetskikh Respublik)
SS	Schutzstaffel, the central organization of the police and security service in Nazi Germany
SSOD	Soiuz sovetskikh obshchestv druzhby i kul'turnoi sviazi s zarubezhnymi stranami (Union of Soviet Societies for Friendship and Cultural Relations with Foreign Countries)
SSR	Socialist Soviet Republic
UEA	Universala Esperanto-Asocio (Universal Esperanto Association)
UK	Universala Kongreso de Esperanto (World Congress of Esperanto)
USSR	Union of Socialist Soviet Republics
VOKS	Vsesoiuznoe obshchestvo kultur'noi sviazi s zagranitsei (All-Union Society for Cultural Relations with Foreign Countries)

List of Figures

Fig. 1.1	The writer Georgii Deshkin spent 18 years in Siberia	6
Fig. 1.2	Grigorii Demidiuk, one of the principal leaders of SEU, survived 18 years of captivity	10
Fig. 1.3	Dmitrii Snezhko was the first well-known Esperantist swept up by the machinery of detentions	12
Fig. 1.4	The actor Nikolai Rytkov—here in the role of Lenin—suffered 17 years in concentration camps because of Esperanto. Having fled to the west in 1965, he worked in the BBC's Russian Service	14
Fig. 2.1	The Estonian teacher and lexicographer Henrik Seppik was one of the Esperantists in the Baltic countries forced into exile for many years	21
Fig. 2.2	Among the Esperantists deported in June 1941 was the Latvian poet Ludmila Jevsejeva	22
Fig. 2.3	The Lithuanian anthropologist Antanas Poška sheltered a Jewish friend from the Nazis during the war; he was arrested after the return of the Soviet army	22
Fig. 3.1	Kurisu Kei, of Japan, at the time a convinced communist, continued lively correspondence with Soviet Esperantists until 1937–38. Only after the war did he gradually find out why they all suddenly went silent	46
Fig. 5.1	E.K. Drezen was the leader of the Soviet Esperantist Union (SEU) for most of its history	64

Fig. 5.2	Among Soviet Esperanto activists liquidated by the régime was N.V. Nekrasov	65
Fig. 5.3	V.M. Kolchinsky, also liquidated by the régime	65
Fig. 5.4	Soviet Esperanto activists R.B. Nikolsky, a victim of the régime	66
Fig. 5.5	V.V. Varankin, author of the Esperanto novel *Metropoliteno* and Esperanto activist, liquidated by the régime author of the Esperanto novel	66
Fig. 5.6	Poet E.I. Mikhalsky, liquidated by the régime	67
Fig. 5.7	I.E. Izgur was persecuted by the Tsarist régime as a communist and liquidated by the Stalinists as an Esperanto activist	67
Fig. 5.8	Maksim Kriukov, Esperanto activist liquidated by the régime	68
Fig. 5.9	Shamil Kh. Usmanov, Tatar writer and activist in the SEU, liquidated by the régime	68
Fig. 10.1	The Chinese poet Armand Su endured years of suffering during the cultural revolution because of his foreign contacts	132
Fig. 11.1	During the world youth festival in Moscow in 1957, Soviet Esperantists were able to meet with foreigners for the first time. Standing, L to R: 2 Liudmila Bokareva, 4 Nikolai Rytkov, 5 Nguyen Van Kinh (Vietnamese Ambassador)	136
Fig. 11.2	Leaders of the semi-legal 'Soviet Esperantist Youth Movement' in 1971: V. Šilas, M. Bronshtein, A. Vizgirdas, A. Goncharov, B. Kolker, V. Arolovich, A. Mediņš	139
Fig. 11.3	At the founding conference of the Association of Soviet Esperantists (March 1979): Aleksandr Korolevich, Vladimir Samodai, Boris Kolker, Magomet Isaev, Dmitrii Perevalov	155
Fig. 11.4	The sculptor Nikolai Blazhkov made this bust of Zamenhof at the end of the 1950s. Because the Soviet authorities did not support him and refused permission to send it to the 44th World Congress of Esperanto (Warsaw, 1959), it remained in the courtyard of his home in the center of Odessa. Only after the fall of the Soviet Union did it become a tourist destination	161

Picture Credits

Hector Hodler Library (UEA), Rotterdam: Fig. 1.1, Fig. 1.3, Fig. 1.4, Fig. 2.1, Fig. 2.3, Fig. 3.1, Fig. 5.1, 5.2, 5.4, 5.5, 5.7, Fig. 10.1, Fig. 11.3, Fig. 11.4
Sennacieca Asocio Tutmonda, Paris: Fig. 2.2, Fig. 5.6, Fig. 5.8
Mikhail Bronshtein, Tikhvin (Russian Federation): Fig. 11.1, Fig. 11.2
Anatolii Sidorov, Saint Petersburg (Russian Federation): Fig. 1.2, Fig. 5.3, Fig. 5.9

Part I

The Death of Esperanto in the Soviet Union

1

The Events of 1937–38

Widely adopted in the early days of the Soviet Union, the international language Esperanto seemed to many of the revolutionaries and their followers to herald a new linguistic era going beyond the narrow divisions of nationalism. The language was embraced by these enthusiasts as the embodiment of international socialism. But, even as the language took hold, tensions emerged—with the workers of the capitalist west, with the guardians of socialist ideology, and, above all, with the growing emphasis on Soviet nationalism as Josef Stalin consolidated his power following the death of Lenin. The 1930s, with their stress on ideological conformism, put many Esperantists, and ultimately the language itself, on the wrong side of the nationalist/internationalist divide, leading ultimately to the purging and annihilation of the Esperanto movement in the late 1930s.

What, then, happened to the Soviet Esperanto movement in the years 1937–38? In our earlier volume we described the demise of the Soviet Esperantist Union (SEU) from the perspective of the members of the so-called Worldwide Non-national Association (SAT) and of the Proletarian Esperantist International (IPE) outside the Soviet Union. The Esperanto journals of the day, particularly *Sur Posteno*, presented a picture of slow, unrelenting decline as fewer and fewer Esperanto publications appeared in the Soviet Union, regular contacts were broken, and finally letters stopped coming from individual Esperantists. For a 20-year period thereafter, no information about Esperanto life in the Soviet Union emerged.

From the country itself, up until 1987–88 there was not even official confirmation that Esperanto was suppressed. Only here and there do we encounter statements to the effect that the movement 'has long been stagnant'. The former secretary of the SEU Committee for the Urals reported that from 1938 until 1957 he read and wrote nothing in Esperanto.[1] About the poet Evgenii Mikhalsky it was noted that he 'died tragically' in 1937.[2]

Early on, rumors circulated of the arrest of Soviet Esperantists. In October 1936 the founder and long-time leader of SAT, Eugène Lanti (see Chap. 5 in our earlier volume), mentioned the case of the veteran Bolshevik and radical non-nationalist Maksim Kriukov, who was imprisoned and shot because he 'dared to express his opinion'.[3] In April 1941 the International Esperanto League announced that the Soviet government had in 1937 'dissolved all independent educational associations, including Esperanto organizations',[4] but in the midst of war this information attracted little attention. Ivo Lapenna, board member of the Universal Esperanto Association (UEA), the principal apolitical Esperanto organization, as late as 1947 publicly denied assertions that in the Soviet Union the Esperanto movement had been harassed.[5] On the other hand, a Bulgarian informed Japanese comrades in 1948 that 'SEU was liquidated. Causes: anarchism, Trotskyism and other harmful isms and sects among Soviet Esperantists'.[6]

---

[1] Jakov Vlasov, 'Ĉe la luna lumo', *Bulgario* 1 (1964) 7: p. vii.
[2] N. Ŝtejnberg, 'Eugen Miĥalski', *Nuntempa Bulgario*, 1968, 6: 45. He was shot on 14 October 1937. See esp. V.A. Kornilov & J.M. Lukaŝeviĉ, 'Eŭgeno Mihalskij. Novaj informoj', *Sennacieca Revuo*, 1993, 121: 24–7; Krys Ungar, 'La vivo kaj pereo de Eŭgeno Mihalski', in Eŭgeno Mihalski, *Plena poemaro 1917–1937*, ed. William Auld, Antwerp: Flandra Esperanto-Ligo, 1994, pp. 9–27; Lucien Bourguignon, 'Pri vivo kaj morto de E. Mihalski', *Sennaciulo* 72 (2001), Jan.: 14–15. On another poet, Vladimir Sutkovoi, see Aleksandro Logvin, *Sur la vivovojo: Poemoj*, La Laguna: J. Régulo, 1964, p. 56. Sutkovoi was shot, along with at least four other Esperantists, in Odessa on 24 November 1937.
[3] Lanti (1940), p. 129.
[4] 'Bulteno de I.E.L.', *Esperanto Internacia* 5 (1941): 37.
[5] During a congress meeting in Berne: *Esperanto* 40 (1947): 133.
[6] Letter from Asen Grigorov to Kurisu Kei, 26 November 1948 (in Kurisu's archive).

Only in the post-Stalinist 'thaw' did more details surface. In 1956 the Swedish Esperantist Erik Ekström, on a visit to the Soviet Union, discovered that 'legally' SEU 'was never disbanded', but at the same time, he brought news of the fate of Ernest Drezen, who for many years had led the Soviet Esperantist Union: 'He was arrested by Beriia's bandits'[7]—as they were described—and died in prison.'[8] East European Esperantists could well understand what was meant when the journal *Pola Esperantisto* informed them that in 1938 the Esperanto poet Georgii Deshkin 'was unwillingly torn away from the Esperanto movement for eighteen years and lived in Siberia'.[9] Little by little, disturbing news of the fate of the Soviet Esperanto movement leaked out. In 1965 the first witness to these persecutions succeeded in fleeing to the West: the Russian actor Nikolai Rytkov, well known for his portrayal of the role of Lenin. An interview with him,[10] along with conversations between Soviet Esperantists and Western visitors, helped, at least in part, to reconstruct the sequence of events in the years 1937–38 (Fig. 1.1).

We should note that groundwork for these arrests did not include direct attacks against Esperanto in the Soviet mass media (which, however, were full of information about enemies of the people, foreign spies and public trials), so it is hard to know whether the mere knowledge and use of Esperanto was dangerous.[11] Indeed it was precisely in the mid-1930s that Soviet Esperantists, like many other ordinary people, experienced something of a reduction in pressure to observe 'class consciousness' compared with the time of the First Five-Year Plan. In this breathing space, the Esperantists looked forward with a certain optimism to a more tranquil

---

[7] Lavrentii Beriia was head of the secret police for 15 years. In 1953, after Stalin's death, he was dismissed and shot.
[8] Erik Ekström, 'Kiel esperantisto-turisto en Sovet-Unio', *La Espero* 44 (1956): 115.
[9] 'Georgo Deŝkin', *Pola Esperantisto* 38 (1958), 1 (Jan./Feb.): 5. See also B.V. Tokarev, 'Georgo Deŝkin', *Impeto '91*, Moscow: Progreso, 1991, 151–8.
[10] The interview was conducted at the author's request by Eleanor Higginbottom in London in September/October 1968. The taped recording was later transcribed in Abol'skaia (1999), pp. 6–33.
[11] The public prosecutor Nikolai Shinkarenko told Lev Vulfovich in February 1989 that in the documented charges Esperanto was never mentioned as a cause of the arrest ('had it been, not one of the Esperantists would have remained alive'): personal communication from Vulfovich, 29 July 1997.

Fig. 1.1 The writer Georgii Deshkin spent 18 years in Siberia

period in which, independently of ideological considerations, Esperanto's practical utility might be recognized. It was no accident that SEU's chief theoretical contribution in this period was publication of a methodology of Esperanto teaching—a work that put particular emphasis on Esperanto's so-called propaedeutic value as an introduction to language study that facilitated the acquisition of foreign languages.[12]

Drezen, probably with a feeling of relief, completely abandoned excursions into the field of Marxist theory and, as of 1932, concentrated on research on the international standardization of technical terms. He helped popularize in his country the pioneering work on that topic, published in 1931 by the Austrian terminologist Eugen Wüster, who— an Esperantist from his youth—argued in favor of the broad use of Esperanto for international language standardization.[13] Drezen himself

---

[12] G.M. Filippov, *Metodika prepodavaniia èsperanto* (Methods of Teaching Esperanto), Moscow: SÈSR, 1935. Cf. Moret (2007), 55–7.

[13] Eugen Wüster, *Internationale Sprachnormung in der Technik, besonders in der Elektrotechnik. Die nationale Sprachnormung und ihre Verallgemeinerung*, Berlin: VDI-Verlag, 1931 (3rd edn., Bonn: Bouvier, 1970); E. Drezen, 'Normigo de la teknika lingvo dum kapitalismo kaj socialismo', *La Nova Etapo* 1 (1932): 161–8 (review of Wüster's book).

produced a programmatic monograph on the standardization of scientific and technical terms.[14] As head of the terminological commission of the All-Soviet Committee for Standardization, he developed a project for establishing an international terminological code derived from the basic principles behind Esperanto. This report[15] was presented by the Standardization Committee in September 1934 to the conference of the International Federation of the National Standardization Associations (ISA) in Stockholm, which accepted it unanimously and commissioned the Soviet Committee to continue its researches. In the following year a Russian translation of Wüster's work was published.[16]

This common interest in giving Esperanto a place in discussions of international linguistic standardization strengthened the relations between Drezen and the neutral movement as of 1934.[17] On 15 March 1936, Drezen wrote to the president of the Universal Esperanto Association Louis Bastien: 'In our country probably sometime soon the work of SEU will be re-energized on probably a somewhat new basis. Among other things our affiliation with UEA will likely be possible.' At the end of May 1936, Drezen sent a postcard to Bastien promising that cooperation between SEU and UEA will be possible 'as soon as a solution is found to a few basic problems relating to Esperanto activity in SEU'.[18] Meanwhile, Drezen stayed in active contact with Wüster. On 28 January 1937 Wüster asked Drezen whether the Soviet Union would be represented in an ISA meeting planned for June in Paris[19] and congratulated him 'that you have

---

[14] Ė.K. Drezen, *Standartizatsiia nauchno-tekhnicheskikh poniatii, oboznachenii i terminov* (Standardization of scientific and technical concepts, symbols and terms), 2nd edn., Moscow & Leningrad: Standartizatsiia i ratsionalizatsiia, 1934.

[15] Esperanto translation of the report: E. Drezen, *Pri problemo de internaciigo de science-teknika terminaro. Historio, nuna stato kaj perspektivoj*, Moscow & Amsterdam: Standartgiz & Ekrelo, 1935 (reprinted Saarbrücken: Iltis, 1983); cf. Smith (1998), pp. 154–6.

[16] Eugen Wüster, *Mezhdunarodnaia standartizatsiia iazyka v tekhnike*, Moscow: Standartgiz, 1935. Wüster deals briefly with his relations with Drezen in the article 'Benennungs- und Wörterbuch-Grundsätze. Ihre Anfänge in Deutschland', *Muttersprache* 83 (1973): 434–40, esp. pp. 436, 439.

[17] Marcel Delcourt & Jean Amouroux, 'Wüster kaj Drezen', *Esperanto* 71 (1978): 197–8.

[18] Jean Amouroux kindly made available to the author, from a collection of General Bastien's correspondence, copies of the correspondence between Drezen and Bastien. A typed copy of Drezen's postcard of 8 May 1936 is in the UEA archive.

[19] No Soviet delegate attended. Drezen's proposal for an international terminological code was finally rejected at a conference in Berlin in 1938.

been chosen as editor-in-chief of the multilingual technical dictionaries'. The last letter from Drezen to Wüster bears the date 9 March[20]; two later letters that Wüster sent to his Soviet colleague brought no reply.

We now know that Drezen was arrested on 17 April 1937. It is not certain whether his imprisonment was primarily motivated by his leading position in the Esperanto movement. As a non-Russian, a former Tsarist officer and early activist in the Red Army, a university professor, a board member of the All-Union Society for Cultural Relations with Foreign Countries (VOKS), a joint founder of Iazykfront and, not least, a frequent traveler abroad, he provided an abundance of reasons to be suspected as a 'spy'. Non-Soviet Esperantists never regarded Drezen as a convincing representative of the Soviet Union—a view apparently confirmed by his mode of presentation at the World Congress in Danzig (1927). Participants in the Congress observed that the SEU leader, ensconced in a first-class railway compartment, wore yellow gloves.[21] Following the Congress, Drezen revealed to a former fellow student 'that he cannot get used to that Russia, and their culture shocks him'.[22] But in 1937 other factors were more important, namely, his extreme loyalty to Stalin's regime and his active participation in ideological campaigns. He engaged in unbridled denunciations of SAT as an anti-Soviet organization and accused the followers of the competing international language systems Ido and Occidental of 'counterrevolution'.[23] There was a certain suicidal quality to the denunciation since the same accusation was eventually turned on him. He was among the chief victims when, as we shall attempt to show, the authorities, probably before his arrest, came to a decision about SEU. The decision amounted to a gag order on the Esperanto movement in the Soviet Union.

---

[20] Wüster kindly gave the author details of his correspondence with Drezen. On his relations with Drezen, see Wera Blanke, 'Terminological standardization—its roots and fruits in planned languages', in W. Blanke, *Esperanto—Terminologie und Terminologiearbeit*, New York: Mondial, 2008, pp. 27–47.

[21] Borsboom (1976), p. 39.

[22] Letter from Roman Sakowicz to Hans Jakob, 2 July 1957. Sakowicz also wrote that Drezen 'was just a careerist who pretended to be a Bolshevik'.

[23] Kuznecov (1991), p. 25; Nikolaj Stepanov, 'Homo de kontrastoj en kruela epoko', *Esperanto* 85 (1992): 184–5.

The sentence was carried out when the Great Purge of 1937–38 began. Following the arrests of Bukharin and Rykov in late February 1937, the Central Committee, meeting from 23 February to 5 March, cleared the way for the launch of Stalin's offensive against all real and imagined opponents. In June the terrorized people learned that Marshal Mikhail Tukhachevsky and other leaders of the Red Army had been shot.

No decision putting SEU on the list of enemies to be exterminated was ever published; it remained uncertain whether Esperanto might still be tolerated as a mere hobby. This uncertainty was entirely in conformity with the tactics of the secret police. The purges were effective precisely because they mostly occurred with no accompanying noise: the individuals were not warned, nor could know beforehand, whether the fate that struck a neighbor, often as a result of denunciation (e.g. for the receipt of letters from abroad), would strike them too. In this way, SEU died slowly—with the gradual disappearance of its functionaries. Drezen's fate was shared by other members of SEU's Central Committee. On the same day as Drezen's arrest, Nikolai Intsertov, SEU's executive secretary,[24] who was particularly active in the spread of Esperanto in the anti-religion movement, was also arrested; on the 10 and 11 February 1938, it was the turn of Demidiuk and Nekrasov, former friends of Lanti, who, during and after the schism, loyally defended Drezen against the attacks of SAT. Added to them was Roman Nikolsky, editor of *Mezhdunarodnyi iazyk* and one of the most revolutionist activists in SEU, who once described the Red Army's role as unifier of the international working class by declaring that 'its targets are the filthy bellies of burgers'.[25] Also imprisoned was the head of the SEU mailroom, Pyotr Gavrilov, along with his technical assistants, and even the designer Evgenii Gurov, who in 1932 designed a sticker with the text 'Support the publication of Lenin's works in Esperanto'. Nor did foreign Esperantists, immigrants to the Soviet Union, escape arrest, for example, the Hungarians József Batta,[26]

---

[24] Cf. Nikolaj Zubkov, 'Nikolaj Incertov—respondeca sekretario de SEU', *Scienco kaj Kulturo*, 1997, 5 (13): 2–4.
[25] R. Nikolskij, 'Esperanta movado en la ruĝa armeo', *Sennaciulo* 2 (1925/26), 29 (81): 6. He was executed on 4 October 1938.
[26] He was arrested in December 1937. His wife later learned from Demidiuk that he was condemned to death. She herself spent eight years in a concentration camp, until 1946: letter from

who until the Nazi seizure of power was the editor of the IPE journal *Internaciisto* in Berlin, and Ferenc Robicsek, son of the Deputy People's Commissar for Postal Services in the Hungarian Republic of Councils of 1919.[27] A German Esperantist, Friedrich Köhncke, who had moved to the Soviet Union in 1931 because of unemployment, was arrested in 1937 as a spy and, after seven months of prison torture, extradited to … the Gestapo (Fig. 1.2).[28]

Fig. 1.2 Grigorii Demidiuk, one of the principal leaders of SEU, survived 18 years of captivity

---

Margit Batta, Budapest, 1 August 1982, in *Internaciisto*, n.s., 8 (1982), 9/10: 2.
[27] Batta and Robicsek were both killed in October 1938.
[28] Letters to Kurisu Kei, 29 September 1955 and 28 October 1955, published in *Nia Korespondo*, journal of Esperanto-Koresponda Studrondo (Tokyo), 1955, 4 (Oct.): 5–8, 12; 1956, 6 (Feb.): 9–12; letter from Köhncke to Semyon Podkaminer, 20 January 1963 (Kurisu's archive). In 1932 Köhncke warned foreign comrades desirous of working in the Soviet Union that they should have understanding for the 'difficult conditions' and not come expecting 'an already fully realized socialist paradise': *Bulteno de CK SEU* 11 (1932): 40–1. In a letter of 21 June 1973 Köhncke wrote to the author: 'When I learned Esperanto (1925), it was part of my communist worldview; in the meantime I have lost my political idealism so I can't even give a reason to be an Esperantist.' He died in Hamburg on 2 May 1974.

For a long time, details of the fate of many Esperantists who suffered imprisonment remained unknown. Rytkov revealed that Drezen was shot in 1937; we now know that the execution occurred on 27 October 1937[29] (again, on the same day as Intsertov). Drezen's wife, Elena Sazonova, also very active in SEU, was arrested on 27 May 1937, a few weeks after her husband. Under interrogation, she acted 'with great dignity', not only refusing to admit guilt but also strongly defending her husband; she confessed to the interrogators that she had confided to her husband the secret of her collaboration with the NKVD, forced upon her in 1932.[30] The journalist Nikolai Nekrasov, who did so much to enrich the literature of Esperanto, was executed on 4 October 1938.[31] A year earlier, on 3 September 1937, the same fate had befallen Viktor Kolchinsky, only 35 years old, who in 1936 had accused Drezen of deliberately slowing the expansion of the Soviet Esperanto movement. Vladimir Varankin also disappeared—author of *Teorio de Esperanto* (1929) and of the original novel *Metropoliteno* (1933), who in 1926 helped to launch the use of Esperanto in international workers' correspondence.[32] The Ukrainian writer Volodymyr Kuzmych, who wrote also in Esperanto, was arrested in Alma-Ata in November 1942.[33] Relatively lucky at first seemed to be the situation of the locksmith Viktor Belogortsev, who in 1932 called for an unrelenting battle against 'putrid liberalism' and efforts to create a distinctive 'Esperanto morality'[34]: He was arrested in 1935, so before

---

[29] Drezen was rehabilitated on 11 May 1957 but readmitted (posthumously) to the Party only at the time of Gorbachev (10 October 1989).

[30] Stepanov (1992), p. 55. Elena Sazonova was shot on 3 November 1937.

[31] On the occasion of the 50th anniversary of Esperanto, so in 1937, Nekrasov looked forward 'very optimistically' to the coming five decades, during which, despite persecution by 'reactionary forces', Esperanto would finally aid the victory of the idea of 'brotherhood among humankind': V. Bleier & E. Cense (ed.), *Ora Libro de la Esperanto-movado, 1887–1937*, Warsaw: Loka Kongresa Komitato, 1937, pp. 213–14.

[32] On Varankin (arrested 8 February 1938, shot 3 October 1938) see Stepanov (1990c). In August 1937 the brilliant linguist Evgenii Polivanov was arrested—known as a critic of Marr's theory. He was executed in January 1938 (rehabilitated 1963). Before the revolution he led a student Esperanto group in Petrograd: Kuznecov (1991), p. 26.

[33] He died in prison in Tashkent (9 October 1943): Cibulevskij (2001), p. 70.

[34] See his Russian-language article in *Bulteno de Centra Komitato de Sovetrespublikara Esperantista Unio* 11 (1932): 61–2.

the great wave of arrests, and condemned to three years in prison. But in 1938 he was not released.[35]

The imprisonment of the leaders brought with it more and more victims, among them not only functionaries at the local level but also large numbers of ordinary members. Up to the last moment there were Esperantists who, trusting to the justice of the regime, continued to use the language, correspond with friends abroad and, as Rytkov continued to do at the end of 1937, accept into their homes guests from capitalist countries. Rytkov reported that, when the first major figure in SEU, Dmitrii Snezhko, was suddenly detained, 'everyone thought "Oh, perhaps he has done something wrong"' (Fig. 1.3).[36] And when Drezen and the IPE executive Herbert Muravkin were arrested, many people suppressed their uneasiness by telling themselves that the Latvian Drezen spoke Russian with a foreign accent and Muravkin had studied in Germany

Fig. 1.3 Dmitrii Snezhko was the first well-known Esperantist swept up by the machinery of detentions

---

[35] In 1940 he died in a concentration camp: Stepanov (1994), p. 22.

[36] Abol'skaia (1999), p. 7. Nikolai Stepanov, who studied the NKVD papers ('Li estis la unua', *Sennaciulo* 63 [1992]: 25, 28–30), said Snezhko was arrested in February 1936 and freed only in 1955. He died in 1957.

for a long time[37] and wore fancy clothing—concluding, then, that perhaps they really did have contact with 'anti-Soviet elements'. Only when Gavrilov and Robicsek, his close friends, were arrested, Rytkov 'understood that something unjust had occurred', but even then he did not stop his Esperanto activities.[38]

Touching evidence of the unconcern of ordinary Soviet Esperantists can be found in the journal *Sur Posteno* of February 1938, published in the midst of the most horrific phase of the Purges. The editors (then based in Paris) printed letters from Soviet readers giving their opinion of the journal. I. Mironov, from Leningrad, expressed a wish that, according to the editors, often came from the Soviet Union: '[…] Publish more puzzles and riddles.' Another Leningrad Esperantist asked that the answers to these puzzles appear not in the next issue but in the issue after that, because he always received the journal, by way of SEU, late. Rytkov also sent a response: he complained that 'the riddles in number 54 were too easy and therefore uninteresting'.[39]

When Rytkov was arrested on the night of 21–22 March 1938 (the secret police also confiscated a suitcase containing letters he had received from abroad) he seriously believed that he was being taken to Lubianka to help with translation. He discovered the true reason only after arrival in that notorious house of torment in Moscow. Like every Esperantist arrested, he heard the same stereotypical accusation: 'you are an active member of an international espionage organization hidden in the territory of the USSR under the name of the Soviet Esperantist Union' (Fig. 1.4).[40]

We will not detail Rytkov's further fate here[41]; it is similar to the Golgotha that many other victims of the Stalinist terror had to suffer

---

[37] Muravkin was born in Berlin (in 1905), where he acquired a doctorate in physics. He was arrested on 26 November 1936. He brought many people down with him through forced confessions and was executed on 11 December 1937: Stepanov (1990a).

[38] Abol'skaia (1999), p. 8.

[39] 'Sovetiaj k-doj pri SP', *Sur Posteno*, 1938, 59 (Feb.): 6. Rytkov also expressed his admiration for a short story, 'Fidela hundo', published in the journal and said 'Soon I will perform it'.

[40] Stepanov (1990b), p. 76.

[41] Until 1943 Rytkov worked as a gold miner. Later, mindful of his profession as an actor, the authorities gave him the task of participating in entertainment shows in various concentration camps in northern Kolyma. From 1946 on, he was no longer confined to a concentration camp,

14   Dangerous Language — Esperanto and the Decline of Stalinism

Fig. 1.4 The actor Nikolai Rytkov—here in the role of Lenin—suffered 17 years in concentration camps because of Esperanto. Having fled to the west in 1965, he worked in the BBC's Russian Service

and generally did not survive. Like Rytkov, many SEU members suffered years of hard labor in Siberian concentration camps. Few returned. The precise number of victims will probably never be known. According to one American researcher, around 5000 Esperantists perished in the Gulag; in another estimate we read that hundreds were arrested.[42] Probably a few dozen were shot. Among those persecuted were also non-Soviet Esperantists. After his return from ten years as a prisoner of war in the Soviet Union, the German journalist Arthur Pankratz indicated that he met many Esperantists in the labor camps: not only Russians

---

but instead received 'permanent exile' in Norilsk, a city within the Arctic circle; there, in 1949, he returned to acting 'in the biggest northern theater in the world'. During more than 17 years of confinement, his ties with Esperanto were not entirely broken: in his place of exile, Rytkov on one occasion unearthed in an attic a copy of Zamenhof's *Fundamenta Krestomatio*—among forbidden books by Trotsky and Bukharin. Cf. Abol'skaia (1999), pp. 14–16. Varlam Shalamov, in one of his well-known tales from Kolyma, writes about a Moscow Esperantist condemned to 15 years in prison: *Kolyma Tales*, trans. John Glad, New York & London: W.W. Norton, 1980, pp. 189–196 (esp. p. 194).

[42] Smith (1998), p. 163; Mikaelo Bronŝtejn, 'Rememoroj aperas…', *REGo*, 2009, 1 (50): 13–19 (esp. p. 14).

and Ukrainians but also Germans, Poles, Finns, Estonians, Tartars, Georgians, Uzbeks and even Japanese.[43] Nikolai Khokhlov, translator of Drezen's major work *Historio de la mondolingvo*, ceased activity in the movement early in the 1930s and perhaps for that reason escaped persecution.[44] Kharkovsky asserts that 'almost everyone who immediately understood the irreconcilability of Esperanto with communism and left the movement' was saved.[45] The anarchist Ioganson Zilberfarb, who translated the Communist anthem 'The International' into Esperanto, similarly survived; he refused to join SEU 'because it conducts police spy operations for the government', and that perhaps saved him.[46] Seldom did an Esperantist suspected by the secret police succeed in avoiding arrest—and even less often was a detainee freed after one or two years.[47] Sergei Mastepanov, who was freed in 1948 after ten years of hard labor, afterward repeatedly changed his place of residence and employment, fearing that he would be arrested again.[48]

Only 24 years old when he was arrested, Rytkov was freed in November 1955, around the same time as Demidiuk.[49] Rytkov soon resumed his Esperanto activity (and also his acting career) with the same enthusiasm that he showed until the night of his arrest.[50] Other returnees also

---

[43] *American Esperanto Magazine* 69 (1955): 52. It is not clear whether they were imprisoned in connection with Esperanto.

[44] Kuznecov (1991), p. 29.

[45] According to Kharkovsky (http://miresperanto.com), among them were the pioneers Aleksandr Sakharov and Sergei Obruchev.

[46] Letter to E. Mikhalsky, 5 December 1926, in Ungar (1994), p. 15.

[47] Viktor Gusev, 'Kelkaj vojkrucoj survoje de la iranto', in Samodaj (1999), pp. 106–25 (esp. pp. 112–13), on Konstantin Gusev, who refused to denounce his Esperantist friend Vladimir Glazunov. The telegraph operator Aleksandr Eriukhin, who often provided his local newspaper in Arkhangelsk with the fruits of his correspondence, was arrested in May 1937 and freed at the end of March 1939.

[48] Sergei Mastepanov, self-educated on account of his poverty, became a German teacher and director of a village school; he learned more than ten languages: see the biographical sketch by Anatolo Ivasenko, *REGo*, 2013, 1 (74): 18.

[49] Sidorov (2005); Blanke (2007b), interviewed April 1982. Demidiuk died at the age of 90 in November 1985. See also 'Mi ne timas persekutojn. Letero de Grigorij Demidjuk [24 Oct.1981]', *La Ondo de Esperanto*, 1997, 2: 26–7.

[50] As of 1956, Rytkov resumed acting in the Lenin-Komsomol Theater and played in Soviet films, radio and television. In 1965, attending the European Esperanto Conference in Vienna, he decided to remain in the West. Later, as he had done earlier in Moscow, he played the role of Lenin in West German television and in a British play. During World Congresses of Esperanto he declaimed,

resumed activity, among them the Ukrainian Aleksandr Logvin. In his early poetry, his acquaintances noted promising talent: 25 years later he returned to Esperanto literature, profiting from the concern of his father, who, 'at the time unfavorable to Esperanto', hid his young son's poems in a beehive.[51]

After so many years of suffering and fear, not everyone immediately trusted the warmer climate: when in 1961 foreigners discovered that Stepan Titov, father of the cosmonaut German Titov, was an Esperantist, and the World Congress of Esperanto, taking place that year in the English town of Harrogate, sent a congratulatory telegram on the success of his son, Titov was at first dismayed. Only little by little was he convinced that the time was over when people were persecuted because they used Esperanto. Fortunately, *Izvestiia* ran a story about Stepan Titov describing him as 'a worthy representative of our rural intellectuals' and mentioned as evidence the fact that Titov in his youth was a 'passionate enthusiast for Esperanto', who corresponded widely with almost every continent.[52] To people in other countries, the survivors dared to allude to their suffering only very guardedly: after the war, Evgenii Melnik, for example, reported to Friedrich Köhncke 'that he was away for several years and breathed the scent of pine trees in Siberia'.[53]

---

among other pieces, the works of Solzhenitsyn. In his final years he worked for the Russian section of the BBC. He died in London on 1 September 1973 from stomach cancer.

[51] Ferenc Szilágyi, 'Renkonto sur la vivovojo', in Logvin, *Sur la vivovojo*, p. 11.
[52] *Paco* 8 (1961), 96: 22.
[53] Communication to the author from Kurisu Kei, who had corresponded with Köhncke (26 June 1973).

2

Esperantists in the Great Purge

The Esperantists of course did not have the caliber of long-time Bolsheviks or high-ranking members of the Red Army. They belonged, in Solzhenitsyn's formulation, to the 'modest, persistent little streams' that were almost lost 'under the overflowing torrents' of people streaming into Stalin's concentration camps.[1] Little was said about the Soviet Esperantists who up to the last moment, as we have seen, remained innocently unaware that destruction was on the way. But today we know that they did not simply disappear anonymously, along with millions of victims of the terror, but that the regime explicitly and systematically destined them for elimination.

Let us try to reconstruct the way in which the persecution of the Esperantists was organized. The Great Purge, launched on a major scale in March 1937, aimed not only at the liquidation of old-time Bolsheviks, whom Stalin regarded as an obstacle to his drive for personal dictatorship,

---

[1] Aleksandr I. Solzhenitsyn, *The Gulag Archipelago, 1918–1956: An Experiment in Literary Investigation*, trans. Thomas P. Whitney, New York: Harper & Row, 1973, vol. 1, p. 59; also mentioned is the fact that Stalin persecuted the Esperantists at the same time as Hitler. Elsewhere (vol. 2, p. 88), Solzhenitsyn cites an official source according to which Esperantists belonged to the (forced) workforce for construction of the Stalin White Sea/Baltic Sea Canal in 1933.

but also, through mass arrests and deportations, at the complete realignment of Soviet society. With this aim, a special Department of the NKVD[2] had lists in which suspicious persons were grouped in the following categories:

AS = anti-Soviet elements
Ts = active members of the church
S = members of a religious sect
P = rebels—that is, those who in the past were drawn into anti-Soviet activity
SI = citizens with contacts abroad[3]

That the Esperantists were assigned to this last category is reinforced by information provided by the Austrian Communist Alexander Weissberg-Cybulski, who, while working in the Soviet Union as a physicist, was arrested in March 1937:

> It was Stalin in person who gave Yezhov [the head of NKVD] his instructions for the Great Purge. It was Stalin himself who indicated the groups which were to be destroyed.
>
> [...]
>
> (5) All people who had lived abroad and had themselves experienced the pre-war period, and all people who had friends and relatives living abroad and maintained correspondence with them; the stamp collectors and the Esperantists.[4]

Weissberg did not indicate his source, but a very similar categorization appears in the only NKVD documents that we have. These are documents that were captured by German troops during the occupation of Lithuania and later fell into the hands of the Americans. They are secret

---

[2] From 1917 to 1922 the secret police were called Cheka, later GPU and OGPU. As of 1934 the office of the People's Commissar for Internal Affairs (NKVD) was responsible for state security.
[3] Conquest (2008), p. 257. On Esperantists as a category in the Great Purge, see also John Arch Getty & Oleg V. Naumov, *The Road to Terror: Stalin and the Self-Destruction of the Bolsheviks, 1932–1939*, New Haven & London: Yale University Press, 1999, p. 481. Generally on the organization of the mass repression see Paul Hagenloh, *Stalin's Police: Public Order and Mass Repression in the USSR, 1926–1941*, Washington, DC: Johns Hopkins University Press, 2009.
[4] Alex Weissberg, *Conspiracy of Silence*, London: Hamilton, 1952, p. 504. Listed are 16 categories in all.

instructions issued in connection with the forced integration of the Baltic States into the USSR in 1939.

Carrying out order number 001223 of the NVKD of the USSR of 11 October 1939, the People's Commissar for Internal Affairs of the Lithuanian Soviet Socialist Republic Aleksandras Guzevičius, required, through the 'top secret' order number 0054 of 20 November 1940, that, on account of their 'widespread contamination' of Lithuania, all 'anti-Soviet and socially foreign elements' should be registered. In all, he listed 14 categories, among them:

> j) Persons maintaining personal contacts and correspondence abroad, with foreign legations and consulates, Esperantists and Philatelists.[5]

Soon afterward came the arrests on the basis of the prepared lists. The task of removing 'anti-Soviet elements' from the Baltic republics to distant regions of the Soviet Union was given to the deputy chief of the Soviet NKVD, Ivan Serov. Deportation began on 6 June 1941, reaching its culmination on the night of 13–14 June. It was interrupted by the German invasion on 22 June. The Nazis continued the work in their own fashion. Among the Esperantists whom they killed were the Lithuanian Esperanto activist Michaelis Dušanskis, the writer Helmi Dresen and the minister of social affairs for the Estonian SSR, Neeme Ruus.[6]

These victims of the Nazis had already seen the end of the organized Esperanto movement long before the German invasion. In November 1940 the Swedish Esperanto journal *La Espero* reported that in the Soviet Estonian parliament 15% of the deputies were Esperantists and that a sympathizer of Esperanto, the writer Johannes Vares-Barbarus, had become the new prime minister[7]; in addition it was revealed that the new Lithuanian transport minister, Jonas Masiliunas, was an Esperantist.[8]

---

[5] *Lithuanian Bulletin* (New York) 7 (1949), 7/12: 18. After the fall of the Soviet Union the order of Guzevičius was published in *Lietuvos gyventojų genocidas*, vol. 1: 1939–1941, Vilnius, 1992, pp. xxvii–xxviii; for this information (25 September 2003) the author thanks Vytautas Šilas. Earlier, the order appeared in *Lietuvių archyvas. Bolševizmo metai* (Kaunas), vol. 1, 1942, pp. 19–21.

[6] Neeme Ruus was an active member of SAT.

[7] *La Espero* 28 (1940): 99. Hilda Dresen translated poems of Barbarus into Esperanto (1931). He committed suicide in 1946, probably fearing arrest.

[8] *Heroldo de Esperanto*, wartime issue, no. 1 (1 December 1940), p. 4.

Only a few months later, however, in April 1941, *La Espero* informed its readers that the Estonian Esperanto journal had ceased publication.[9] Rein Kapper, former president of the Estonian Esperanto Association, who in 1944 successfully fled to Sweden, also testified that the banning of Esperanto radio broadcasts and closing of Esperanto groups took place before 'the most terrible, satanic night of the 13th and 14th of June 1941'.[10] Arrested on that night were, among others, two well-known Latvian Esperantists, the poet Ludmila Jevsejeva and, with his family, Tālivaldis Indra, for many years president of the Latvian Esperanto Society.[11] Not until 1954 did it become known abroad that the former president of the Lithuanian Esperanto Association, lawyer and noted pacifist Balys Giedra, compiler of an Esperanto-Lithuanian dictionary and the verse anthology *Violetoj*, died 'somewhere in Siberia'.[12] Many Lithuanians, however, noting that the Russian Esperantists had already been silenced, ceased their Esperanto activity in good time and for the most part broke off postal contact abroad. In this way they escaped arrest (Figs. 2.1, 2.2 and 2.3).[13]

If 'socially foreign elements' were not tolerated in the Baltic countries, evidently they were not tolerated and were earlier removed in the Soviet Union itself. Thus Weissberg's categories would seem to carry a high grade of authenticity. They seem credible not only because of

---

[9] *La Espero* 29 (1941): 26. According to the Latvian Esperantist Teodors Arbergs, in his country in 1941 the Esperanto groups 'were liquidated along with other private societies': *La Pacdefendanto*, 1955, 48 (Dec.): 5. The Lithuanian Esperanto Association lost its registration at the end of June 1940.

[10] Rein Kapper, 'Memoroj kaj impresoj de estona rifuĝinto', *Malgranda Revuo* 2 (1944), 4: 12.

[11] A. Zigmunde, 'Forpasis duonjarcento…', *Latvia Esperantisto*, 1991, 12 (Aug.): 4–5. Indra perished on 8 December 1942 in Solikamsk, in the Urals.

[12] *Esperanto* 48 (1955): 12. Giedra died of starvation in 1942 on the Arctic Sea. Among the Lithuanian Esperantists who survived many years of captivity was the teacher Eduard Levinskas, popularizer of the ideas of Tolstoy in Lithuania, who in 1945 was exiled to Tajikistan with his whole family and was allowed to return home only in 1955, and the anthropologist Antanas Poška (Paškevičius), who was arrested in 1945 in part because of his activities as an Esperantist. He was able to return to Vilnius only in the summer of 1959 (Vytautas Šilas, 'Kavaliro de la verda stelo', *Litova Stelo* 13 [2003], 3: 3). A well-known Estonian Esperantist, forced to remain in Siberia for ten years with his family, was the teacher Henrik Seppik. Ludmila Jevsejeva was able to return to her homeland in 1957 (see Nikolao Stepanov, 'Ludmila Jevsejeva, esperantistino kaj poetino', *Sennacieca Revuo*, 1994, 122: 29–31).

[13] Vytautas Kalasauskas, 'Renaskiĝo de Esperanto en Litovio', *Litova Stelo* 7 (1997), 1: 22.

2 Esperantists in the Great Purge

Fig. 2.1 The Estonian teacher and lexicographer Henrik Seppik was one of the Esperantists in the Baltic countries forced into exile for many years

their similarity to the Lithuanian documents but also because of two other similarities. First, the assumption that Esperantists were put into the same category as philatelists is supported by the testimony of Rytkov, who remembered that, when SEU was destroyed, the same fate descended on the association of philatelists. Also the historian Roy Medvedev mentions persecution of stamp collectors and Esperantists in the same context.[14]

The other similarity is even more interesting. The name of Nikolai Ezhov, the NKVD head, had been long since mentioned in connection with Esperanto. A little before the mid-1930s Nikolai Intsertov, SEU's executive secretary, wrote to his Japanese comrade Kurisu Kei, that Ezhov had begun to explore the situation of Esperanto in the Soviet Union; as a result of these researches, Intsertov anticipated that, thanks to Ezhov's intervention, the position of SEU would improve.[15]

---

[14] Roy A. Medvedev, *Let History Judge: The Origins and Consequences of Stalinism*, New York: Knopf, 1972, p. 352.
[15] Personal communication from Kurisu Kei, 4 August 1971.

Fig. 2.2 Among the Esperantists deported in June 1941 was the Latvian poet Ludmila Jevsejeva

Fig. 2.3 The Lithuanian anthropologist Antanas Poška sheltered a Jewish friend from the Nazis during the war; he was arrested after the return of the Soviet army

Intsertov's testimony was neither the first nor the only indication that the highest Soviet authorities had been scrutinizing Esperanto. In fact, SEU, in 1930 and later, several times announced efforts to win more support from the authorities—evidence that makes it painfully obvious that SEU's actions all too often ran into resistance because of the Party's lack of explicit recognition of its usefulness.

In mid-1930 Drezen expressed the conviction that soon SEU would reach a decisive turning point. While relations with SAT went steadily downhill, he informed the members that, because 'the whole system of the various public organizations in the Soviet Union is being studied', SEU could expect concrete proposals on how best to adapt its activities and organization to 'social needs'. Drezen prepared the members for several possibilities, among them the possibility that SEU would be dissolved and its place taken by Esperanto centers in trade unions at the all-union and local levels.[16] Awaiting a party directive, SEU several times delayed the opening of its Fifth Congress, originally planned for July 1930. But the directive did not come. When the Congress finally took place, in November 1931, Drezen announced that SEU would 'again' present the question of Esperanto to the Communist Party Central Committee.[17] In the years following, SEU was again kept waiting, noting its concern at a certain 'immobilization' among its members, and that the ability to recruit for Esperanto was impeded because the Association was 'not officially recognized by the Soviet authorities'.[18] And there were unsettling precedents. In September 1932 came the dissolution of the Society for Proletarian Cinematography and Photography—which seemed to attest to a general intention by the Party to reduce the number of 'voluntary' associations.

The fragility of SEU's position is revealed with rare clarity in a report presented in 1935 to the Second Congress of IPE in Antwerp. In this report SEU's organizational problems are directly tied to the nonexistence of a guiding decision from the higher authorities:

---

[16] E. Drezen, 'La vojoj de SEU – organizo kaj evoluo', *Bulteno de CK SEU* 9 (1929/30): 117–22.

[17] '5-a Kongreso de Sovetrespublikara Esperantista Unio', *Bulteno de CK SEU* 10 (1931): 135. On this occasion Drezen mentioned the negative effect of the opinions of Bukharin, Krupskaia and Ulianova, who 'hindered us from winning over the press'.

[18] 'Pli da atento al membrovarbado', *Bulteno de CK SEU* 12 (1933): 17–18 (quotation p. 17).

To understand the specific conditions in which SEU operates, the irregular publication of journals, the reduction of publishing activity etc., we must understand the position of the Esperanto movement in Soviet social life. The Esperanto movement is a so-called 'voluntary movement', so not state-supported. No central agency has been seriously concerned with the problem and therefore has also not supported generally or in principle the work of Esperantists. Certainly, individual regional committees of the Communist Youth, of the Red Cross and of trade unions have supported the work of PEK [Proletarian Esperanto Correspondents] and to that extent it has produced striking results. There also exists a supportive recommendation from the Central Committee of the Ukrainian Communist Youth and of the cultural department of the all-Soviet organization of trade unions. A few well-known comrades, such as Lozovsky and Manuilsky[19] are sympathetic to our movement, but that is not enough. The lack of a decision in principle or a recommendation on the part of the central authorities certainly hinders local work, because the local authorities often lack the courage to take the initiative and thus much depends on the [whims of] changing functionaries. Dependent on all of this is the provision of paper to the SEU department of publishing, a function that is centralized for all organizations. In line with our categorization as a third-level organization, we receive paper only in extremely small quantities.

The report concludes:

We expect in the near future a principled and more general solution to the problems of our movement which will finally give us a basis for rapid progress.[20]

In its campaign for an authoritative decision, SEU also mobilized an old friend of the revolutionary Esperanto movement, the French writer

---

[19] A. Lozovsky (Solomon Abramovich Dridzo) was a high-ranking official in the Red Trade Union International and, from 1929 to 1946, deputy minister for foreign affairs. Arrested in 1949 for 'Jewish nationalism', he was the principal figure among those accused in the trial against the Jewish Antifascist Committee in 1952; he was executed along with several others. Dmitrii Zakharovich Manuilsky, among other functions a member of the presidency of Comintern 1924–43, was one of the few old-time Bolsheviks to survive the Purges. On the contact of Drezen and Muravkin with Manuilsky see Fayet (2008), pp. 9, 20.

[20] *Sur Posteno* (international edition) 3 (1935): 184–5. SEU's report formed part of the 'organizational report of the IPE Center' presented to the congress by A. Respe, IPE general secretary.

Henri Barbusse, who in mid-1935 was living in Moscow. In a conversation with two representatives of SEU and IPE,[21] Barbusse promised to write an article on Esperanto for *Pravda* and do what he could to counter 'our difficulties, the ignorance and lack of understanding, which we often encounter among the authorities in the national and international labor movements'.[22] But a month after his meeting with the Esperantists, Barbusse died.

In spite of everything, SEU did not lose courage. In December 1935, a few months after the Antwerp congress and the conversation with Barbusse, the internal newsletter of the IPE Center in Leningrad provided a glimpse of SEU's way of dealing with the authorities. When failure to receive its paper quota prevented it from publishing textbooks and its journal, the association, to expedite a decision, presented the authorities with a simple alternative: that 'it disband or that it become a subsidized organization'. Explaining its tactic, SEU asserted that, in fact, after the Party Central Committee established a department of voluntary associations, 'our problem received more attention', that several bodies, including the Komsomol Central Committee, affirmed SEU's right to exist and that, as a consequence, 'in no way could they think of the disbanding or death of SEU'. Knowing that its request 'is already under study', SEU assumed that 'perhaps in one or two months' the authoritative, definitive decision would come. And it did not doubt that the decision would be positive.[23]

Jean-François Fayet discovered evidence in a Moscow archive that in March 1936 Drezen and Muravkin turned directly to Stalin. Their letter was audacious in its wording:

> It seems to us – for its utility, particularly in the defense of the USSR – that SEU should find itself in a position if not better, then at least normal, in comparison with the working conditions in capitalist countries. But the situation is such that our enemies abroad are beginning to compare the conditions of the USSR Esperantists with those in fascist Germany.

---

[21] They were Herbert Muravkin and Vladimir Varankin.
[22] Homo (Muravkin), 'Henri Barbusse mortis', *Sur Posteno Klasbatala*, 1936: 2. Barbusse was, in absentia, Honorary President of the IPE congress in Antwerp.
[23] 'Pri nuna stato de SEU-movado', *Informilo. Interna organo de la IPE-centro*, 1935, 3 (Dec.): 14.

Drezen and Muravkin declared politically unacceptable the existence of an organization with foreign connections whose situation was at one and the same time official but only semi-legal. They therefore asked Stalin 'not to postpone a solution to our questions to some future time'. A reply came from Comintern: it required the disbanding of IPE, whose national sections should join the neutral organizations linked to UEA.

According to Fayet, Drezen found this requirement 'unsuitable',[24] which seems difficult to reconcile with the already mentioned discussion of collaboration with UEA. We do not know the details, but soon after, on 25 August 1936, Drezen was relieved from 'responsibility as General Secretary because of too much work'.[25] Elected as his successor was Pavel Shumilov.[26] Was Drezen still hopeful, at this stage, that in the near future 'a few problems' in SEU's activities would be solved, as he had written to Bastien in March and May 1936? Perhaps his departure was connected with the criticisms of Kolchinsky and others, that Drezen had ceased to accord importance to recruitment for Esperanto. But a more likely reason was his awareness of an approaching threat, as Kuznetsov suggests,[27] and indeed only three months later came the arrest of a key figure, Herbert Muravkin. This terrible blow led, as we now know, to many arrests.[28] Yet SEU still remained in existence; as late as 1937 its Central Committee continued to meet. Kuznetsov summarizes: 'At the 24 January meeting, the committee members adopted changes to the SEU constitution; at the 6 March meeting they called on Esperantists "to join with the Communist Party, which has smashed the Trotskyite-Fascist gangs"; on 24 March they fixed the date to celebrate the 50th anniversary of Esperanto (14 July 1937); on 6 April they noted the failure of the

---

[24] Fayet (2008), p. 22.

[25] Cited in Kuznecov (1991), p. 28; cf. Fayet, p. 23.

[26] Shumilov, former Red Army commandant, was arrested on 20 February 1938. He survived some 18 years of hard labor. Following his death in 1972, an obituary referred to his protracted suffering in these terms: 'During his entire life he remained faithful to the international language and to proletarian internationalism through all the storms and blizzards of our unsettled times.' See N. Sulje, 'Veterano forpasis', *Paco* 20 (1973), 1: 12.

[27] Note that Drezen resigned right after the first extensive Moscow trial, namely, that of Zinoviev, Kamenev and others (19–24 August 1936).

[28] See this volume, p. 13, note 37.

membership campaign for SEU.' This was the last meeting attended by Drezen: 11 days later he was arrested.[29]

SEU waited; the hoped-for decision did not come. But there is no doubt that the authorities, this whole time, continued their scrutiny of the organization, even if slowly. They seem to have done their work thoroughly. Lev Kopelev, as a schoolboy an enthusiastic SAT member, though he later lost much of his interest in Esperanto, one day received instructions to revive it. Required to prove his 'class awareness', Kopelev, at the time a student in the Moscow Foreign Language Institute, was given the task of going to meetings of Esperantists and noting the regular attendees. Among the matters particularly interesting to Kopelev's handlers was information on mail received from abroad.[30]

All this was in 1936 or a little later. Kurisu no longer remembered the exact year in which Intsertov sent him his hopeful letter about Ezhov's researches. But we know that at some point following the proclamation, early in 1933, of the need for a full examination of the Party's membership, Ezhov became a member of the examining commission. The following year, during the 17th Congress in January–February 1934, he was named deputy head of the Party Control Commission, and in February 1935, less than three months after the assassination of the Leningrad party secretary Kirov, he took full leadership of this commission. Around the same time he launched a campaign against foreign influences.[31] The signs of terror rapidly intensified. In mid-1935 came the disbanding of the Society of Old Bolsheviks and the Association of Former Exiles (whose records Ezhov acquired for examination). At about the same time the Komsomol was fundamentally reorganized with the goal of eliminating 'enemies' of the Party, and in 1936, the Communist Academy, a center for Marxist scholars, was closed.

In late September 1936 Ezhov was promoted to the position of People's Commissar for Internal Affairs, commissioned by Stalin to speed up the unmasking of Trotskyists and Zinovievists. Now, as head of the NKVD,

---

[29] Kuznecov (1991), p. 29. On 18 May 1937 the remaining committee members discussed publication of the leaflet 'What the Trotskyist Saboteurs Said to the Workers'.
[30] Lev Kopelev, *Khranit' vechno* (To Preserve Forever), Ann Arbor: Ardis, 1975, p. 278.
[31] Jansen & Petrov (2002), p. 38.

he transformed the secret police into a suitable instrument for the terrors to come. Early in 1937 preparations for the Great Purge were complete. Also made, finally, was a 'decision in principle' about SEU. What that decision was became known to the Esperantists only when they were arrested. In the Lubianka basement they heard the verdict: 'You are an active member of an international espionage organization'.[32]

---

[32] The party secretary of the Foreign Language Institute told Kopelev one day: 'You don't need to visit the Esperantists anymore. Their leaders are arrested as enemies of the people and the entire shop is closed.' (Personal communication from Kopelev, 15 April 1984.) The SEU office was probably closed on 21 February 1938, following the arrest of the last staff member, the bookkeeper Aleksandr Samoilenko (shot on 4 October 1938, the same day as Nekrasov and Nikolsky). More than 50 years later, Russian Esperantists learned from the office of the military prosecutor of the USSR that the court investigators of the NKVD imputed to the SEU board the organization of a 'Trotskyite-Esperantist spy center' (Nikolaj Zubkov, 'La restarigo', *Moskvaj Novajoj*, provnumero, April, 1989: 13–14, quotation p. 13). In the tribunal records for 1937–38 there were frequent references to a 'counterrevolutionary fascist-Trotskyite group of Esperantists'.

3

The Emergence of Soviet Patriotism

Before coming to a final analysis of the reasons why the Soviet Esperantists were chosen for 'purging', we must return once again to the relationship between socialism and an international language. As we explained in an earlier chapter, around 1932 the Esperantists ceased participation in the short-lived but vigorous theoretical discussion about the future of language under communism because they realized that they were getting locked into the sensitive area of the nationalities problem. Their claim to be forerunners of the distant goal of a universal language was negatively related to the practical politics of the moment, which was focused on the 'flowering' of nations in the transition period. As long as Stalin supported Lenin's position that Great-Russian chauvinism was the principal threat to the harmony of the peoples of the Soviet Union, and thus that full equality of rights among all nations and nationalities seemed to be a key part of Soviet policy, the Esperanto movement continued to feel encouraged to participate in the search for a compromise between the principle of equality of language rights and the necessity for international communication. But once the socialist, supposedly 'supranational' content was filled with Russian symbols and Stalin as of

1934 identified 'local nationalism' as a greater danger, it was no longer useful for the Esperantists to continue using as a justification for their activities theories still officially valid but no longer favored. In fact it seemed dangerous to rely on those theories and thereby demonstrate its lack of attention to current political priorities.

The disconnect between theory and practice increased during the Great Purge, when pressure on the non-Russian peoples reached its culmination. This pressure was perhaps nowhere clearer than in the linguistic field. In the 1920s, providing all peoples of the Soviet Union, if possible, with their own literary language was considered a priority. Serving as a basis for this effort was the Latin alphabet, adopted also by nationalities already possessing their own written tradition. Behind this choice, in addition to practical considerations, lay the view that Latinization would lead to the rapprochement of the peoples. The Latin alphabet was described not only as 'a powerful instrument of cultural revolution' in the Soviet Union but also as 'the alphabet of world communist society',[1] and for the non-Russian peoples it symbolized freedom from Great-Russian oppression. A few enthusiasts, for example, Anatolii Lunacharsky, even called for Latinizing Russian.[2]

Not surprisingly, language policy activities in the non-Russian republics attracted lively interest among the Esperantists. A few became activists themselves in alphabetization and language planning. In Azerbaijan, where a movement for Latinization was begun in 1922,[3] one activist attempted to create a writing system based on the Esperanto alphabet because—as he wrote in *Izvestiia*—it was 'the most rational of all alphabets'.[4] Later, Esperantists participated in the creation of new words or the development of alphabets, for example, in Armenia,[5] Turkmenistan[6] and

---

[1] Isayev (1977), pp. 244, 249; Smith (1998), pp. 121–42.
[2] Martin (2001), p. 196.
[3] Isayev (1977), p. 238; cf. Smith (1998), p. 110.
[4] R. Mencel, 'Esperanta alfabeto kaj orientaj lingvoj', *Esperanto* 18 (1922): 176–7 (on an article by Mamed Shakhakhtinsky in *Izvestiia*).
[5] The Armenian linguist Gurgen Sevak, member of the Esperanto Academy from 1971 until his death in 1981.
[6] The SAT member Aleksandr Potseluevsky was a member of the State Scientific Council of Turkmenistan: S. Bojev, 'Latina alfabeto en Turkmenio', *Sennaciulo* 3 (1926/27), 144: 5.

the northern Caucasus.[7] In early 1930, when the transition to the Latin alphabet among peoples formerly using the Arabic script was complete, SEU's theoretical journal published several articles on writing reform demanding, with all the fervor of the cultural revolution, the introduction of the Latin alphabet for Ukrainian.[8]

But, as of the beginning of 1933, the signs increased that Latinization no longer had support from the top.[9] Articles unfavorable to Latinization began to appear, for example, in *Pravda*. Culturally 'derussifying' the Russian proletariat now became a major political crime.[10] In August 1936 the All-Union Committee for the New Alphabet was criticized for insufficient attention to the growing significance of Russian as a pan-Soviet means of communication; particularly sharply condemned was the view 'that the Russian alphabet carries within it remnants of a feudal and patriarchal character'.[11] In February 1937 the Soviet of Nationalities decided to introduce the Cyrillic alphabet for the languages of the northern peoples. In the following three years the majority of non-Russian peoples, who in many cases had just a few years earlier adopted, after much preparation, the Latin alphabet, were required to switch to the Cyrillic.

To justify this change of direction in language policy, it was explicitly stated that strengthening the common socialist content of the languages of the Soviet Union required that appropriation of technical and scientific terms from Russian be made easier and that, instead of the communication-restricting Latin alphabet,[12] better conditions needed to be created for learning Russian. In 1937 a Congress of the Communist Party of Kyrgyzstan named knowledge of Russian a prerequisite for integration of the Kyrgyz population into the all-Soviet culture; similarly, the

---

[7] The linguist Lev Zhirkov: Isayev (1977), p. 245.

[8] E. Chikhachev, 'Latinskuiu azbuku ukrainskomu iazyku' (Latin alphabet for the Ukrainian language), *Mezhdunarodnyi iazyk* 8 (1930): 36. See also D. Snejko, 'Ĉu esperanta alfabeto povas esti akceptata kiel internacia?', *Sennaciulo* 6 (1929/30): 241; V. Kolchinsky, 'Za issledovanie "iskusstvennosti" v iazykakh SSSR' (For research on 'artificiality' in the languages of the Soviet Union), *Izvestiia Ts.K. SESR* 6 (1928): 328–30.

[9] Martin (2001), p. 416; further details in Smith (1998), pp. 143–60.

[10] Yuri Slezkine, 'The Soviet Union as a communal apartment, or How a socialist state promoted ethnic particularism', *Slavic Review* 53 (1994): 415–52 (quotation p. 443).

[11] Isayev (1977), p. 250.

[12] Isayev, p. 268.

Uzbeks were advised to learn Russian, 'the language of Bolshevism, the means of communication with the other peoples'.[13] The effort came to a head with a decree by the Party and government declaring the Russian language a required subject in all schools in the Soviet Union.

This decree was published on 13 March 1938—on the same day as Bukharin and Rykov were condemned to death. Even if this was mere coincidence, the persecution of non-Russian party leaders, running parallel with the Russification policy, formed an essential part of the Purge. The battle against 'nationalist deviations' intensified around the middle of 1937. Following familiar practice, criticism of the culprits was soon followed by their ouster, accusation and execution. In the public trial of Bukharin a number of leaders of non-Russian party organizations played a role. The new party functionaries installed by Stalin in the various republics of the Union began their work with campaigns for the Russian language. From this time on, a non-Russian communist sought to prove his or her loyalty to Moscow by fluency in Russian.

Precisely what the theorist Efim Spiridovich feared, back in 1930, now occurred.[14] In response to Mykola Skrypnyk, the Ukrainian People's Commissar of Education, he had warned that the Esperanto movement 'can move forward only on the basis of the broader development of national cultures and languages'. To believe that matters would develop differently 'would be to rely on the idea of the assimilation of nations, and therefore also their languages, by more powerful nations'. And, if that were so, 'the need for an international auxiliary language would cease to exist'.[15]

Eight years later, that was the precise state of affairs. In Ukraine, which saw the first signs of the move to repressive policies against non-Russian peoples, the call went out in 1938 for a relentless battle against the 'bourgeois, nationalist, Trotskyist and Bukharinist enemies' who were trying

---

[13] Isayev, pp. 263–4.
[14] On Spiridovich, see our earlier volume, chapter 7.
[15] E.S., 'Ésperantizatsiia vytekaet iz ukrainizatsii' (Esperantization derives from Ukrainization), *Mezhdunarodnyi iazyk* 8 (1930): 217–22; trans. Spiridoviĉ (1932), p. 159.

'to drive the noble Russian language out of our schools and universities'.[16] This statement adds support to the supposition, already mentioned, that Skrypnyk, in criticizing the link between 'Esperantization' and 'non-nationalizing' was covertly attacking Russification and centralization. Not only Spiridovich but also Drezen alluded to the connection, confessing that he did not see a difference between substituting Esperanto for Ukrainian in the schools and the suppression of Ukrainian by the Russian language.[17]

Neither Skrypnyk nor Drezen lived to see the day (and Spiridovich was in prison[18]), when intensive teaching of Russian began in Ukraine. By 1937–38, the advance of all-Soviet patriotism, strongly promoted as of 1934[19] and accentuating the common interest of all Soviet peoples for the building of socialism and the victory against internal and external enemies, could no longer be halted. The Russian language was raised to the rank of common language for all Soviet peoples. It was now officially considered 'the language of a great people, who have created the world's richest socialist culture, with Leninism as its greatest achievement'. Such were the words of *Pravda* in mid-1938. Much as the place of worldwide revolutionary expectations was taken by a nationalist Greater-Russian brand of Soviet patriotism, so in the field of language policy internationalist traditions had no right to exist if they contradicted the newly defined role of Russian: 'Russian will become the international language of socialist culture, much as Latin was the international language of the higher levels of early medieval society or French the international language of the 18th and 19th centuries.'[20]

---

[16] *Kommunisticheskaia partiia Ukrainy*, Kiev, 1958; quoted in Hans-Joachim Lieber & Karl-Heinz Ruffmann (ed.), *Sowjetkommunismus. Dokumente* II, Cologne & Berlin: Kiepenheuer & Witsch, 1964, p. 124.

[17] E. Drezen, 'Al esperantistoj!', *Mezhdunarodnyi iazyk* 9 (1931): 271.

[18] Spiridovich was condemned to eight years in prison, then to permanent exile. He died in 1958 in a Siberian home for the aged. (Personal communication from Nikolai Stepanov, 10 August 2003.)

[19] For an early Esperanto-language warning about Soviet patriotism, see Lanti & Ivon (1935), p. 36 (quotation from *Pravda*, 19 March 1935); cf. Moret (2010), p. 182.

[20] *Pravda*, 7 July 1938; quoted in Erwin Oberländer (ed.), *Sowjetpatriotismus und Geschichte. Dokumentation*, Cologne: Wissenschaft und Politik, 1967, pp. 26–7.

The context was abundantly clear when a writer in *Pravda* railed against 'enemies of the people' who, under the mask of militant internationalism, spread 'national nihilism'.[21] The disappearance of Esperanto at the same time as the arrival of Soviet cultural hegemony by way of Russian accordingly makes sense.[22] In the system of all-Soviet patriotism, which had banished even the 'revolutionary' Latin alphabet, there was no place for a neutral international language. Stalin, aiming at a single all-encompassing state, ceased tolerating the free development of languages and nations during the so-called period of transition, and he 'forgot' Lenin's important axiom—that the confluence of nations had to occur voluntarily, that there was an irreconcilable conflict between socialism and national suppression and that no language could be privileged over others. And the Esperantists, who were proud of their position in the vanguard of the formation of world communism, who had worked tirelessly for the model achievements of the Soviet Union, who faithfully noted the prophecies of Stalin about a worldwide language, who greeted Ezhov as a savior: they were now, in the middle of these developments, silently swept away, without warning or discussion. Lacking a legal basis and lacking the possibility of defending themselves against concrete accusations, they were now simply deported to oblivion, if not immediately killed, along with, for example, the lovers of such an innocent pastime as the collection of stamps. The feats of intellect by which Drezen and others sought to put Esperanto at the service of proletarian internationalism brought the Esperantists no privileged treatment when Stalin decided to embark on the Great Purge against all 'enemies of the state'.

This all took place even while officially the old international ideology of the Bolshevik revolution remained in place—that 'extremely favorable platform for the advancement of the Esperanto movement'.[23] Although after 1932 the Esperantists made no further attempt to reinforce their

---

[21] *Pravda*, 31 August 1938; quoted in David Brandenberger, *National Bolshevism: Stalinist Mass Culture and the Formation of Modern Russian National Identity, 1931–1956*, Cambridge, MA, & London: Harvard University Press, 2002, p. 92. In calling for the persecution of non-Russian nationalities, the party secretary for Krasnoiarsk believed he was following an order from Ezhov, to the effect that it was necessary 'to end the game with internationalism': Jansen and Petrov (2002), p. 98.

[22] Cf. Slezkine (2004), pp. 276, 279.

[23] Drezen (1991), p. 326.

position by appealing to the theory of a single-language future under communism, the theory itself went unchanged; nor were the Esperantists explicitly asked to reduce their activities or to cease drawing inappropriate conclusions from Stalin's initiative in support of a universal language. On the contrary, if previously the Soviet Esperanto movement had not depended on the Party's language policy guidelines, it could, after its short but enthusiastic excursions into theory, maintain its confidence that the practical dissemination and application of the language in accordance with Soviet conditions would lead to success.

Because the Esperanto movement, accentuating the language's practical side, had made considerable progress in the 1920s, it saw a chance to continue on this path and, as we have seen, was still capable, after 1932, of demonstrating a living Esperanto community. SEU did not lack for optimistic views of the future, nor for opportunities for official support, for example, from trade unions. By the mid-1930s, the members even felt encouraged to rediscover the pleasure of using Esperanto as they pleased. After almost two decades, during which the pressure for political conformity steadily grew, it suddenly seemed possible to emphasize the aesthetic side of Esperanto and to use the words 'revolution' and 'proletariat' with a certain irony.

And yet, shortly after the seeming relaxation of outside pressure came the deathly blow against SEU. It struck the organization, as we have shown, in the midst of the Great Purge, putting an end to the activity of which it was most proud. We will discuss these developments further in the next chapter.

4

International Correspondence

Almost from SEU's beginning, one activity to which the organization devoted a great deal of energy was international correspondence. For Esperantists generally, letter writing has always been a favorite means for the practical application of the language; in the Soviet Union, it was particularly important because of its double function, both as a traditional Esperantist activity and as a means of advancing the cause of international education as defined and proclaimed by the Soviet leadership. Unlike Esperantists in many other countries, who could also use Esperanto for travel and international meetings, for Soviet Esperantists international correspondence was virtually the only means of putting the language to practical use. The exchange of letters brought a great deal of satisfaction to individual Soviet correspondents, since it gave them an understanding of living conditions in other countries, and such concrete experience of internationalism touched them emotionally. Given that correspondence was at the same time officially recommended as a contribution to worldwide worker solidarity, the Esperantists could also see themselves as conforming to the generally approved principle of promoting the international education of the 'Soviet masses'. In fact, they became more and more convinced that, in this way, Esperanto would achieve a recognized position in Soviet society, since it was such an effective means of gathering information through individual correspondence that could then be circulated through newspapers.

We can accordingly say that correspondence in fact constituted the very reason for the existence of the Soviet Esperanto movement.[1] Numerous local successes and several endorsements by central authorities increased the Esperantists' conviction that they were engaged in an activity valuable to the entire country. There seemed to be little reason for concern about occasional negative or indifferent attitudes by party leaders. The more such letters from other countries, with their recognition of the building of socialism in the Soviet Union, were publicized in the press, the more Esperantists began to hope that their chief handicap—the absence of a world-language perspective in Marxist theory—would lose its significance and disappear in the face of the facts.

A precondition of continued progress along this line was, first, that correspondence aimed at international education would continue to enjoy official support, and, second, that Esperantists would continue to have the opportunity to participate in such correspondence, earning respect as suppliers of interesting reports and thereby drawing positive attention to their language.

As for the first precondition, the support of party authorities for bringing workers closer together through correspondence survived the changes in political priorities, more precisely the change characterized by what was defined as the goal of 'building socialism in a single country'. Stalin's transition to policies that depended less and less on expectations of world revolution did not signify a reduction in internationalist slogans nor abandonment of the exploitation of what seemed the natural sympathy of communist movements in other countries for the Soviet Union. When in 1930 the 16th Party Congress once again underlined the importance of promoting international education,[2] the Esperantists had become 'virtual monopolists' in this activity,[3] causing them to intensify their efforts still further.

---

[1] Correspondence is 'the basis of our entire work', remarked a delegate during the 5th SEU Congress: *Bulteno de CK SEU* 10 (1931): 134.
[2] N.I., 'Antaŭ grava etapo', *Bulteno de CK SEU* 9 (1929/30): 171.
[3] A. Marti, 'Dnepropetrovsk ne povas resti trankvila', *Bulteno de CK SEU* 9 (1929/30): 10. See also *Bulteno de CK SEU* 9 (1929/30): 170 (on Moscow).

It was less easy to fulfill the other condition, namely, to demonstrate to the authorities the usefulness of Esperanto. One negative factor was the fact that the Soviet movement seemed to be growing far faster than the Esperanto movements in other countries; quite early on, the view was expressed that the Soviet Union was in danger of 'creating more Esperantists than the capacity for international correspondence outside the Soviet Union'.[4] But even more problems arose from the contents of the letters themselves.

From the beginning, the letter writing was so various and diverse that it resisted all efforts to give it a unified direction. Ideally, western comrades would report on the revolutionary struggle in their own countries, and their Soviet counterparts would report on the post-revolutionary achievements of the Soviet Union—in other words, the exchange of letters would reciprocally stimulate a desire to continue the common struggle for the emancipation of the proletariat. But in practice the range of topics was much broader and more nuanced. Correspondents did not limit themselves to mutual enthusiasm. Soviet correspondents made it clear that their everyday lives were not entirely filled with deeds of heroism, and they confused their counterparts with reports indicating that labor unions in the Soviet Union no longer recognized the right to strike, that salaries and living costs were lower than in the western European countries, even though the latter were currently plagued by economic crises, and that, in sum, certain basic imperfections still prevailed in the workers' and peasants' state. If, then, such contradictions within the Soviet Union, which party declarations sought to obscure, were less easily hidden in correspondence, foreign letter writers delivered to Soviet citizens an unfiltered description of living conditions in their countries which supposedly confirmed the political pressure of the ruling classes and the accompanying social injustice but were not always suited to affirming the thesis of Soviet propaganda that capitalism stood on the verge of collapse.

Beginning in 1928, problems arising from correspondence began to become public knowledge. Insistent questions about political persecution and economic crises flowed into the Soviet Union, and an even greater flow of information moved in the opposite direction making it clear that

---

[4] L. Revo, 'Kelkaj rimarkoj pri malproporcio en nia movado', *Sennaciulo* 3 (1926/27), 133/134: 9.

not everything reported in the bourgeois press was mere lies. As a result, SEU confessed publicly that such correspondence was not without its abuses and warned its members about such dangers. To avoid losing the positive results expected from the use of Esperanto in correspondence, SEU increased its emphasis on the need to go over to collective letter writing, because it believed—not entirely incorrectly—that 'incalculable risk' lay in the widespread use of purely interpersonal correspondence.

By the end of 1927, rumors were circulating in other countries of the existence of a state Esperanto office that censored letters leaving the Soviet Union, or even created its own.[5] SEU denied it. But, after that, when the official organ of workers' and peasants' correspondents published an attack on the lies promulgated through Esperanto and on petty-bourgeois influence in the movement, it was obliged on its own account to strengthen its supervision and to launch a campaign aimed at raising worker consciousness and guaranteeing the ideological purity of its members. To promote collective correspondence, it organized at the end of 1929 a system of Proletarian Esperanto Correspondents (PEK), requiring that in each local group someone take responsibility for making sure that the contents of letters accurately reflected the official point of view—that replies to questions from outside be fully conformable with what the Party wished foreigners to know. Furthermore, this system aimed to supply 'fully trustworthy addresses', namely, those of foreign communists with whom Soviet Esperantists could safely correspond without the risk of falling under the influence of unorthodox ideas.[6]

Consistent with such thinking, SEU began at about the same time to prescribe directly the topics that should dominate the letters of its members. They were instructed to communicate statistics on the growth of Soviet industry under the Five-Year Plan and to report on the successful struggle against 'saboteurs' and kulaks and above all to obtain from their correspondents information on the technical achievements of developing capitalist countries, so that they could be applied to advance the building of socialism.

---

[5] Perhaps linked with this is Batta's observation (in a letter to Lanti, 25 May 1927), that social democrats 'are not too eager to correspond' with Soviet Esperantists.
[6] Jakov Vlasov, 'Pli da klasbatalo en nian laboron', *Kunligilo* 1 (1929/30): 4.

The success of such efforts to exercise full control over correspondence was limited. The request that western comrades convey technical knowledge to their correspondents seemed odd, and most often exceeded their capability. In a report on their activities in 1932, Esperantists in Stalino (Donetsk) confessed that that part of their work, described as 'importation of American and European technology', had failed. On the other hand, under the heading 'exportation of our experience of revolutionary struggle and the building of socialism' the document reported 'a host of successes'.[7] On that point the official recipients of the report had a different view. Among communists outside the Soviet Union, who did indeed wish to profit from the experiences of the revolutionists, criticism of the new productivity-oriented form of correspondence continued to grow, along with complaints about the annoying contents of letters from the Soviet Union, and a feeling of anger that Soviet comrades were delivering mere statistics or facts already well known.

If the western PEK collaborators were confused, it was even more difficult to bring the many individual correspondents in other countries round to the requirements set by SEU—requirements dictated to it under the guise of a 'sharpening class conflict'. Questions continued to arrive from abroad, resulting from a natural curiosity but embarrassing to those at whom they were directed, namely, the Soviet Esperantists. To arm its membership with arguments, SEU published leaflets under the title *La vero pri Sovetio* (The Truth about the Soviet Union), to be enclosed with letters. But this effort, and direct requests to SEU members, did not solve the problem. Furthermore, foreigners asked questions 'to which not even every communist could reply', so that—to avoid serious political errors in the letters—it proved necessary to arrange consultation with local party committees. The awkwardness of the questions was demonstrated by the fact that western correspondents increasingly found that their initial letters written in response to would-be correspondents went unanswered.

The SEU's efforts to conform to party guidelines were accompanied by the fear that a large part of its membership, accustomed to using the services of SAT to find correspondents in other countries, would not

---

[7] A. Jurgensen, 'Internacia korespondado estas parto de la socialisma konstruado', *Bulteno de CK SEU* 12 (1933): 10.

accept separation from that organization without protest. The schism in the workers' Esperanto movement not only represented an organizational and ideological break between SAT and SEU but also profoundly influenced personal relations between SAT members outside the Soviet Union and the Soviet Esperantists themselves, especially those who, simultaneously members of SAT, in fact represented the most active (and linguistically most competent) core of SEU.

The SEU leaders had long feared the dangers of schism, but when it occurred they did not hesitate—given the pressure of outside circumstances and also the efforts of SAT to separate leaders and members—to defend vigorously their right to silence all opposition. Following the schism, instructions on preferred contents of letters were raised to a further level, by putting pressure on those Soviet Esperantists who continued to maintain relations with SAT. They were subjected to exploratory questioning by the Central Committee[8]; depending on the results, they were made to suffer censure, expulsion and public pillorying. The mere fact that someone corresponded only with individuals and not collectives could now render that person suspect.

This process of increasingly intrusive supervision and of threats against deviant behavior finally led to arrests. In 1927, Lev Levenzon, an office worker in Shakhty, was attacked for his letter-writing contact 'with Hungarian police, Italian priests, the whore *Heroldo*, and other neutralist scum'.[9] After this denunciation, Levenson vanished without trace.[10] At this stage, at issue was only active correspondence with 'neutralists'. But matters later became more perilous when the battle against SAT was added to the agenda. Calling for the elimination of lackeys and renegades in its ranks, SEU made perfectly clear what model it planned to follow:

> The working class of the Soviet Union has uncovered the conspiratorial work of the 'Industrial Party', the Menshevik center that has been carrying out detrimental (obstructionist) work using money from the Second

---

[8] 'Fragmento el protokolo de kunsido de la sekretariaro de CK de SEU, la 18-an de aprilo 1931', *Sennaciulo* 7 (1930/31): 303.

[9] 'Al ĉiuj SEU-organizajoj', *Biulleten' TsK SESR* 6 (1927/28): 1–2; R. Nikol'skii, '"Sinjoro Levenzon—upolnomochennyi dlia SSSR"' ('... representative for USSR'), *Biulleten' TsK SESR* 5 (1926/27): 118–19 (quotation p. 119).

[10] [Aleksandr Kharkovsky], '1931–1937: SEU survoje al infero', http://miresperanto.com.

International and French imperialism. The worker Esperantists of the Soviet Union have similarly succeeded in unmasking and accurately assessing the 'publicity' work of 'Soviet SAT members', who are helping Lanti to poison the workers' movement outside the Soviet Union with doubts profiting only capitalism.[11]

Thus SEU took aim primarily at those individuals whose letters, critical of Drezen and the Central Committee, were published anonymously in *Sennaciulo* under the title 'Voĉoj el Sovetio' (Voices from the Soviet Union). They were able to identify some of them, and, hardly surprisingly, to condemn them as traitors and spies. Among them was the locksmith Viktor Diatlov, who had, among other things, provided SAT with a translation of the internal minutes of the Central Committee meeting of 7 August 1930. He was expelled from the SEU and finally sentenced to prison.[12] Of the others hit with a verdict of counterrevolutionary behavior because of links with SAT, we know only that, as of the year 1931, they went silent. The last sign of life from one of them was a despairing plea for help: 'I ask that, in the event of my arrest, […] you help me. Otherwise, I will have to "pay a visit" to some rather distant parts of the USSR. I don't want to perish there.'[13]

After the schism, contacts between SAT and a few former members in the Soviet Union could be maintained only with extreme caution. Lanti himself gave western European SAT members advice on such correspondence, for example, ways of getting around the censors. He recommended that questions be 'entirely specific':

> If you are sufficiently patient and persistent, I assure you that after a year or two you will have collected material giving you an entirely different picture of the life of workers in the Soviet Union from the one disseminated across the world on a vast scale and at great expense by the Stalinist propaganda machine. In this way you will put the language to practical use.[14]

---

[11] 'Sovetio sukcese plenumas kvinjarplanon', *Bulteno de CK SEU* 10 (1931): 18.

[12] N. Incertov, 'Por ke SEU estu forta necesas forigi el niaj vicoj la fremdulojn', *Bulteno de CK SEU* 10 (1931): 13. According to *Sur Postena Klasbatala* (1935: 10), Diatlov was condemned because he apparently 'stole a typewriter and books from the office of the SEU Central Committee' and 'wrote letters asking for money from foreign Esperantists'. See also note 38, below.

[13] Letter of Nikolai Shchegolev, journalist from Barnaul, to Lanti, March 29, 1931.

[14] E. Lanti, *Absolutismo*, Paris & Amsterdam: SAT & FLE, 1934, p. 16.

Freed from a leadership position in SAT, Lanti no longer hesitated to publicize letters received from the Soviet Union. As of 1935 he founded, as organ of the 'Nationless Section' (Sennacieca Frakcio), the journal *Herezulo* (Heretic),[15] in which he confessed that he had long been subject to 'pangs of conscience' because for many years, in order to conserve the unity of SAT, he had 'tolerated the publication of misleading articles on the Soviet Union and sidelined those that spoke simple truth'.[16] In the new journal Lanti began to publish current articles from the Soviet Union which, in his opinion, presented an unfiltered picture of the situation.

The letters contained, for example, information on salaries and prices in Moscow, next to which Lanti presented similar figures for Paris.[17] On the basis of this comparison of costs of living, one Soviet correspondent concluded that 'French workers live in what looks like a paradise of a country'.[18] Another wrote that he did not even regard the lower standard of living in the Soviet Union as the chief evil. He was more upset by the lack of 'freedom of speech and assembly' and, most of all, the realization that people were beginning to grow accustomed to its absence: '[…] in truth—and this will perhaps be the most terrifying news to you—the people here are increasingly losing the desire for freedom; the younger generation doesn't even understand what constitutes freedom for you and for me.'[19] All these published letters uncompromisingly described the sociopolitical situation under the reign of Stalin: that failure to denounce someone resulted in punishment of ten years' imprisonment; that the police used torture to secure confessions; that, according to a new decree, even 12-year-old children could be condemned to death[20]; that a new class had come into being, 'of the privileged, of exploiters', while 'socialist ideology little by little is ceasing to play a role'.[21]

So the letters gave an extremely negative representation of Soviet reality. They painted a picture of repression, fear and misery—of a 'place of deadening orthodoxy', in which a highly perfected system of state

---

[15] Subtitled 'Sendependa revuo por batalado kontraŭ ĉiajn dogmojn', *Herezulo* appeared quarterly for two years.
[16] E.L., 'Ĉu "Herezulo" estas necesa?', *Herezulo*, 1935: 17.
[17] *Herezulo*, 1935: 63–4.
[18] Letter to the French Esperantist S. Brun, 6 April 1936, *Herezulo*, 1936: 48.
[19] Letter to Lanti, 15 November 1935, *Herezulo*, 1935: 60.
[20] The decree, aimed at fighting criminal activities by minors, was published on 7 April 1935.
[21] Letter to Lanti, 20 May 1935, *Herezulo*, 1935: 20–1.

capitalism had enslaved the very workers who were once to have been freed.[22] The letters were written by people who themselves had done battle with the Tsarist regime and hoped that the revolution would bring an end to exploitation, only to see their hopes cruelly dashed. With broken hearts they confessed that even the persecutions of the Tsarist regime paled by comparison with the system of terror established by 'the jackals who now rule over us', and that the battle for the liberation of the working class 'has entered a blind alley'.[23]

Lanti, who at the latest by mid-1933 lost what was left of his belief that the Soviet Union was 'still a revolutionary factor in the battle of the proletariat for its emancipation',[24] considered the letters confirmation that the assertion that the Soviet Union was building socialism was a myth that had to be demolished.[25] According to Lanti, that country's system of rule could only be characterized as 'red fascism'.[26] This conclusion put Lanti completely at odds with the adulations of the writer George Bernard Shaw, who, in a BBC broadcast in October 1931, asserted that there reigned in the Soviet Union an 'atmosphere of such hope and security for the poorest as has never before been seen in a civilized country on earth'.[27]

Only Lanti published letters in which 'Esperantist revolutionaries'[28] openly described the circumstances in the Soviet Union, but certainly such outpourings of disillusionment reached many people in the west who were less forthcoming than Lanti.

One wrote that communists in other countries would be amazed if they knew the truth about the Soviet Union: 'Only comrades occupying

---

[22] Letter to Lanti, 15 November 1935, *Herezulo,* 1935: 59, 62.

[23] Letter, signed by 'Ruĝa Ribelulo' (Red Rebel), to Lanti, *Herezulo,* 1935: 11, 13.

[24] Letter to Jan Willem Minke, Amsterdam, 30 June 1933, in Lanti (1940), p. 64. This change of perspective was influenced not only by letters but also by testimony of people who had lived for years in the Soviet Union. For example, the French SAT member Robert Guiheneuf returned to France in early 1934 after over ten years in the Soviet Union; see letter to Hermann Wagner, Stuttgart, 19 February 1934, in Lanti (1940), p. 111.

[25] See also Lanti & Ivon (1935).

[26] 'La ruĝa faŝismo', *Herezulo,* 1936: 8–10.

[27] Quoted by David Caute, *The Fellow-Travellers: A Postscript to the Enlightenment,* London: Weidenfeld & Nicolson, 1973, pp. 66–7.

[28] Letter to 'Ruĝa Ribelulo', *Herezulo,* 1935: 13.

well-paid positions could write so enthusiastically of the Soviet Union; but the majority live in misery and do not dare to write anything about their real condition.'[29] And, for their part, the Soviet Esperantists would be amazed if they knew what the British socialist Beatrice Webb noted in her diary in May 1932, during a journey through the Soviet Union: 'Instead of the despairing apathy or cynical listlessness of capitalist countries there is enthusiasm and devoted service on the part of millions of workers in Soviet Russia.'[30]

A particularly interesting experience, also of the risks that writers exposed themselves to, was that of the Japanese IPE member Kurisu Kei (Fig. 3.1). He had written a letter to the SEU in which he expressed admi-

Fig. 3.1 Kurisu Kei, of Japan, at the time a convinced communist, continued lively correspondence with Soviet Esperantists until 1937–38. Only after the war did he gradually find out why they all suddenly went silent

---

[29] Letter from Jean Wutte, Strasbourg, to Lanti, 28 September 1930 (quoting from a letter by a Soviet Esperantist).

[30] 'Diary of Beatrice Webb', typewritten transcript, p. 5313; http://digital.library.lse.ac.uk/objects/lse:nut827hel/read/single#page/84/mode/2up.

ration for the building of socialism in the Soviet Union, described his difficult life under the attentive eye of the Japanese police and asked that SEU find for him suitable Soviet Esperantists as correspondents. SEU circulated Kurisu's letter and as a result he received several letters—and also a packet containing an old French-language Esperanto grammar.³¹ Opening the book, Kurisu found that a Soviet Esperantist had written a message in it—namely, that throughout the entire 165-page book every odd-numbered page contained, in the margin next to the binding, handwritten sentences. The handwriting was barely decipherable:

> My dear comrade, Your good opinion of our country is only a beautiful dream and a self-deception. There is no happiness here. Freedom and plenty exist only on paper. In fact, as in all other countries of the world, people are hungry and suffering and are cruelly, even more cruelly than in capitalist countries, exploited by their new overlords. [...] Here the Esperanto movement is under great pressure to avoid giving Russian labor direct contact with foreign workers. [...] Delegates who travel here from abroad are chosen in advance by the Soviet government and, when they arrive, are taken without charge to all of the resorts and receive various gifts. No foreign worker can directly talk with Russian workers unless accompanied by plain-clothes agents. [...]
> Dear comrade and friend, I fully understand your terrible situation in capitalist countries, but, believe me, here it is no better. I myself was extremely active as a Red Guard and for many, many years fought for the workers with a full heart, but now everything has changed completely. [...] Dear friend, I write these lines with my worker's blood. If you now begin to believe me, this will be a terrible disillusionment for you. [...] I have become a most unhappy wretch. [...] I have fought against untruth, but what have I gained? Nothing; no hope.
> My dearest comrade, I deeply regret your situation, but believe these words, written in blood. Your happy opinions about the Soviet Union are simply a beautiful dream, like visions of paradise to a religious believer. I still do not know where one must look for happiness for the workers.³²

---

³¹ Namely, *Langue internationale Esperanto. Manuel complet avec double dictionnaire*, traduit sur l'ouvrage russe du Dr. L. Zamenhof par L. de Beaufront, troisième édition, Paris: H. Le Soudier, 1897.

³² Kurisu provided me with copies of this grammar. As best he could remember, he received the book from a Latvian, living perhaps in Moscow, sometime around the end of 1933 or the begin-

We must assume that there were more than a few people who had the courage to write openly about Stalinist excesses in letters to their foreign correspondents; such is also the observation made in a meeting of the SEU Central Committee in September 1934, that 'counter-revolutionary elements have penetrated the organization and instigated the delivery of such information to other countries'.[33] Letter writing had become dangerous. The Siberian teacher Vladimir Bazhenov, having sent 'anonymous postcards to Austria and France' describing 'certain "horrors" of hunger and "misery"' in the USSR, was publicly denounced as a 'traitor'.[34] Lanti himself experienced such a situation when two of his correspondents were subjected to persecution because the Soviet censorship discovered the source of the letters that had been sent to him.[35] But correspondence was dangerous also because of a factor that the Soviet letter writers had not included in their calculations. This led to a particularly dark chapter in Soviet Esperanto history.

As we have noted, as early as the end of the 1920s, SEU publicly discussed topics that were touched on in the correspondence of Soviet Esperantists with other countries. SEU members often turned to the organization to ask for advice on how to present their arguments. But it also happened that foreigners on occasion turned directly to SEU for confirmation of what their correspondents had told them about the role of trade unions, about the results of agricultural collectivization or about salary distribution. As Stalinism expanded, the number of politically problematic topics continued to grow, so that this practice of turning to the SEU for advice, originally derived from the understandable curiosity of western comrades, caused the SEU leaders increasing embarrassment and led to disagreeable consequences for the members whose letters were thus revealed.

---

ning of 1934. A fuller version of the notes appeared in his essay collection: Kurisu (2010), pp. 101–3.

[33] 'Plenkunsido de CK SEU', *Sur Posteno Klasbatala*, 1934: 129–30 (quotation p. 130, contribution to the discussion by Fyodor Kosushkin).

[34] V. Dereguzov, 'Predatel' iz Chity' (A traitor from Chita), *Mezhdunarodnyi iazyk* 10 (1932): 188; 'Historio de unu perfido', *Bulteno de CK SEU* 12 (1933): 6–7.

[35] Letter to Horace Barks, 23 May 1932, in Lanti (1940), pp. 97–8.

This danger was less predictable than the dangers resulting from the vigilance of the censors. Lanti explained the problem—namely, the risk of being denounced from outside the country—in a speech to the Dutch worker Esperantists. Offering advice on how to continue correspondence with Soviet Esperantists under these increasingly difficult conditions, he pointed out that 'it is all the more necessary that you gain their confidence; they have to be certain that their letters will not be sent to the Central Committee of SEU, as has already happened on the part of comrades who undoubtedly supposed that such letters were written by dangerous counter-revolutionaries'.[36] Early in 1936, Lanti touched this sore point even more directly, if in private:

> Imagine what has occurred. Comrades outside the Soviet Union have caused the imprisonment of their Soviet correspondents because, receiving letters that spoke the truth, these comrades chose to believe that only 'counter-revolutionaries' could write such letters. So they communicated these statements to the SEU Central Committee—and nothing more was ever heard from or about these unfortunate letter-writers.[37]

Lanti was not exaggerating. In 1931, the letters of two Soviet SAT members, sent to Paris, were published in facsimile in SEU's Russian-language journal.[38] Speculating on how such a thing could happen, SAT expressed the suspicion that one of the three members of its Control Commission had broken a written pledge not to reveal the names of Soviet correspondents. The Control Commission had received a file from the SAT office containing letters from Soviet Esperantists in connection with the response to Drezen's charge of 'defamation' by the SAT Directorship.[39] Suspicion of having betrayed precisely the people who accused Drezen of

---

[36] Lanti, *Absolutismo*, p. 16.
[37] Letter to Raymond Laval, 2 February 1936, in Lanti (1940), p. 119. Similarly: letter to Minke, 30 June 1933, Lanti (1940), p. 68.
[38] 'Dvurushnikov—k otvetu!' (Two faced—explain yourselves!), *Mezhdunarodnyi iazyk* 8 (1930): 271–5 (facsimiles p. 274). The two people thus unmasked were Aleksandr Lapovenko and Viktor Diatlov. The issue in question appeared in April 1931, but Lanti had already learned in February that Diatlov was in danger because SEU had acquired photocopies of some of his writings.
[39] 'Kiu rompis sian honorvorton?', *Sennaciulo* 7 (1930/31): 336; see also Lanti's clarifications: *Protokolaro pri la XIa Kongreso en Amsterdamo, 2–7 aŭgusto 1931*, Paris: SAT, 1931, p. 25.

dictatorial behavior fell on the Belgian communist Henri Jeanneret, who in late December resigned from his function as a member of the commission and went over to the opposing camp.[40]

At the Amsterdam congress, the communist opposition explicitly justified the breaking of the pledge[41] and greeted the public reading of anonymous letters from the Soviet Union with cries of 'White Russian!' or 'Counter-revolutionary!'[42] Given such a frame of mind, we need little imagination to understand how faithful followers of the Soviet Union in the west reacted when Soviet Esperantists occasionally poured their hearts out and revealed facts that foreign party members could not or would not believe. Kurisu recalls that he in no way wanted to believe his correspondent's marginal notes and only out of instinct chose not to write to SEU about them. Even some readers of *Herezulo*, and therefore members of SAT's Nationless Section, greeted the shocking contents of the published letters with doubts: according to Lanti, they 'tended to think that only "whites" and "counter-revolutionaries" could talk in this way about "the fatherland of worldwide labor"'.[43]

The openness of the Soviets and the orthodoxy of their western partners frequently led to their breaking their letter-writing connections. About the unhappy fate that awaited those whose letters were sent back to the Soviet Union from the west there is unfortunately no question: beyond all doubt, the SEU Central Committee to whom the letters were sent agreed to carry out the task that the Party required of all Soviet citizens. Its willingness to serve is all too evident in the style of its language, suffused with the prevailing attitudes of Stalinism at its most militant.

---

[40] *Internaciisto* 1 (1930/31): 73. Jeanneret was directly identified as responsible in a letter from Lanti to the Paris comrades in October 1936: see Lanti (1940), p. 129. Four months later, the secretary of the Control Commission, Léon Bergiers, also from Belgium, resigned. In the course of a quarrel whose details need not concern us here, he threatened to publish the names of all Soviet informers *(Protokolaro Amsterdamo,* p. 14). We do not know whether he in fact did so. In June 1932, he was expelled from SAT.

[41] *Protokolaro Amsterdamo*, p. 25.

[42] *Protokolaro Amsterdamo*, p. 20; see also pp. 29, 58.

[43] 'El k pri la ruĝa faŝistejo', *Herezulo*, 1936: 22. Others acknowledged the possibility that the reports were true, but expressed the fear that 'reactionaries might use them to oppose communism', *Herezulo*, 1936: 57.

We must increase our working-class vigilance. Using Esperanto for the goals of the revolution, we must prevent kulak agents from exploiting Esperanto for counter-revolutionary goals. We must drag these agents of world capital out of their hiding holes; we must shatter their will to continue their work, whose essential direction is preparation for capitalist war against the Soviet Union. We must loudly declare to the worldwide worker Esperantists: see how, through contact with the oppressive and exploitative capitalist forces, the renegade Lanti and his fellow-agents in the Soviet Union are working.[44]

One outcome of this servile attitude was the fact that SEU informed its superiors about cases of 'class enemies using Esperanto to link up with hostile circles abroad'.[45] With their expressed desire to demonstrate their 'working-class vigilance' and their willingness to drag 'agents' out of their hiding places, SEU inevitably fed the doubts and suspicions of those in power. SEU could not have understood that such denunciation of weakness in its ranks equaled suicide.

But also the opposite occurred. Letter-writing contact was sometimes broken off because of an unbridgeable gap between western correspondents, who, as socialists, judged developments in the Soviet Union with disapproval, and Soviet Esperantists who staunchly defended their country against all forms of criticism. That an epistolary friendship extending over many years could come to an abrupt end in this way is revealed in the following example. F.A. Chavenon, a French letter writer from Clermont-Ferrand,[46] carried on a long correspondence with a Soviet counterpart whose father perished fighting against the Whites in the civil war, and who himself 'was always fervently devoted to the Soviet regime'. Chavenon regularly informed him of 'the bad reputation' of the Soviet Union in France, and the Soviet correspondent insistently communicated 'the truth' to his friend in France. For a while, the Soviet correspondent was 'unjustly' imprisoned, but even then his loyalty to the regime remained unshaken.

---

[44] G.D., 'Pri iu "amiko de Sovetio" kaj liaj amikoj el Sovetio', *Bulteno de CK SEU* 12 (1933): 38–9 (quotation p. 38).

[45] Quoted by Fayet (2008), p. 22.

[46] Chavenon, a former gendarme who became an anarchist, worked as a nightwatchman after his retirement (communication from Raymond Laval, 25 November 1981).

In October 1936, Chavenon sent a postcard to his 'dearest friend' that read as follows:

> Both of our regimes are capitalist, either in the form of state capitalism or private capitalism, but, either way, oppressing the people; thus they cannot support the Spanish proletariat, whose victory would be a death blow to capitalism. […] People say that Stalin is sick; he could die; he has already done evil enough by betraying the October Revolution.

A few weeks later, a reply arrived. Chavenon was addressed as 'Sir' and read in the letter, among other things, the following:

> For the past several years of our acquaintance you have told me that you are a socialist, but I have the impression from the content of your letters that there is very little of the socialist in you—and today I have finally understood, with the receipt of your postcard, that you are a Trotskyite.

There followed a detailed explanation of the viewpoint of the Soviet Union concerning the Spanish civil war, which sought to prove that only the Soviet Union was providing the Spanish people with effective help. His Soviet correspondent advised Chavenon to read *L'Humanité* more often—'then you will have a more accurate point of view'—but immediately gave up any hope that Chavenon would change his opinion. The letter ended as follows:

> […] given your lack of affection for our much-loved Comrade Stalin, I can only conclude that your head has drowned in the filthy bog of Trotskyism; thus you stand in the ranks of the fascists, in the ranks of the enemies of peace.
> We can fight for peace together with socialists, anarchists and even Catholic workers in a united front, but we cannot unite with Trotskyites, all of whom we should shoot dead like mad dogs.[47]

---

[47] Chavenon, 'Fruktoj de korespondado', *Sennaciulo* 13 (1936/37): 22.

5

Silence Descends

It is not difficult to understand that, in correspondence between the Soviet Union and other countries, addressing issues of political ideology had become, by the mid-1930s, more and more impossible (not to say dangerous). Despite the employment of various kinds of indirection, Lanti's contact with Soviet correspondents also became sporadic after 1935.[1] But the question remains as to whether such relations came to an end simply because Soviet correspondents were unmasked, western socialists asked provocative questions and communists outside the Soviet Union denounced their Soviet comrades. In other words, should we attribute the death of the Soviet Esperanto movement primarily to the fact that anti-Soviet tendencies began to dominate their letter writing?

There can be no doubt that, as of the beginning of the 1930s, numbers of people were arrested because of the contents of letters that they sent to the west, and perhaps also because of communications with 'unorthodox' content that they received.[2] As a consequence, Soviet Esperantists became

---

[1] 'El k pri la ruĝa faŝistejo', *Herezulo*, 1936: 22.
[2] According to Lanti, Esperantists in the city of Simferopol were imprisoned 'simply because they had received unorthodox communications in Esperanto from other countries'. *Herezulo*, 1935: 67.

far more attentive to such matters. In essence, there were three ways in which they could adapt: by cutting off correspondence, by continuing it and remaining attentive to the party line, or by limiting their correspondence to non-political topics.

The first option, then, was simply to avoid all risk by abandoning further communication. Even in earlier years, foreign correspondents often experienced a situation in which a Soviet Esperantist, having announced his wish to correspond, failed to reply to their first letter. There could be various reasons for this, but evidently in the 1930s such silence resulted, more and more frequently, from embarrassment at the leading questions of foreigners.

On the other hand, letter writing was so firmly linked with Esperantism that it was hard to give up. Furthermore, SEU considered participation in collective correspondence a requirement of its members—which would seem to point to the second option of faithfully following the party line. When complaints began to arrive to the effect that efforts to connect Soviet and foreign factories and organizations had failed, SEU severely admonished its members not to undermine its work: 'We remind you that failure to respond to the questions of foreign correspondents is a major political crime, in no way forgivable!'[3] And when in 1933 SEU received acknowledgment from the All-Union Central Council of Trade Unions of the value of using Esperanto in 'international inter-factory correspondence', it even acquired a guarantee that the unions would punish any Esperantist factory-worker who neglected his responsibility to organize correspondence.[4]

That problems remained following the pressure to move to collective correspondence was evident also to party officials. Aleksandr Shcherbakov, responsible for cultural activities in the Party Central Committee,[5] remarked in a report on SEU in 1936 that 'the correspondence of Soviet Esperantists with other countries has taken on a relatively large dimension', particularly along the western border. He expressed uneasiness

---

[3] 'Kial iuj sovetiaj kamaradoj perfidas la laboron', *Bulteno de CK SEU* 11 (1932): 17.

[4] 'Pli da disciplineco en niaj vicoj', *Bulteno de CK SEU* 12 (1933): 33–4.

[5] Shcherbakov was also secretary of the writers' association. During the war he was the highest-ranking political general in the Red Army.

that lack of organization on the part of local SEU sections was causing this exchange of letters to take place 'without any kind of supervision' and that many Soviet Esperantists were continuing to correspond individually with members of SAT. Shcherbakov expressed a general lack of confidence in the SEU membership, 'whose situation and social origins have not been examined and whose linguistic skills are as little known to us as their political qualifications'.[6]

This all goes to show how the energy had gone out of the letter-writing activity launched earlier with such enthusiasm; the threats and warnings were symptoms of what had now become an arduous task—namely, the composing of irreproachable responses to workers outside the Soviet Union. Yet the fact remained that correspondence, particularly collective correspondence, continued as an important part of SEU's work. Although, as Drezen observed in 1932, its relative importance had declined, it had still not encountered principled opposition from the authorities.

In the absence of official discouragement, many Soviet Esperantists, with a clear conscience, chose the other approach: to continue their correspondence. Since the principle of advancing international workers' education still prevailed, they wished to maintain their relations with the rest of the world and show the authorities that Esperanto could help bring the worldwide proletariat together. The price to be paid was strict adherence to the framework of those forms of expression prescribed to its citizens by the Stalinist regime. The result, as we have seen, was increasingly stereotyped letter writing. The letters were full of enthusiastic reports about the achievements of the Five-Year Plan, fulsome praise for the Party and its beloved leader Stalin and fiery expressions of the conviction that the Soviet Union was 'the strongest, most powerful state in the world' and that 'here we live a good and varied life, but the future will be even better'.[7]

---

[6] Quoted by Fayet (2008), p. 22., Shcherbakov was disquieted by the work of Esperantist cells 'in several war factories and, more importantly, defense enterprises, for example, in Sebastopol, Leningrad and Moscow' and insisted on 'strict surveillance, particularly because of their active contact with other countries'.

[7] Several such letters from Soviet Esperantists, especially from the years 1935 and 1936, were printed in *Kolekto de Esperanta internacia korespondado*, compiled by Ganglin (Zhou Zhuangping) and Kroji (Zheng Zhuyi), two vols., Shanghai: Aŭroro, 1936; see quotations in vol. 2, pp. 43, 45. Their contents are reminiscent of Stalin's famous statement that 'Life has become more beautiful,

Such correspondence could succeed only if adequate responses arrived from abroad—responses that could be published in the Soviet Union as striking proof of the value of Esperanto as conveyer of foreign admiration. This was what was expected from the PEK system, and to some extent it clearly succeeded in producing the desired results. But, as we have seen, the patience of even the best-intentioned PEK collaborators was severely tested by the tendency of Soviet correspondents to communicate reports and statistics documenting major successes, but not the kinds of things that really interested their western comrades. The westerners continued to prefer a division of labor between the Soviet Union and other countries, namely, that one side should describe post-revolutionary achievements and the other the revolutionary struggle. In 1936, the PEK branch in Moravská Ostrava (Czechoslovakia) stated once again what was expected from comrades in capitalist countries like themselves: they should write 'about their struggle, about the creation of a united front, about strikes, prison life, the life of the unemployed [...], preparations for war against such hardships [...]'. At the same time they formulated very precise questions to which they expected replies from their Soviet correspondents:

> What was the life of workers formerly like, and what is it like now? Housing then and now? How many hours a day do workers work, and under what conditions? What are the salary differences among young people, and between men and women? Do workers receive coal without charge? How much? What kind of social security do they have, and who pays it? What support is given to sick workers? For as many days as they are sick? What support do the incapacitated receive if they are handicapped or aged? How much do widows and orphans receive if their husbands or fathers are killed? Are there frequent unhappy incidents in factories? How long is the vacation period of workers, and how do they spend this time? How do workers spend their free time? In factories, how are workers, specialists, engineers, etc., punished? What are the relations like among these three groups? What

---

comrades; life has become happier' (1935). The Fritz Hüser Institute (Dortmund) preserves several letters sent by Esperantists from various parts of the Soviet Union in 1932 to comrades in Dortmund, mostly in extremely neat handwriting. Other examples of stereotyped letters can be found in: *Arbeiter-Esperantist* (Berlin) 18 (1932), 5: 3; *Arbeider-Esperantisten* (Oslo) 13 (1937), 7: 4–5; *La Laborista Esperantisto* (Manchester), 1936, Jan./Mar.: 9–11.

opportunities are there for study? What does a worker eat? (This question is very important for our workers.) What about the beautification of cities, national minorities [...]?

And this was not the end of the Czechs' curiosity. Perhaps they overestimated the degree of social progress in the Soviet Union, but clearly they did not stop wondering. Pointing to the campaign launched after the miraculous achievements of the miner Aleksei Stakhanov in 1933, they added these further questions:

> [...] Why are Stakhanov Days held? (Is it a method, a system? If you can do it once, you should be able to keep doing it, suggested one of our comrades). Do Stakhanov workers get paid in proportion to their production? Don't they have their salaries lowered, as happens here?[8]

We do not know whether the Czechoslovakian PEK group ever succeeded in eliciting a reply and, as they intended, passing it on to Czech workers' newspapers, thereby giving impressive demonstration of their ability, thanks to Esperanto, to provide an authentic glimpse of the daily life of Soviet workers. The stereotyped nature of the communications sent at the time by PEK correspondents leads us to doubt whether a satisfactory response was ever received, because the actual social situation and the conditions of everyday life in the Soviet Union were already so hedged about with secrecy and taboos barely hidden under platitudes and bombastic statistics.[9]

If and when they arrived, the letters from the Soviet Union were full of such generalizations that even communists would have difficulty digesting them. Sometimes, a concrete question was answered, but with a response bordering on the absurd. In the middle of 1935, basing his information on an article published in *Izvestiia* on May 9, according to which some Ukrainian manager received a monthly salary of 3300 rubles, the Frenchman Raymond Laval wrote to the PEK contact person in Minsk to request clarification. Here is her answer*:*

---

[8] 'Kelkaj vortoj al korespondantoj', *Sur Posteno*, 1936, 42 (Apr./May): 3.
[9] On this topic, see Koestler (1983), pp. 131, 147–8, 160.

Your question: Is it true? Reply: No, it is not true. I looked through *Izvestia* for the entire month and did not find the report. First, it's not true; secondly, it couldn't be. No such salary could exist, according to Soviet laws.[10]

In sum, continued participation by Soviet Esperantists in what was apparently officially sanctioned correspondence did not protect them from risk. They constantly had to contend with the endless curiosity of their foreign partners, whose probing questions could be answered only by clumsy sidestepping and propagandistic slogans—or greeted by silence.

But a third approach remained available to Soviet Esperantists: they could consciously avoid any engagement with topics other than Esperanto or matters easily connected with it, like stamp-collecting. In fact, a tendency to focus on entirely non-political, not to say banal, subjects had always been a feature of the correspondence. For several years such trivialities were barely tolerated. But when, in the mid-1930s, the regime declared the class battle no longer necessary, and actually moderated, at least on the surface, its insistence on revolutionary fervor, the Esperantists, in their turn (as in the examples of Blinov and Rytkov) once again came to believe that it was legitimate to use Esperanto in less serious ways.

The foreign admirers of the Soviet Union were just as displeased with this new way of conducting correspondence. For example, the PEK branch in Madrid complained that the Soviet PEK teams failed to reply 'to serious sociopolitical questions about Soviet life. There are even some individuals who prefer postcards and philately to serious topics'.[11] But of course there were some who understood the situation of their Soviet correspondents and the fact that, wary of the risks entailed in any serious exchange of opinions, they were forced to resort to banalities. The newsletter of the Swiss worker Esperantists directly counseled westerners to contain their curiosity if they wanted to maintain contact with their comrades in the Soviet Union. It would be better if they did not move from 'general questions about technology, literature, or even the weather' to questions about politics or the regime, 'because that could lead to the cessation of correspondence'.[12]

---

[10] The letter, of 20 July 1935, was printed in *Herezulo*, 1936: 11. See also *Herezulo*, 1935: 20; Lanti (1940), pp. 115, 117–19 (four letters to Laval); Valo (=Laval), *Sepdek jaroj sub la verda stelo*, Laroque Timbaut: Cercle espérantiste de l'Agenais, 1980, pp. 49–50.

[11] *Sur Posteno*, 1934: 4.

[12] 'La interkorespondado kun kamaradoj en diktatore regataj landoj', *La Semanto*, 1937, 39 (Oct.): 1.

In truth, it was increasingly apparent in the west that exchanges of letters with the Soviet Union were not working. It was not that the Soviet Esperantists voluntarily stopped writing; several, after a required hiatus, even resumed correspondence, as is shown in a letter from Voronezh dated December 1, 1936, to a Swedish Esperantist:

> In January 1933 I was arrested and condemned to five years in prison because of an arrogant letter addressed to M. Gorky. In September of this year I was freed and returned home. As a prisoner, I worked on the construction of the Moscow-Volga Canal. I have memories of interesting moments from that period, but I'm not ready to risk writing about it. For the above reason, all my Esperanto materials, collected over a period of twenty years, were lost.[13]

In this instance, the occasion of the arrest seems not to have been linked with Esperanto. But we also know of a Swedish Esperantist's similar experience of at about the same time. His Soviet correspondent, who always preferred 'to write about general, day-to-day affairs', suddenly went silent. One day, however, he reappeared. Evidently, he had been condemned to two years in Siberia for what the Swedish Esperantist suspected was his 'only crime', namely, 'his Esperanto correspondence with people in other countries'. Caution no longer helped. These Swedish friends were obliged to conclude that, although 'we avoided all involvement in politics in our letters', correspondence from the Soviet Union was gradually drying up. One of them described a particularly heart-wrenching example of a recent cessation of contact:

> A comrade in our group here recently received a card from Russia. It was from a Russian friend who, while in transit to Siberia, was able to send a secret final greeting to his Swedish friend. The card was almost illegible because, perhaps through the lurching of the train, or numbness in his

---

[13] A copy of this letter was graciously provided by Pelle Persson, Farsta (Sweden). The original, with a Swedish translation, can be consulted at http://www.arbark.se/2004/01/sista-brevet-fran-stalins-sovjet/. The letter was written by Andrei Sidorov, who in December 1927 had called for realistic reporting in *Sennaciulo*. Early in 1956 Sidorov resurfaced—with the information that he knew nothing about the Esperanto movement over the past 18 years: *La Pacdefendanto*, 1956, 50 (Feb.): 4.

fingers, or overpowering emotion, the text was written with such trembling handwriting that it was very hard to make out its contents. Now this Esperantist has gone silent—perhaps forever, perhaps only for a time? To that question we have no response. The Russian government is silent, and Siberia is also silent, about all its victims.[14]

Let us pick out just one month in the most terrible period of the Purges: October 1937. The most active correspondent in Kharkov was Ivan Reznichuk, a factory supervisor. He had 80 contacts in 31 countries. He was arrested in that month. In his NKVD file we read the following note after his arrest:

> [...] he is linked with other countries through correspondence, writes letters to people abroad, doubtless with counterrevolutionary contents, discredits the Soviet regime.[15]

Also in October 1937 the Swiss Esperanto newsletter cautioned against dangerous curiosity, and *Sennaciulo* reported the news from Thomas Aldworth that all his correspondents had gone silent. This was no temporary pause. The silence was, in most cases, forever.

So foreigners had to conclude that their letter-writing relations with Soviet Esperantists would be broken off even if both sides tried to avoid touching on sensitive topics. Caution was no longer useful because in the end the essential problem was not how to correspond but whether to correspond at all.

That that was the problem is evident from the fate of what seems to have been the last significant campaign launched to advance international workers' correspondence through Esperanto. In February 1937 the British Communist Party newspaper, the *Daily Worker*, began to call, under the slogan 'Hands across the Sea', for the linkage of British and Soviet workers through correspondence. The newspaper published addresses of people in the Soviet Union looking for correspondents—addresses delivered in part by the British Workers' Esperanto Association (BLEA). BLEA at once enthusiastically proposed its services for the transmission and translation

---

[14] 'Kio okazas al niaj amikoj en Ruslando?', *Laboristo. Organo por esperantistoj senŝtatanoj* (Stockholm) 3 (1936), 27 (Nov.): 1–2.
[15] Cibulevskij (2001), pp. 58, 67. Reznichuk was freed in 1946.

of letters. Having long undertaken similar work in the context of PEK, the Association saw in the campaign a unique chance to recommend itself to the Party in an indispensable role. In fact, Esperanto was more often used in this correspondence than English, and the *Daily Worker*, which every week published a column with addresses and reports about the state of the campaign, admitted that the success exceeded its expectations.[16]

But in less than a year the campaign was halted—with no public clarification. Aldworth was the first to report on the matter in *Sennaciulo*. On the causes of the cancellation he wrote:

> [...] The correspondence bothered those supervising the flow of letters. Too many insistent questions arrived about conditions, wages, etc., and, as every Esperantist knows, the Russian correspondents write only in generalities. When anyone asks for details, the correspondence stops.[17]

After that, BLEA tried to clarify the matter. It listed the following two causes:

> First, the British Communist Party felt that it had already done enough to set up the correspondence and needed the space for other purposes. Secondly, and more importantly, there is an agreement between the Soviet and English governments that one will not propagandize in the other's country; and the British Party did not want to provide the British reactionaries with a chance to say that the Soviet government had broken the agreement by publishing the letters of Soviet citizens in an English newspaper.[18]

This second argument unintentionally reveals the essence of the matter. It asserts that correspondence equals propaganda, that it has to submit to political considerations and, regardless of its content, interferes with state interests. In other words, the problem is not misuse of correspondence but the correspondence in itself. So the correspondence is a nuisance and needs to be stopped. The argument is quite clear on the matter, and misleading only about the identity of the entity objecting to the correspondence. This was not the British but the Soviet government.

---

[16] *Ruĝa Esperantisto*, 1938, 68 (Jan.): 2.

[17] *Sennaciulo* 14 (1937/38): 43.

[18] E.P. Ockey, in *Sennaciulo* 14 (1937/38): 59. In *Ruĝa Esperantisto*, BLEA's journal, which regularly reported on the campaign, no information was given about its cancellation.

Were the Esperantists, before so many of them disappeared into labor camps, aware of this 'desire' on the part of the Soviet government? This is difficult to establish with concrete facts. As an American researcher was told after the war by a former Soviet citizen, at the end of the 1930s it became known in the Soviet Union that it was dangerous to pursue Esperanto correspondence; Esperanto, he said, had 'silently and quietly' died because private correspondence was no longer possible with Esperantists in Europe and America.[19] In this regard, the experience of the British Communist Esperantist E.A. Evans is noteworthy. In 1937 he forwarded a letter from Kurisu Kei, smuggled out of a Japanese prison, to his correspondent in Kharkov, Abram Klimovsky. Evans himself also exchanged letters with Klimovsky over several months, but: 'Then he told me that he could no longer write to me. Friends of mine who corresponded with other Soviet citizens received similar letters. It seems that the Soviet Esperanto Association advised its members that correspondence with foreigners should stop.'[20] A Hungarian exiled to New York, Ralph Bonesper, who, along with other people from his town, had over 100 correspondents in the Soviet Union before 1937–38, indicated that the contact ended not only because of censorship but because, from that time on, 'it was a hundred per cent (or almost a hundred per cent) forbidden to correspond with foreigners'. He explained that this ban concerned correspondence in all languages, not just Esperanto, though 'Esperanto itself was distinctly disfavored'.[21] Indeed, if correspondence was forbidden, the ban had to hit Esperanto hardest because, as the former Central Committee member of SEU Lucien Laurat pointed out, certainly with little exaggeration,

---

[19] Springer (1956), pp. 14, 32 (quoting a letter from Nicholas Poppe, 23 August 1954).

[20] Kurisu, who was arrested by the Japanese police in May 1937, learned about the affair only after the war, from a letter from Evans, 13 May 1948 (from which our quotation was taken); see Kurisu Kei (T. Kurisu), *Onaji taiyō ga sekai o terashite iru/La sama suno lumigas la mondon*, Kyoto: Kitaōji shobō, 1949, p. 132. Klimovsky was also arrested, but survived: Cibulevskij (2001), pp. 48–9, 62–6.

[21] Letter from Ralph R. Bonesper to Boris I. Sokolov, 30 March 1954, in *Informilo de Esperanto-Koresponda Studrondo* (Tokyo), 1955, 3 (Sept.): 11. The French communist William Gilbert wrote, in 1952, that '95 out of 100 Esperantists in our country were quite certain that a real ban [on the Esperanto movement] existed in the Soviet Union'. He also observed that in communist periodicals 'you never found requests for correspondence, not in Russian, not in French, not in any other language': *La Pacdefendanto*, 1952, 11: 1.

Esperanto was practically the only foreign language by which Soviet workers could easily relate with foreigners.[22]

With that we come to the conclusion that in the years 1937–38 Esperanto ceased to be tolerated because it was an effective instrument by which Soviet citizens could correspond abroad, and such officially supported correspondence had lost favor with the Soviet regime because in all its aspects it contained risks:

- The correspondence did not fulfill its goal of serving the interests of the Soviet Union as these were defined by the Party.
- The letters arriving in the Soviet Union from abroad, at first welcome if they encouraged the builders of socialism, carried too much information about life in the capitalist countries, which instead of producing positive stimulation, invited unfavorable comparisons with the Soviet regime.
- Letters from abroad contained too much nagging curiosity about the actual political and social situation within the Soviet Union, which official propaganda diligently sought to hide.
- It was no longer possible to use the correspondence simply to describe socialist achievements in the Soviet Union. Even organized correspondence resisted complete uniformity because the element of spontaneity could not be eliminated from letters.
- Nor did the idea of correspondence as a hobby give any guarantee against failure to observe taboos, because correspondence, which, in line with the formerly proclaimed principle of the internationalist education of the masses, was regarded as a political instrument, could not be simply reduced to the level of a hobby.

Given that the risks associated with correspondence were overwhelmingly negative, it had to be shut down. Thus the Esperanto movement, which lived by correspondence, lost its right to exist.

The Soviet government never officially explained why it suppressed the Esperanto movement. But an understanding of its motives can be gleaned from Drezen's attempt at analysis, published in 1932:

---

[22] Laurat (1951), p. 85. A German Esperantist noted the following statement by a Soviet officer (an Esperantist) in the eastern zone of Germany: 'The language itself is not banned, only foreign correspondence.' (Sepp Hönig, 'Trans la kurteno', *Heroldo de Esperanto* 25 [1949], 10 [1107]: 1.)

[...] It is evident that the world bourgeoisie is beginning to do everything in its power to prevent the penetration of Esperanto into the working masses. Even a brand-new worker Esperantist, even if he has come to Esperanto through some Catholic or 'non-nationalist' organization, is at risk, with Esperanto's help, of becoming educated, understanding the essence of the class struggle, actively joining in international workers' correspondence, which is entirely in the hands of class conscious proletarians; and thus, as a result, he risks becoming an active, organized opponent of the present social order.[23]

Drezen was correct in his assertion that there were governments that turned against Esperanto because their citizens, with its assistance, risked 'becoming educated' and abandoning the prescribed framework of loyalty. But he could not have foreseen that five years later the same idea would occur to a government to which he himself and thousands of Soviet Esperantists, among them 'class conscious proletarians', showed loyalty to the bitter end (Figs. 5.1–5.9).

Fig. 5.1 E.K. Drezen was the leader of the Soviet Esperantist Union (SEU) for most of its history

---

[23] Ė. Drezen, *Problema mezhdunarodnogo iazyka na tekushchem ėtape ego razvitiia/Problemo de la internacia lingvo en nuna etapo de ĝia evoluo*, Moscow: SEU, 1932, p. 51.

5 Silence Descends 65

Fig. 5.2 Among Soviet Esperanto activists liquidated by the régime was N.V. Nekrasov

Fig. 5.3 V.M. Kolchinsky, also liquidated by the régime

Fig. 5.4 Soviet Esperanto activist R.B. Nikolsky, a victim of the régime

Fig. 5.5 V.V. Varankin, author of the Esperanto novel *Metropoliteno* and Esperanto activist, liquidated by the régime author of the Esperanto novel

Fig. 5.6 Poet E.I. Mikhalsky, liquidated by the régime

Fig. 5.7 I.E. Izgur was persecuted by the Tsarist régime as a communist and liquidated by the Stalinists as an Esperanto activist

Fig. 5.8 Maksim Kriukov, Esperanto activist liquidated by the régime

Fig. 5.9 Shamil Kh. Usmanov, Tatar writer and activist in the SEU, liquidated by the régime

Part II

Esperanto Reborn

6

After the Second World War: The Great Silence in Eastern Europe

With the exception of Czechoslovakia, the Esperanto movement in the eastern European countries between the two world wars found itself in an almost constant struggle against the disapproval or even persecution of the authorities. This was particularly so for workers' Esperanto organizations, often compelled to act semi-legally or operate entirely underground. Later, the Nazi advance completely exterminated Esperanto life in Poland, and in the remaining countries it threatened to extinguish the modest remains of the neutral movement that the right-wing governments were prepared to tolerate. Many Esperantists, particularly in Bulgaria and Yugoslavia, gave their lives in partisan battles against local or foreign fascism.

It is therefore more than understandable that the end of the war lifted a heavy burden from the hearts of many Eastern European Esperantists; the destruction of fascism seemed to signal a new dawn also for the ideal of a common language. Several worker Esperantists, formerly persecuted by the authorities, assumed important functions in the newly established socialist states, where they hoped to create, through these responsible positions, unprecedented opportunities for the Esperanto movement.

Esperanto activities resumed most quickly in Bulgaria. Immediately following the establishment of an anti-fascist government on 9 September 1944, local Esperanto groups were reborn. As early as August 1945, the monthly *Internacia Kulturo* began publication as organ of the Bulgarian Esperantist Association (BEA). In its first issue the editor, Asen Grigorov, a long-time veteran of the workers Esperanto movement,[1] noted with pleasure that 'thanks to the powerful support of the Red Army' the Esperanto groups were once again 'centers of burning cultural life' and that correspondence with neighboring countries, including the Soviet Union, was newly permitted.[2]

The new BEA claimed that the former class-based separation of Esperantists into neutral and workers organizations was no longer necessary; such separation would now bring only divisiveness and so 'would serve only reactionaries'.[3] In their enthusiasm for the new political order, the leaders of the Bulgarian Esperanto movement went even further, suggesting, rather unsettlingly, that anyone who did not support 'the people's government' was 'an enemy of Esperanto':

> [...] if any Esperantist exists who is not also a supporter of the truly democratic F.F. [Fatherland Front] government, he is a supporter of the reactionary fascist regime, a supporter of the idea of liquidating our democratic international language Esperanto as a 'dangerous' language—so he has no right to call himself an Esperantist.[4]

BEA sought to apply, in the international Esperanto movement as well, the same model of a united anti-fascist front that it applied at home. To this end, the association soon turned its attention to coordinating activity among the national associations in the People's Democracies. Beginning with the May–June issue of 1946, *Internacia Kulturo* carried the subtitle 'Cultural Review of the Esperanto Associations of the Balkan

---

[1] From late 1945 Grigorov was for a time secretary to Georgi Dimitrov.
[2] Asen Grigorov, 'Nia kongreso', *Internacia Kulturo* 1 (1945/46), 1: 3.
[3] Nikola Aleksiev, 'El la historio de la laborista Esperanto-movado en Bulgario', *Internacia Kulturo* 1 (1945/46), 7 (Mar. 1946): 12.
[4] M. Conkovski, 'La esperantistoj kaj la balotoj', *Internacia Kulturo* 1 (1945/46), 1 (Aug. 1945): 13.

Countries',⁵ and at the end of August, delegates from Bulgaria, Romania and Yugoslavia met in Asenovgrad for a Balkan Esperanto Conference. On this occasion the International Esperanto League and Universal Esperanto Association were criticized for their 'inconsistently democratic' attitude ('a passive, neutral attitude to fascism and reaction').⁶ Shortly thereafter, in April 1947, after the new UEA was established as a unified organization for the neutral movement, eight national associations⁷ presented to the 32nd World Congress in Berne at the end of July a draft resolution that required that all Esperantists 'ceaselessly and energetically fight against the remnants and the new hotbeds of fascism' ... 'unmask the preparers and provocateurs of new war; actively support all democratic, peaceful trends'.⁸

The resolution was defeated by an approximately three-quarters majority. Even those Esperantists who agreed that, after the experience of fascist hostility against Esperanto, the earlier understanding of neutrality required revision, voted against a resolution that would in practice have tied the Esperanto movement to one side of the incipient Cold War, namely, the politics of the Soviet Union.⁹

The efforts of the Bulgarian and Yugoslav Esperantists to engage in common action for the 'democratization' of UEA were a failure. The failure was due not only to the resistance or disinclination of the majority of Esperantists outside the People's Democracies but also to a basic handicap confronting the East European protagonists of an anti-fascist UEA: the non-existence of a movement in the Soviet Union. In 1947 *Internacia Kulturo* mentioned receipt of a few letters from Soviet Esperantists, but

---

⁵ The associations were initially the Bulgarian, Yugoslav and Romanian organizations. Later they were joined by those of Hungary, Poland, Austria and Czechoslovakia. They appointed representatives to the editorial committee of *Internacia Kulturo*, whose subtitle was changed in September 1948 to 'Cultural and Social Review of the Danube-Region Esperanto Associations'.
⁶ 'Decidoj de la Unua Balkana Esperanto-Konferenco [...]', *Internacia Kulturo* 1 (1945/46), 9/10 (May–June 1946): 20. See also Ivo Lapenna, 'Neŭtraleco kaj "neŭtraleco"', *Internacia Kulturo* 2 (1946/47), 3 (Nov. 1946): 3–5.
⁷ The associations of Yugoslavia, Bulgaria, Romania, Hungary, Czechoslovakia, Poland, Austria and Palestine.
⁸ For details see Lins (2008), p. 82.
⁹ More than 30 years later, Lapenna still expressed pride in the resolution, whose draft he developed, specifying, however, only its homage to the victims of Nazism: *Horizonto* 5 (1980): 23–4.

they evidently did not contain any relevant information,[10] although we now know that from 1940 until 1950 a few Moscow Esperantists met in the home of a courageous woman, Nina Nikiforova, and that in 1943–44, also in Moscow, Mikhail Gishpling taught himself Esperanto, without having the chance to use it until 1957. Also in 1947 news came of obstacles to the Esperanto movement in the Soviet zone of Germany,[11]—news contributing to the negative reaction to the draft resolution in Berne. Even in Communist media outside the People's Democracies unfavorable opinions of Esperanto were voiced, as a French SAT member reported at the beginning of 1947. Referring to various aspects of the attitude of the French Communist Party, for example, lack of permission to organize a course in a district section of the Party in Paris, he let it be known that 'the party authorities are boycotting our activities' because they 'have no wish for the proletarians to maintain free relations with brother workers in other countries'.[12]

The year 1948 brought intensification of the Cold War between the USA and the Soviet Union. In February the Communist Party assumed power in Czechoslovakia, so that now all of Eastern Europe had fallen under the influence of the Soviet Union. The western states were alarmed at the danger of a further Communist advance, all the more so when, in June, the Soviet Union blockaded the land routes between West Berlin and the western zones of Germany. Growing attention in the West in turn persuaded Moscow to solidify its rule over the People's Democracies. At the end of June, Yugoslavia, resisting Soviet oversight, was expelled from the Cominform. To avoid similar disobedience in other countries controlled by a Communist Party, there followed an intense campaign against all real and supposed deviations from the required loyalty to the Soviet Union. In August Władysław Gomułka was driven from his position as first secretary of the party in Poland. As of 1949, a far worse fate befell functionaries in Bulgaria, Hungary, Romania and Czechoslovakia.

As the suffocating atmosphere of Stalinism continued its spread across Eastern Europe, the Esperanto spring in these countries, having barely

---

[10] *Internacia Kulturo* 2 (1946/47), 13/14 (Sept./Oct. 1947): 32.
[11] *Heroldo de Esperanto* 23 (1947), 16 (1075): 2; *Sennaciulo* 18 (1947), 10: 7.
[12] Hector Cachon, 'La komunistoj k Esperanto', *Sennaciulo* 18 (1947), 3: 2.

blossomed, came to an abrupt end. The Esperantists in the eastern region of Germany, who had tried to re-establish their movement, experienced difficulties from the beginning, as an activist in Mecklenburg reported: 'Here [in the eastern zone] we dare not make the first approach to the public because, given the unpredictability of the Russians, we are afraid of disagreeable consequences. Esperanto activity is partly permitted, partly forbidden, depending on the opinion of the commandant.'[13] The situation was totally confusing. In May 1947 the Saxon government banned Esperanto groups. In February and September 1948 decrees allowing activity were published; in October the Berlin administration denied that activity was banned. But up to the end of 1948 the dissolution of local groups increased, and on 12 January 1949 came a decree that left no further doubt: it required the dissolution of 'artificial-language groups' and the immediate cessation of Esperanto columns in the press.[14]

This decree created consternation among the East German Esperantists. They found it not only completely incomprehensible but also 'a powerful attack on personal freedom'.[15] Particularly shocked were the veteran worker Esperantists who had suffered so much during the Nazi period and now were forced to recognize that the victorious Soviet army was disposed to such drastic action. They flooded the SED—the ruling party—with messages of complaint. When the trade union received some 40 protest letters, uncertain how to react to such anger, it turned to the Party for help in providing arguments. The Party was uncompromising, referring to 'a campaign by reactionary forces'. Responding to the protesting Esperantists, the Party called the ban 'a temporary necessity', as if carried out to prevent the misuse of Esperanto by international organizations, but internally it alluded to the 'political danger' that 'many fascist elements have attached themselves [to it] in search of ideological refuge'.[16]

---

[13] Speech of Gustav Streblow in a conference in Stralsund, 16 October 1948; cf. Hans-Joachim Borgwardt, 'Zwischen Verbot und Misstrauen', *Esperanto aktuell* 11 (1992), 3: 12–13.
[14] *Zentralverordnungsblatt* (Berlin), 1949, 7 (10 Feb.): 67–8.
[15] Letter from ten Esperantists to the board of FDGB (Free Trade Union Federation), 1 May 1949, Bundesarchiv, SAPMO, DY 34/1228.
[16] Note on a telephone conversation with Kaufmann, SED, 10 May 1949, Bundesarchiv, SAPMO, DY 34/1228; letter from the Control Commission to five Esperantists, 20 May 1949, Bundesarchiv, SAPMO, DY 30/IV 2/4/25, fol. 84.

Even though they lacked full knowledge of these offensive internal judgments, the Esperantists vented their anger. One wrote to the Cultural League to the effect that throughout the history of Esperanto repression, it had always been based only on political motives and that 'the opponents of Esperanto, in spite of their assurances of peace are in fact not in the least interested in international collaboration on the basis of equal rights'.[17] Nothing changed after the founding of the German Democratic Republic (7 October 1949). Protest letters continued to arrive, the party leadership naming them attacks by 'Esperanto fanatics' who would do better to direct their energies to establishing courses in Russian, and defending the decree as necessary because of the 'anti-Soviet effect' that 'American propaganda has already had among all life- and language-reform groups'.[18] In January 1950 a district party committee asserted that 'today Esperanto is exclusively used by Tito for activities undermining the [people's] democratic countries'.[19] The bitterness of the Esperantists is well illustrated by a letter that one of them wrote to the Party Control Commission:

> Nothing surprises me anymore. We must accept that *our* country, along with fascist Portugal, is the only one that bans Esperanto. My thoughts are clear. As Hitler, Mussolini, Franco and the rest were not interested in having workers of all nations understand one another with the help of an easily acquired interlanguage, so, here, we also have no interest. We are not being told the truth. [...] They can talk about discipline and so on all they like. That no longer touches me. [...] It's impossible that anyone could be so stupid as to not want to understand how important we Esperantists might be in the battle against the USA imperialism [...]. But much as in the 12-year Reich it proved impossible to exterminate the idea of Marxism-Leninism, so today they cannot exterminate the Esperantists.[20]

---

[17] Letter from Gustav Streblow, 29 September 1949 (copy provided by Hans-Joachim Borgwardt, Stralsund, 7 July 1992).
[18] Board of SED to board of FDGB, 6 January 1950, Bundesarchiv, SAPMO, DY 34/1228.
[19] Letter of 18 January 1950, Bundesarchiv, SAPMO, DY 30/IV 2/4/25, fol. 153. Cf. Frank Hirschinger, *'Gestapoagenten, Trotzkisten, Verräter'. Kommunistische Parteisäuberungen in Sachsen-Anhalt 1918–1953*, Göttingen: Vandenhoeck & Ruprecht, 2005, p. 269.
[20] Letter from Walter Dietze, 25 March 1950, Bundesarchiv, SAPMO, DY 30/IV 2/4/25, fol. 43; cf. Hirschinger, pp. 270–1.

6 After the Second World War: The Great Silence in Eastern...

Under the circumstances it was almost progress when the Ministry of Internal Affairs, putting aside ideological accusations, stressed in October 1950 that because of historical developments since 1945 an artificial language no longer had the same significance as it did before 1933.[21]

In Romania too the renewed blossoming of the movement was short-lived. In 1947 the Romanian Esperantists joyfully reported on a 'historical moment'. They were referring to the fact that the Romanian Esperanto Society, founded in 1907, had just acquired recognition as a legal entity for the first time.[22] But in the following year a 'profound silence' descended on Romania[23] and not until January 1990 could the Society be re-established.

It was the turn of the Bulgarians. Ominous signs came in the form of intensified efforts by the BEA to discipline its membership. In August 1948 its youth section demanded 'the definitive annihilation of the senseless ideas still alive in some Esperantists of "a new feeling" [*nova sento*], "the internal idea" [*interna ideo*] or some special divine mission for Esperanto'.[24] A year later came the eventful summer of 1949. In early July Georgi Dimitrov died; in September Bulgaria was forced to break its contract of friendship with Yugoslavia. The 32nd Bulgarian Esperanto Congress, to take place in Vratsa from 21 to 23 August, was canceled at the last moment.[25] *Internacia Kulturo* was obliged to strike the Yugoslav members from its editorial committee, among them Ivo Lapenna.[26]

At around the same time the Hungarians also experienced a disagreeable change in their external circumstances. After the war their activity began under similarly promising circumstances to those of the Bulgarians. In the spring of 1948 the education minister permitted the teaching of Esperanto as an optional subject in elementary schools, as a result of

---

[21] State Secretary Hans Warnke to the Cultural League, 11 October 1950 (copy provided by H.J. Borgwardt).
[22] 'La movado en Rumanio', *Internacia Kulturo* 2 (1946/47), 11/12 (July/Aug. 1947): 17.
[23] *Heroldo de Esperanto* 25 (1949), 6 (1103): 4.
[24] N. Nikolov, '3-a konferenco de la Junulara Fako ĉe Bulgara Esperanto-Asocio', *La Estonto Esperantista*, 1948, 6 (Oct.): 44; cf. 'Niaj pozicioj', *Internacia Kulturo* 5 (1950), 1/2: 25.
[25] Ivan Sarafov, *Skizo de la historio de bulgara Esperanto-movado*, Sofia: Bulgara Esperantista Asocio, p. 37.
[26] They appeared for the last time in the August number of 1949.

which 104 Members of Parliament, among them 34 Communists, supported extending the decree to middle schools as well.[27] At a conference of delegates of Danube-region Esperanto associations in Budapest in July, the delegates heard encouraging words from party and government representatives and solemn promises for the further support of the movement. The president of the Hungarian Parliament, Imre Nagy, declared that 'Esperanto must rise above the life of a sect and must be disseminated among the broader levels of the population',[28] while Mátyás Rákosi, the party leader, said, during a reception of conference delegates, that he did not need interpretation because he himself had once learned Esperanto.[29]

Only a few months later the optimism disappeared. A membership meeting of the Hungarian Esperanto Society (HES) noted in early 1949 that the movement 'finds itself in crisis' because it 'has not established for itself a program identical with the interests of the nation'. In a fashion already observed in Bulgaria, the blame was attributed to the ideological backwardness of the members, who, as a result, were exhorted 'to put aside useless neutralist politics' and 'give up their ideas of pacifism'.[30] The further stages in the development of the Hungarian movement ran parallel to the Stalinist purge in the party. In May 1949, László Rajk, Minister of Foreign Affairs, was arrested for 'nationalist deviation' and 'spying for imperialism'; the journal *Literatura Mondo*, rich in tradition, revived in 1947, ceased publication with its July–August issue, officially 'because of financial obstacles'[31]; and in October, the month of Rajk's execution, the Esperanto broadcasts of Radio Budapest were discontinued. On 6 April 1950 the last committee meeting of HES took place. A proposal was presented to the 15 people present that the society 'temporarily interrupt its activity'. After intense discussion a vote was taken: 10 accepted the proposal, one opposed it and one abstained.[32] So began a period which the Hungarians later called 'The Great Silence'.

---

[27] *Heroldo de Esperanto* 24 (1948), 7 (1085): 1; *Internacia Kulturo* 3 (1948), 8: 11.
[28] *Internacia Kulturo* 3 (1948), 10: 19.
[29] 'Danubregiona Esperanto Konferenco en Budapest', *Internacia Kulturo* 3 (1948), 8: 12.
[30] 'Landa kunsido de HES', *Hungara Esperantisto* 4 (1949), 1 (Jan./March): 5–6 (quotation p. 5).
[31] *Sennaciulo* 21 (1950), 2 (537): 7. At the same time *Hungara Esperantisto* also ceased publication.
[32] 'Ĝustigo', *Hungara Esperantisto* 7 (1967), 3: 15.

The longest resistance to suppression came from Czechoslovakia. Between the two world wars the Esperanto movement in Czechoslovakia was among the strongest in Europe. It was never hit with persecution, except during the Nazi occupation. As a result, when the ruling power in this country—a country that had experienced true functioning democracy—was transferred to the Communist Party, it had an effect on the Esperanto movement quite different from that in, for example, Bulgaria and Hungary. Because a strong workers' Esperanto movement was missing, under the new political regime the leadership of the movement remained in the hands of representatives of the neutral movement. Thus it was the task of the already established board of the Esperanto Association in the Czechoslovakian Republic (EAĈSR) to adapt its work for Esperanto to the changing political circumstances. During the first year under Communist rule it seemed that the traditionally favorable attitude of the authorities would continue. The Ministry for Information and Education supported the publication of a propaganda magazine, *Esperanto-Servo*, dispatched abroad in several thousand copies.[33]

On the other hand, as of the end of 1948, it was no longer possible to send money abroad for individual membership in UEA or to purchase Esperanto books.[34] Soon EAĈSR also felt obliged to emphasize its loyalty to the regime more explicitly, which resulted—along the lines already observed in the other People's Democracies—in insistent calls by the leadership for ideological conformity among the members. These calls were directed not only against the traditional 'neutralism' but also against the ideas of SAT, which a considerable number of worker Esperantists supported. At the beginning of June 1949 a resolution accepted during the Seventh Czechoslovakian Esperanto Congress in Liberec proclaimed the Esperantists should 'pitilessly unmask nests of reaction and fascism and bring along with us those who are fixated on "Esperanto for Esperanto's sake"' that is, those 'who make of Esperanto a mere amusement'. At the same time the resolution attacked 'a tendency of

---

[33] This 'current information bulletin from Prague' (*aktuala informa bulteno el Praha*), as its subtitle read, began publication in October 1948. It was edited by the president of EAĈSR, Adolf Malík, who also assumed the function of supervisor of the Esperanto subsection at the Ministry of Information and Education.

[34] *Esperantista* 4 (1949): 4.

the international capitalist reactionaries to misuse the world Esperantist movement for deceitful imperialist aims hidden under the false device of cosmopolitanism'.[35] To the members of SAT, who themselves had always disapproved of the use of Esperanto for 'personal goals', it was clear that the attack on 'cosmopolitanism' was aimed at them. Rudolf Burda, a veteran of SAT, noted bitterly that 'the rigidly neutral ladies and gentlemen' who until February 1948 'collected pretty stamps and insulted us as "communist Esperantists"' are now denouncing the members of SAT as 'cosmopolitan and anti-state' to demonstrate their fidelity to the regime.[36]

For a time it seemed that the opportunism of the former 'neutralists' would be enough to guarantee the continued existence of the movement. At the end of May 1950, the Eighth Czechoslovakian Congress in Brno attracted a record number of almost 1000 participants. But in that same year the Czechoslovak movement suffered two blows: on 17 September, exactly five years after they started, the popular Esperanto broadcasts of Radio Prague were discontinued,[37] and at the end of 1950 EAĈSR cancelled its affiliated membership with UEA because UEA 'is too clearly influenced by reactionary imperialist politics and by Titoism'.[38]

In the second half of 1951 the Stalinist infiltration of the political life of Czechoslovakia reached a climax. In September Rudolf Slánský, general secretary of the Communist Party of Czechoslovakia, was expelled from the Party; in November he was arrested under the no longer original charge of serving as a hidden agent of imperialism and Titoism.[39] At the end of the year the Czechoslovakian Esperanto periodicals had to cease publication. At this point EAĈSR was already in a state of disarray. At a meeting

---

[35] *Esperantista* 4 (1949): 42; *Internacia Kulturo* 4 (1949), 8: 14.

[36] R. Burda, 'Pri la Ĉehosl. neŭtralaj esperantistoj', *Sennaciulo* 21 (1950), 7 (542): 7. See also *Sennaciulo* 22 (1951), 6 (553): 2.

[37] *Esperantista* 5 (1950): 62.

[38] Adolf Malík, 'Sur novan vojon!', *Esperantista* 6 (1951): 2. The letters from EAĈSR to UEA, 31 December 1950 (declaration of resignation) and 5 May 1951, indicated, as the main reason for the decision to disaffiliate, the refusal of UEA to work 'actively' for peace. See also 'Eksiĝo de E.A.Ĉ.S.R.', *Esperanto* 44 (1951): 130–1. An article in *Esperantisto Slovaka* (6 [1951]: 1) confessed that the decision was made 'with a heavy heart', reminding readers, among other things, of 'the sympathy shown by UEA to ĈSR during the German-Nazi occupation'. The resignation occurred on the advice of the Ministry for Foreign Affairs, orally conveyed by Malík: Kamarýt (1983), p. 177.

[39] In December 1952 Slánský was executed.

of the Central Committee of the Communist Party of Czechoslovakia in July 1952, the Association's delegates were obliged to take note of the recommendation 'not to propagandize and not to teach Esperanto, even if it helps in the battle for peace and socialism, because the peoples understand one another in these matters and are equally united without an international language'. The representative of the Party further noted 'the dangerous nature of Esperanto' because it facilitated subversive activity by class enemies.[40] On 19 August the Ministry of Internal Affairs voiced an order that EAĈSR should 'voluntarily' liquidate itself.[41] On 6 September the Association's committee met in extraordinary session. The majority (23 votes) yielded; 18 abstained. Rudolf Burda and two others voted against the self-liquidation of EAĈSR, preferring to await its compulsory dissolution.[42]

The feelings shared by probably the majority of Czechoslovakian Esperantists after the liquidation of their association were expressed by one of their number in the following terms:

> If it weren't a fact that it happened, I would not believe it! Never in my life had I imagined that there would come a time when the Esperanto movement would be liquidated—by a socialist government.[43]

Esperanto in Czechoslovakia was no longer wanted—not even to publicize abroad the work of a 'national hero': the Esperanto translation of *Notes from the Gallows* by the Czech Communist Julius Fučík, executed by the Nazis, was already fully typeset in 1951 but, under the pressure of the authorities, never reached book form.[44]

---

[40] R Burda, 'Uzu fiakriston, ĉar aŭtomobilo estas burĝa', *La Pacdefendanto*, 1952, 8 (Aug.): 3.

[41] 'Ĉu la batalo fin[iĝ]is', *La Pacdefendanto*, 1952, 10 (Oct.): 1.

[42] *La Pacdefendanto*, 1952, 10 (Oct.): 1–2; cf. Kamarýt (1983) pp. 177–8.

[43] Letter from Hejda, *La Pacdefendanto*, 1952, 11: 4.

[44] Also, EAĈSR planned to publish a book on the Nazi atrocities in the village of Lidice; it, too, did not appear 'because of technical difficulties': *La Pacdefendanto*, 1952, 5: 5. The translation of Fučík's *Notes from the Gallows* appeared only in 1979, under the title *Riporto skribita en la pendumila maŝo*; cf. Kurisu (2010), p. 77.

Czechoslovakia was the last of the European People's Democracies to adopt the Soviet model also regarding the Esperanto movement.[45] When the life of EAĈSR came to an end, there remained only one country in the Soviet sphere of influence that was for the moment spared from the wave of disapproval of Esperanto: the Chinese People's Republic. In Beijing in March 1951, in the presence of government representatives, the Chinese Esperanto League (ĈEL) was founded, with the veteran Esperantist Hu Yuzhi as its president. As head of the Publishing Administration, Hu was able, in a little more than six months after the founding of the Chinese People's Republic, to arrange for the Foreign Language Publishing House to begin publishing a monthly magazine in Esperanto, *El Popola Ĉinio*. For some time it was the only Esperanto-language periodical by which the Esperantists of Eastern Europe could satisfy their urge to read; in Czechoslovakia the magazine had around a thousand subscribers. At the end of 1953, however, when the post offices in the German Democratic Republic refused to accept the Chinese journal because of its 'undesirable propaganda for cosmopolitanism',[46] it ceased to appear, and its publishers chose to send its former subscribers in the People's Democracies (and even the USA) the equivalent magazine in the Russian language.[47]

As in the Soviet Union, and therefore in all the countries at that time regarded as its satellites, the Esperantists lost all possibility of public activity. However, the suppression of Esperanto was not absolute in the communist bloc; it varied from country to country. In Romania and Hungary the movement was almost completely blocked. In Bulgaria the situation was no better. Its print run already reduced, in 1950 the journal *Internacia Kulturo* stopped production after publishing a further four issues[48]; in the spring of 1952 the Esperanto broadcasts of Radio Sofia were also terminated.[49] But the Bulgarian Esperanto Cooperative could, if only

---

[45] In Albania no action was taken against Esperanto because there was no Esperanto movement there.

[46] *TKKE Informas*, 1956, 2: 3 (supplement to *Bulteno de Esperantista Klubo ĉe Osvětová beseda en Praha* 2 [1956], 34/35 [Jan./Feb.]).

[47] Letter from Ralph R. Bonesper to Boris I. Sokolov, 30 March 1954, in *Informilo de Esperanto-Koresponda Studrondo* (Tokyo), 1955, no. 3 (Sept.): 10.

[48] After a break of over a year, in January 1952 one further issue of *Internacia Kulturo* was published, definitively the last.

[49] *Heroldo de Esperanto* 28 (1952), 7 (1159): 4.

modestly, continue to function. In the German Democratic Republic, despite severe oversight by the authorities, many Esperantists met in secret, organized communal excursions to practice the language and kept contact with Esperantists in the Federal Republic and other countries by the exchange of letters.[50] The Czechoslovakian Esperantists were relatively fortunate because they were able to function at the local level under the umbrella of educational or trade union clubs. A subtle form of recruitment for Esperanto were exhibitions where material obtained through the language reported on strikes in the West; Esperantists also organized the collection of money for persecuted peace activists in capitalist countries, for example, Japan. Stenciled bulletins appeared semi-legally,[51] the most remarkable being the bulletin *La Pacdefendanto*, appearing in Plzeň as of January 1952 and edited by Rudolf Burda. Its significance was later felt also beyond the borders of Czechoslovakia.[52]

Less strict were the limits in Poland. Although the Esperanto broadcasts of Polish Radio ceased in August 1950 and one after the other the local groups were liquidated (of 30 such groups, only those in Warsaw and Wrocław remained), the Association of Esperantists in Poland (AEP) retained its office and published, in the form of 'exercise material for a correspondence course', a very modest-looking newsletter, *Tra la Mondo kaj Literaturo*. But AEP was not allowed to publish paid announcements of its correspondence course and only on the occasion of the anniversary of the death of Zamenhof two Warsaw journals published paid obituaries framed in black, announcing a meeting at the grave of the creator of that language which was now almost anathema in its own country.[53]

---

[50] P.G. (Paul Glöckner), 'Raporto el Saksio', *Heroldo de Esperanto* 29 (1953), 17 (1187): 2; Ewald Ebmeier, 'Esperanto vivas malantaŭ la Fera Kurteno', *Esperanto-Post* 6 (1953): 113, 124.

[51] Details of the youth bulletins and related activity: Kamarýt (1983), pp. 88–9, 179–83.

[52] See pp. 108–111.

[53] 'Al niaj legantoj', *Pola Esperantisto* 37 (1957), 1 (Sept./Oct.): 1; I. Dratwer, 'Strato Marszałkowska 81', *Pola Esperantisto* 42 (1962), 5/6 (Sept./Dec.): 13; letter from Isaj Dratwer, *Esperanto* 61 (1968): 85.

7

Stalin Against Marr

Around the same time as the Esperanto movement was silenced in the People's Democracies, a debate on linguistic questions was launched in the Soviet Union that attracted considerable attention also in the West. On 9 May 1950 *Pravda* began publication of a series of articles on the situation of Soviet linguistics, in which, surprisingly, the Japhetic theory of Marr was strongly criticized. On 20 June, quite unexpectedly, Stalin himself entered the discussion, raising what was at first sight a purely linguistic dispute to the highest political levels.

Stalin was clearly partisan—against Marr; he disapproved of the essential principles of Marr's 'new teaching'. While, for Marr, language—like art—was a category in the ideological superstructure and all changes in language depended on changes in the economy, Stalin denied that language belonged to the superstructure. For him, language was something independent and more durable than superstructure or base. Against Marr's position that language is always a class language and that there is no national language uniting the various classes in a society, Stalin insisted on the existence of a unifying national language; the language of an entire people was barely influenced by the individual classes, and it would be unhelpful if the class struggle limited linguistic unity. The Soviet leader, then, pulled language out of the scheme of base and superstructure, attributed to it a class-transcending character and accented its significance as an instrument linking society through many centuries and epochs. Stalin explained that language serves both bourgeois and socialist culture, constituting the unchanging national *form* of the changing cultural *content*. In other words, the interest of nation ranks above that of class.

The implications of the break with Marr's theory were particularly clear on the matter of the future unifying language of humanity. In 1930, Stalin—much like Marr—asserted that in the era of communism the national languages would meld into a single common language which 'will be neither Great Russian nor German, but something new'. But now, 20 years later, Stalin wrote in *Pravda* that it would be 'quite wrong to think that the crossing of, say, two languages results in a new, third language which does not resemble either of the languages crossed and differs qualitatively from both of them'. In fact, 'one of the languages usually emerges victorious from the cross [...] while the other language [...] gradually dies away'. By this prognosis, language development is not such that the various languages 'flower' equally and mutually enrich one another, finally flowing together in a united language; that was what Stalin proclaimed in 1930. Now a new principle applied, namely, that whenever languages meet, there is always a battle, ending only with conquest or defeat. Stalin gave an example of the victory of one language over another:

> Such was the case, for instance, with the Russian language, with which, in the course of historical development, the languages of a number of other peoples crossed and which always emerged the victor.

In this process the vocabulary of Russian was enriched, but its 'specific national individuality [...] did not suffer in the slightest'.[1]

Stalin's initiative against Marr, whose authority as the creator of a new, materialistic science of language had until then seemed untouchable, created a sensation both inside and outside the Soviet Union. Among those noting Marr's dethronement with particular interest were the Esperantists.

---

[1] J.V. Stalin, *Marxism and Problems of Linguistics*, Peking: Foreign Languages Press, 1972, p. 28.

Because Esperanto-language studies had, both earlier and again in 1950, asserted proximity between the teaching of Marr and the aims of the Esperanto movement,[2] there seemed to be a connection between Stalin's articles in *Pravda* and the difficulties that Esperantists faced in the countries under Soviet influence. However, in truth the Eastern European Esperantists were already deprived of organization, or anticipated that such a fate awaited them, long before Stalin intervened in the linguistic debate. A general guideline to the effect that all state support for the Esperanto movement should end was probably decided in the autumn of 1949 at the latest—more than six months before the discussion in the columns of *Pravda* began. When on 2 October 1949 Lajos Kökény arrived in the studio of Radio Budapest as usual, he was informed that the station would no longer broadcast in Esperanto. 'From now on, that's the line', he was told.[3]

This 'new line' was not a precursor of the attack on the Marrists. On the contrary, precisely in mid-1949 the short period marked by tentative attempts to break out of the increasingly confining frame of Japhetic theory came to an end. As early as October 1948, Marr's disciples reinforced their position, launching an attack on deviators. They accused colleagues in the field, who, for example, argued for a revival of the comparative method in linguistics, of being under the influence of 'reactionary and idealistic currents of foreign bourgeois linguistics'. By occasional allusions to the dispute with Iazykfront in the early 1930s, the Marrists indicated that they aimed—as on that previous occasion—to reassert their monopoly on Soviet linguistics, and in fact on 21 July 1949 the Academy of Sciences issued an official declaration confirming the continued exclusive validity of the theories of Marr.[4]

Is it mere chance that Esperanto lost favor in the East European countries precisely when the Marrists occupied a dominant position similar to that in the mid-1930s, enjoying full official support and having

---

[2] See my summary presentation 'Stalin kontraŭ Marr: la sekvoj por Esperanto', in I. Stalin, *Marksismo kaj lingvoscienco*, trans. Aleksander Korĵenkov, Ekaterinburg: Sezonoj, 1992, pp. 3–6. A good overview is provided by Moret (2005), pp. 205–7.
[3] Lajos Kökény, 'Esperanto en Hungario, 1945–1949', *Hungara Vivo* 10 (1970), 2: 19.
[4] Lawrence L. Thomas, 'Some notes on the Marr school', *The American Slavic and East European Review* 16 (1957): 323–48 (esp. p. 347); Slezkine (1996), p. 856; Smith (1998), pp. 81–102.

just overcome their critics? It was one of the leading Marrists, Timofei Lomtev,⁵ who declared at the beginning of 1949:

> The current apologists of imperialism are engaging in intense propaganda for cosmopolitanism, a reactionary ideology of the imperialist bourgeoisie. They are using as an ideological weapon the ideas of the renegade Kautsky concerning ultra-imperialism, the blending of the nations and their languages in the period of capitalism and imperialism and the creation, in the present era, of a single universal language.⁶

The Bulgarian Esperantist Atanas Lakov attempted to adapt himself to this line, writing in December 1949:

> [...] The future common language of communism leads by way of the development of national languages under socialism. Efforts to remove national languages by inserting Esperanto will result only in cultural decline for the nations that are suppressed under capitalism. An effort to impose Esperanto as a universal language in the present, in its now largely European form, would represent the forced liquidation of the cultures and languages of the peoples outside Europe and signify the establishment of Esperanto as a tool of imperialist exploitation.⁷

What ought to be the language policy in the present time had already been proclaimed by Soviet linguists and writers before the initiative of Stalin against Marr. In its New Year issue of 1949 *Literaturnaia gazeta* repeated what *Pravda* had written in 1938: To each historical era a single 'world language' can be assigned—to ancient times Latin, to the feudal era French, to the capitalist era English and, finally, to the era of socialism, Russian.⁸ The Academician Nikolai Iakovlev explained in

---

⁵ Lomtev was formerly a member of Iazykfront.
⁶ T.P. Lomtev, 'I.V. Stalin o razvitii natsional'nykh iazykov v ėpokhu sotsializma' (J.V. Stalin on the development of national languages in the socialist era), *Voprosy filosofii*, 1949, no. 2; quoted from Laurat (1951), pp. 80–1.
⁷ A. Lakov, 'Josif Visarionoviĉ Stalin', *Internacia Kulturo* 4 (1949), 12: 3–4 (quotation p. 4).
⁸ David Zaslavskii, 'Velikii iazyk nashei ėpokhi' (The great language of our era), *Literaturnaia gazeta*, 1 January 1949; quoted from Kucera (1954), p. 25. Cf. 'Ekspansio de la rusa lingvo', *Sennaciulo* 21 (1950), 2 (537): 7.

November 1949 that the long-term perspective is already present because the Russian language 'is not only the language of the USSR but also the international language of the People's Democracies'.[9] And Lomtev took a further step, naming the Russian language 'the instrument of the most advanced civilization, of socialist civilization, of the most progressive science' and 'the language of peace and progress'.[10]

Praise of the Russian language, which began in the mid-1930s and culminated in the 1940s, in no way fit the ideas of Marr, for whom every language was formed by class and not by nation. Marr always refused to treat languages ('so-called national languages') as units, as national legacies, but considered them a combination of various class languages or remnants of such languages. As he saw it, with economic and political progress and the disappearance of class differences these languages would intermingle and, finally, in the worldwide classless society, yield their place to an entirely new, universal language. That left no possibility that one of the present languages would emerge victorious from a battle of languages. On the contrary, Marr lauded his own theory because it 'gives equal consideration to all languages' and 'shatters the pseudoscientific, ideological principle of the autocracy of the Russian language'.[11]

Despite Marr's view, the Soviet Union under Stalin followed a policy of Russification. The Japhetic theory, still the leading school in Soviet linguistics, had to serve that policy, regardless of the policy's distance from the original ideas of Marr (who died in 1934). If the Marrists had not obediently cast themselves as instruments of the regime from the beginning, they would have been quickly prevented from drawing conclusions from their theories that ran counter to the politics of the Party.

But finally Stalin understood—admittedly late—that to justify a policy that systematically favored a national language, Russian, and utilized a national tradition, the Russian tradition, with the goal of forging Soviet patriotism, it was no longer appropriate to rely on Marrist theory.[12] The Marrists' counteroffensive of 1948–49 probably provided this

---

[9] *Vestnik Akademii Nauk SSSR*, 1950, no. 2; quoted from Laurat (1951), p. 80.
[10] Quoted from Laurat, p. 73.
[11] Quoted from Kucera (1954), p. 27.
[12] Cf. Smith (1998), pp. 164–73; Valerii Grechko, 'Mezhdu utopiei i "Realpolitik". Marr, Stalin i vopros o vsemirnom iazyke' (Between utopia and 'Realpolitik'. Marr, Stalin, and the problem of a

new opening. Their attacks on the use of traditional linguistic methods, particularly their refusal to accept the traditions of bourgeois Russian linguistics, was an almost heretical act if we consider that at the same time the state propaganda machinery was giving prominence to everything Russian and to the continuity of Russian science. Accordingly, Stalin personally intervened, encouraged by the leader of the Party in Georgia, Kandid Charkviani, to whom the linguist Arnold Chikobava had turned with complaints about Marr.[13] Using his authority as the highest leader of the Party, Stalin decreed that language was not a class phenomenon and not a part of the superstructure. In support of his view, he pointed out that from the time of Pushkin the Russian language had remained unchanged 'in all essentials', serving as a common national language for all classes in the progression through feudal, capitalist and socialist eras.

Removal of the tension between Marr's theories and the Great-Russian coloration of all-Soviet patriotism was not the only motive causing Stalin to mount the stage of linguistic science. The fact that Soviet linguistics had been so dependent on Japhetic theory had produced a host of negative phenomena. This dependency had retarded more effective language teaching in schools, caused stagnation in Russian philology and, through rejection of the comparative method, impeded historical research on the relationship of Russian and the other Slavic languages. But, however useful it was to saddle the Marrists with the blame for all omissions and errors in Soviet linguistics, the significance of Stalin's verdict against Marr lay primarily in the fact that it removed one of the last remnants of the revolutionary romanticism dating from the pioneer period of the Soviet state. The way was open for the uninterrupted development of the 'great Russian language'.

This judgment of Stalin's motives also is not altered by the fact that in the course of the linguistic debate Stalin relativized his idea of a 'victorious' language. As his response to Comrade A. Kholopov, published in *Pravda* on 2 August 1950, shows, he was asked about the reconcilability of that thesis with his formulation of 1930. Stalin denied that there was a contradiction. Just as, back then, when he was reminded about his

---

world language), *Russian Linguistics* 34 (2010): 159–72.
[13] Pollock (2009), p. 112.

earlier (in 1925) disapproval of the prognosis of Kautsky, Stalin 'solved' the contradiction by declaring that he was making a distinction between the different eras to which his remarks applied, so now, the idea of the victory of a stronger language related, as Stalin explained, to the period before the worldwide victory of socialism—'when the conditions necessary for the peaceful and friendly co-operation of nations and languages are as yet lacking; when it is not the co-operation and mutual enrichment of languages that are on the order of the day, but the assimilation of some and the victory of other languages'.

Under such conditions there could only be winning and losing languages. The situation would be quite different in the era following the victory of socialism on a worldwide scale, namely, 'when the cooperation of nations has been established, and it is possible for national languages freely to enrich one another through their cooperation'. At that point, what Stalin meant in his declaration of 1930 could finally come about, namely, the melding of the languages into a single common language. In the era of socialism it would no longer be a matter of winners and losers:

> Here we shall have not two languages, one of which is to suffer defeat, while the other is to emerge from the struggle victorious, but hundreds of national languages, out of which, as a result of a prolonged economic, political and cultural cooperation of nations, there will first appear most enriched unified zonal languages, and subsequently the zonal languages will merge into a single international language, which, of course, will be neither German, nor Russian, nor English, but a new language that has absorbed the best elements of the national and zonal languages.[14]

Once again returning to the question of world revolution, Stalin nonetheless did not resolve the following contradiction: How could the peaceful melding of languages occur if beforehand they were locked in battle?

---

[14] Stalin, *Marxism and Problems of Linguistics*, p. 51. The thesis concerning the formation of 'zonal languages' (regional languages) as a preparatory step to the creation of the world language had already appeared in Stalin's article 'The National Question and Leninism' (*Works*, vol. 11, p. 364). This article was published in 1949, with a note that Stalin wrote it in 1929. This seems hardly credible when we consider the fact that in his Congress speech of 1930 he made no mention of zonal languages (cf. Thomas, 'Some notes', p. 343, note 77).

The answer is that Stalin was not much interested in what would happen in the distant future. His primary intention was to offer a theoretical justification for the current course of events in the Soviet Union. Accordingly, he condemned the internationalist doctrine of Marr, accented the class-transcendent role of Russian and named the marginalization of smaller languages a sign of historical progression. His statement about a future world language, in the meantime, seems almost an afterthought.[15] With the phrase 'on a worldwide scale' he avoided having his prophecy compared with present reality in the Soviet Union, in which (unlike the rest of the world) socialism was already victorious and 'the mutual distrust of nations' was long since liquidated. In fact, Stalin's anticipation of a future postnational world language seems almost irrelevant in the context of his linguistic ideas because it could lead to the conclusion that the Russian language would not achieve a 'final victory'. It would be more likely that the Russian language, steadily victorious in the battles of the past and now serving the peoples of the Soviet Union as a uniting force, would continue its conquests, enlarging its territory also beyond the Soviet Union and, as a powerful regional language, having a major influence on the future world language.[16] This interpretation of the role assigned to Russian is supported by the fact that in the People's Democracies the language was being touted as the international language of socialism and that Soviet linguists were polemicizing furiously against English, the language of 'Anglo-American imperialism'.[17]

Outside Stalin's consideration remained the question of why, in the conditions of trust prevailing among the peoples of the Soviet Union, the Russian language should expand its sphere of usage at the cost of other languages and why work for the preparation of a future transnational language should not proceed. Stalin himself never clearly discussed whether the process of linguistic unification might somehow be accelerated, but

---

[15] Cf. Ernst Nolte, *Deutschland und der Kalte Krieg*, Munich & Zürich: Piper, 1974, p. 342.

[16] As early as 1945, the linguist Viktor Vinogradov openly declared that the privileged position of Russian in the Soviet Union 'is creating suitable conditions which, in the future, will shorten the path to one single language for all mankind': V.V. Vinogradov, *Velikii russkii iazyk* (The great Russian language), Moscow: OGIZ, 1945; quoted from Kucera (1954), p. 29.

[17] Edward F. James, 'Soviet linguistic policy and the international language movement', *International Language Review* 1 (1955), 1 (Oct./Dec.): 6–16 (esp. p. 12); Goodman (1970), pp. 723–4.

his compatriot, the aforementioned Chikobava, who with Stalin's support had launched the discussion in his May article in *Pravda*, did so. Criticizing Marr, he directed his argument to Marr's theory of a common language for future humanity. At first sight, wrote Chikobava, Marr seemed in agreement with Marxist-Leninism, but in fact, even here, his position was 'incorrect, non-Marxist'. Citing Marr's assertion that 'mankind, proceeding toward economic unity and a classless community, cannot help applying artificial means, scientifically worked out, in order to accelerate this broad process', Chikobava referred to earlier statements by Stalin:

> As is known, Marxists understand this matter differently. They hold that the process of withering away of national languages and the formation of a single common world language will take place gradually, without any 'artificial means' invoked to 'accelerate' this process. The application of such 'artificial means' would mean the use of coercion against nations, and this Marxism cannot permit.[18]

Although Chikobava's main intention may have been to shift blame to the Marrists for shortcomings in the alphabetization and standardization of non-Russian languages in the Soviet Union, the thesis, which he condemned as 'non-Marxist', was in fact an essential point in the teachings of Marr—one that the Esperantists had used in Marxist circles to justify their activities.

The fact that Stalin spoke of a future postnational world language evoked among the harried Esperantists in the People's Democracies the hope that Esperanto could be considered a kind of 'trial version of the world language anticipated by Stalin'.[19] But this was the reaction of Esperantists who had grown up in the bourgeois tradition and who were

---

[18] A.S. Chikobava, 'O nekotorykh voprosakh sovetskogo iazykoznaniia' (On certain problems of Soviet linguistics), *Pravda*, 9 May 1950; English translation in *The Soviet Linguistic Controversy: Translated from the Soviet Press* by John V. Murra, Robert M. Hankon, and Fred Holling, New York: King's Crown Press, 1951, pp. 9–19 (quotation p. 13).

[19] P. Balkányi, 'La Stalina lingvoscienco kaj Esperanto', *La Esperantista Laboristo*, n.s., 1951, 26 (Mar./Apr.): 1. According to Balkányi, 'many Esperantists greeted Stalin's statements with joy and anticipation'. Parts of Stalin's contributions have been translated into Esperanto: *Esperantista* 6 (1951): 10–12, 33; *Internacia Kulturo* 5 (1950), 7/8: 13–14.

not attuned to Stalin's dialectic—in fact probably were not aware of the theoretical discussions in the Soviet Union in the early 1930s. A better sense of the touchiness of the topic can be found among the communist Esperantists in Bulgaria, to whom, even before the discussion in 1950, it was clear that the path to a unified language could only proceed by way of the development of national languages; they explicitly warned against the illusion that Esperanto 'can be the future language of humanity (that is, of communism)'.[20] The same conclusion was reached, after 1950, by the party ideologists in Eastern Europe, called on to interpret Stalin's contribution to the linguistic debate. On the character of the future world language they explained 'that it [...] will not be Esperanto or Ido or any other artificially thought-up language, but a new living language, created by the masses of the socialist nations in their common work for the development of the communist society'.[21] (Stalin himself did not mention Esperanto, but in reaction to his contributions letters arrived asking about the usefulness of an international language like Esperanto.[22] We know about one Esperantist, a veteran Bolshevik named Jakob Kokushkin, who wrote to Stalin and boldly criticized his position on Esperanto.[23])

Long before 1950 there was no place for Esperanto in the development process leading to a universal language. In this sense, Stalin's intervention brought nothing new. He delivered, somewhat late, a theoretical basis for the glorification of Russian, the oppression of minorities and the long-established discrimination and persecution directed at the supranational language collective of Esperantists. But the fact that Stalin, abandoning his thesis on the equal flowering of nations, presented a fundamentally new formula for the conditions prevailing before the worldwide victory of socialism, complicated the situation of the Esperantists—because, if Stalin defined as a characteristic of the contemporary scene the fact that national languages would compete to establish which was strongest,

---

[20] Lakov, 'Josif Visarionoviĉ Stalin', p. 4.

[21] Fred Oelssner, *Die Bedeutung der Arbeiten des Genossen Stalin über den Marxismus und die Fragen der Sprachwissenschaft für die Entwicklung der Wissenschaften. Teil 1*, scientific supplement to *Forum*, no. 15 (3 August 1951), p. 11.

[22] Pollock (2009), p. 130 (relying on papers from the erstwhile Central Party Archive in Moscow).

[23] Kimura Hiroshi, *Roshia bungaku no shūhen* (Around Russian literature), Tokyo: Yomiuri Shimbun-sha, 1971, pp. 307–8. Kokushkin received no reply.

that implied that all citizens of states under Soviet influence, including the Esperantists, had to work together for the victory of Russian. Thus died any hope that still remained, despite the theoretically insecure position of Esperanto, namely, the hope that through a modest demotion of Esperanto to 'the conditional function of an auxiliary language for international communication by persons possessing that language'[24], the movement in Eastern Europe could survive.

---

[24] Lakov, p. 4.

8

The Needs of the Present

Viewing the problem of Esperanto through the lens of the debate on theories of language can easily cause us to pay less attention to the political background that led to a ban on Esperanto activity. The essential point is this: if the movement was suppressed in the Soviet Union, its ability to survive in countries under Soviet influence would inevitably come to an end sooner or later.

In the summer of 1949, when the Esperanto movement in the People's Democracies faced serious obstacles, the Soviet pursuit of alleged allies of Tito's Yugoslavia was in full cry, manifested particularly acutely in the sequential uncovering and liquidation of 'enemies of the Party'. It was accompanied in these countries by a furious campaign against cosmopolitanism. The latter was interpreted as 'an instrument for the realization of the desire for world hegemony by American imperialism', but in fact it served as a collective term to condemn all undesirable ideas from the West that seemed to undermine the stability of the socialist states. Warnings against the cosmopolitan threat were a useful pretext for discouraging citizens from all contacts abroad.

In the Soviet Union, the leading party functionary for cultural affairs, Andrei Zhdanov, began, like some medieval inquisitor, to clamp down on intellectual and cultural life while striving to re-establish party control everywhere where there were signs of softness caused by the wartime alliance with capitalist states. Artistic and intellectual circles, in which, for the moment, fresh winds were blowing, were accused of 'groveling' to the bourgeois culture of the West, of 'rootless cosmopolitanism' and of insufficient respect for traditional Russian achievements. At the end of 1948 and beginning of 1949, the anti-cosmopolitan campaign was augmented by a particularly disagreeable component, namely, anti-Semitism, disguised as a move against 'Zionists' plotting with Western provocateurs. All publications in Yiddish were banned, and even assimilated Jews were persecuted. Jews were objects of suspicion as members of the intelligentsia, as Jewish nationalists and, at the same time, contradictory though this may be, as world citizens.[1]

With the growth of the Cold War (NATO was founded in April 1949) and of the conflict with Yugoslavia, the Soviet Union insisted that the People's Democracies immediately adopt this campaign so as to protect themselves against influences from the outside world. This also had consequences for the Esperanto movement. Lev Kopelev recalled that, in prison shortly after the end of the war, he read a magazine article on cosmopolitanism that mentioned among 'the dangerous instruments for ideological subversion with cosmopolitan ideas' 'the Zionist discovery of artificial languages'.[2] In late December 1949 the followers of Marr were also entrapped by the campaign against cosmopolitanism. The Georgian party secretary, Kandid Charkviani, labeled Marr himself a 'cosmopolitan' and, to prove it, cited his statement that the principal task of Soviet linguists was work for the future world language.[3]

As we know, the Soviet model did not foresee a place for Esperanto. Accordingly, the fact that the language had become so popular in the

---

[1] Cf. Benjamin Pinkus, 'Soviet campaigns against "Jewish nationalism" and "cosmopolitism", 1946–1953', *Soviet Jewish Affairs* 4 (1974), 2: 53–72; Frank Grüner, *Patrioten und Kosmopoliten. Juden im Sowjetstaat 1941–1953*, Cologne: Böhlau, 2008, p. 447; Brown (2009), p. 219. Before 1917, Russians on the radical right, like Stalinists afterwards, regarded cosmopolitanism as a danger to Russian patriotism: Frank Grüner, '"Russia's battle against the foreign": the anti-cosmopolitanism paradigm in Russian and Soviet ideology', *European Review of History* 17 (2010): 445–72.
[2] Personal communication from Lev Kopelev, 15 April 1984.
[3] Pollock (2009), p. 112, who examined the relevant papers, notes that Stalin read the letter from Charkviani very carefully.

Eastern European countries and that even party and state authorities supported the movement would hardly allow the Soviet examiners to stand idly by. Even more odious, in fact downright provocative, was the fact that the Danube-region Esperanto associations had opted for close collaboration outside the control of Moscow, that the Czechoslovaks were calling for Esperanto letter writing and travel contacts between workers in their country and the Soviet Union,[4] that Soviet Esperantists who had escaped from persecution could read in *Internacia Kulturo* about the liveliness of Esperanto life in the new socialist states[5] or that a Leningrad Esperantist had appealed to the worldwide community of Esperantists in that same journal for help in reviving the Esperanto movement in the Soviet Union, thereby burying the Soviet Foreign Language Publishing House under requests for Esperanto-language publications.[6]

A brake had to be applied. A prime consideration was fear of unsupervised contacts through Esperanto—as in 1937–38 in the Soviet Union and in 1941 in the Baltic states. What drove the regimes to limit or ban the spread of Esperanto, then, was less the question of fidelity to some official linguistic doctrine than political considerations: concern about internal security.

To justify the measures accompanying this fear the battle cry against cosmopolitanism proved eminently suitable. The ban on Esperanto groups in the Soviet zone of Germany, for example, was motivated by the idea that these groups were being used 'for cosmopolitan efforts and the activities of agents of American imperialism'.[7] A Party periodical in the GDR explained that the cosmopolitanism propagated by the USA, aiming to paralyze proletarian internationalism, was using Esperanto ('the so-called world language'), 'whose center and headquarters are in America'.[8]

---

[4] William Solzbacher, 'It happened in Prague', *American Esperanto Magazine* 66 (1952): 36.
[5] For a short time, in 1947–48, a few Esperanto letters from the Soviet Union reached other countries, even western countries: *Heroldo de Esperanto* 23 (1947), 13 (1072): 2; *Sennaciulo* 19 (1948), 11: 5; 20 (1949), 4: 2.
[6] Anatol Syromjatnikov, 'Kreu amasan kulturan kontakton kun Sovjet-Unio!', *Internacia Kulturo* 3 (1948), 4: 16.
[7] Ebmeier, 'Esperanto vivas', p. 113 (quoted from information from the Education Ministry).
[8] *Leipziger Volkszeitung*, 1 December 1950; quoted from *Heroldo de Esperanto* 26 (1951), 1 (1136): 2.

Esperanto did not disappear in Eastern Europe at a single blow. The rapidity and intensity of the suppression were dependent on the differing internal conditions in the People's Democracies. In the places where the Soviet authorities were least concerned about local autonomy, they could carry out their wishes quickly. That explains why in East Germany, at that time under the control of a Soviet military administration, a decree could be published as early as the start of 1949, with arguments that closely tracked the Soviet viewpoint; and for the same reason the circle closed last in distant China, namely, at the end of 1953, when the journal *El Popola Ĉinio* ceased publication. The Esperantists in Bulgaria and Czechoslovakia, because they could easily prove their anti-fascist credentials, held out longest against immediate identification as Zionists and cosmopolitans; furthermore, in Bulgaria former leaders of the once illegal workers' Esperanto movement occupied senior party and government positions. Nor were the conditions worse in Hungary, but there, perhaps simply because of a casual recommendation by a high party official 'to abandon this unnecessary movement',[9] the HES vice president, a party veteran, immediately obeyed by pushing the HES committee members to accept her proposal for provisional discontinuance of the society's operations.[10]

A similar fate threatened the Bulgarian movement. The Central Committee of the Bulgarian Communist Party one day concluded that the Bulgarian Esperantist Association was a superfluous organization and that accordingly it should dissolve itself. The most fervent followers of the party line were ready to obey.[11] But the president and a few others stalled, arguing that only an association congress could decide on dissolution. They were successful in that BEA continued its formal existence.[12]

---

[9] Personal communication from Ervin Fenyvesi, 10 May 1981.

[10] That is, Borbála Szerémi-Tóth. She declared that 'Now there are much more important tasks, particularly for the party members, and so it would be proper to terminate the activities': Paŭlo Balkányi, 'El Budapeŝto', *l'omnibuso* 10 (1973), 5 (57): 11.

[11] Although in Poland government pressure against the movement was weakest, there, too, there were Esperantists who—unsuccessfully—counselled the board of the Association of Esperantists in Poland to disband the organization: Bogdan Sadowski, 'Dek jaroj de la Esperanto-movado en Popola Pollando', *Bulteno de Asocio de Esperantistoj en Pollando*, 1955, 12: 2.

[12] Atanas D. Atanasov, *Kelkaj rememoroj*, 9-page unpublished manuscript (received in early 1975), pp. 5–6.

Until 1955, however, public activity for Esperanto was completely impossible: Esperantists in Bulgaria were obliged to submit to the official line that dedication to more urgent tasks than cultivating the international language was now required—that during the building of socialism there was simply no place for Esperanto.

The proposition that attention to Esperanto drew people away from the priority of socialist construction paralleled the campaign against cosmopolitanism and soon began to supersede it, continuing in force in the first years after Stalin's death (in March 1953), until the inhibiting effect of propaganda warning against foreign enemies began to wear off.

The line of argument is well summed up by a document from Czechoslovakia—a three-page English-language letter, 'Answer to a Japanese Friend', allegedly written by a Czech Esperantist (unnamed)[13] and appended to a letter (dated 22 September 1953) from Dr E. Carminová, head of the section for relations with Japan in the Czechoslovak Ministry of Culture. The document attempts to provide a response to Kurisu Kei, who had asked the ministry why Esperanto was suppressed in a country whose literature had been introduced to Japan through Esperanto and whose Esperantists had shown solidarity with Japanese comrades suffering in prison by providing them with assistance. Because the ministry could not simply ignore the arguments of Kurisu, given his position—at the time he was the most active advocate for Czech literature and culture in Japan[14]—we today have a rare example of a detailed official effort to justify the anti-Esperanto policy of a Stalinist regime.

From the outset, the letter explicitly exculpates the Czechoslovakian Esperantists of an accusation used in the Soviet Union and East Germany:

> It is true that Esperantists in Czechoslovakia proved themselves to be patriots who used Esperanto in a progressive manner. There has not been one case of its having been used against the interests of the people and the state. This was due to the conscious and patriotic leadership of the Esperantists,

---

[13] Kurisu Kei provided me with a copy of the letter (4 Aug. 1971). He supposed (communication of 12 March 1973) that the letter was written by Adolf Malík, the last president of EAĈSR.

[14] Kurisu was also a member of the Central Committee of the New Japan Literary Society (Shin Nihon Bungakkai). This organization of leftist authors had an agreement with the parallel body in Czechoslovakia for reciprocal translation and publication of literary works in both countries.

who showed how to use Esperanto for the benefit of the state. Our people suffered overwhelming grief in its national tragedy during the period of the Hitler occupation. The Esperantists did not disappoint the nation and put their knowledge of Esperanto into the services of the country. Their activities were favorably evaluated by the government. Their modest efforts bore good fruit.

After praise like this, it might seem difficult to explain why, in the present time, Esperanto could no longer serve the people, but by a series of mental acrobatics, the ministry came to the conclusion that under the current changing conditions the efforts of the Esperantists could no longer satisfy the great tasks defined by the Party and government. The new social needs, the letter suggested, had brought about a kind of natural death of the Esperanto movement. In 1950 a new law on associations had been published, by which EAĈSR, along with others, should have affiliated with one of the large mass organizations,[15] but no one wanted to go along with it. Stressing that 'Esperanto is not required in the higher phase of the development of international relations', the letter concludes:

> In the capitalist countries, in the hands of progressive people, it [the Esperanto movement] still has an important function and should work hand in hand with the defenders of peace. If that does not happen, then it becomes cosmopolitanism 'for export' and therefore the Czechoslovak people and the state must protect themselves for reasons of their own existence.

That the use of Esperanto in capitalist countries for 'progressive' goals could not be very effective if it lacked the possibility for communication with defenders of peace in socialist countries was evidently beyond the ministry's powers of imagination.

What was meant by 'the higher phase of the development of international relations'? That was something that the authorities preferred to explain in detail only for in-country use. On 5 September 1952, a day before the 'self-liquidation' of EAĈSR, Rudolf Burda dispatched a letter of protest to the prime minister, Antonín Zápotocký (24 October 1952), asking him to clarify why Esperanto—a language which in Burda's opinion

---

[15] On this law see Kamarýt (1983), pp. 177–8.

was supported even by Lenin—was now no longer tolerated. The reply from Zápotocký's office could not be criticized for lack of concreteness:

> Since the time when Comrade Lenin emphasized the significance of Esperanto for the working class, a great deal of time has elapsed. In the meantime the great fatherland of socialism, the Soviet Union, has been constructed, and the building of socialism has spread to an ever greater number of countries, who see the Soviet Union as a model and draw abundantly on its experiences. This motive has caused hundreds of thousands of workers in those countries, and outside them, to learn the mother tongue of that pioneer of socialism – Russian. With this massive spread of the Russian language, the significance of Esperanto, which is in any case an artificial language and therefore not a language in the true sense of the word, has naturally been pushed into the background. [...]
>
> We believe that at the present time it would be much more useful to put the strengths, organizational resources and energy devoted to Esperanto to the service of further dissemination of knowledge of the Russian language.
>
> This has nothing to do with any official ban on Esperanto, as you suggest in your letter. It has to do with the fact that all comrades should be aware of the changed situation and the resulting lowering of the significance of Esperanto.[16]

Disregarding the fact that Lenin never expressed himself in favor of Esperanto, it is remarkable that a Czechoslovakian official, without attempting to contest Lenin's alleged statement, had no scruples in ignoring its validity in the present. He was perfectly willing to repudiate apparently eternally sacred theory in favor of the current agenda.

The question of the relationship between theory and practice brings us back to the linguistic discussion of 1950. When *Pravda* gave space to an extensive treatment of problems in linguistics, in the course of which Stalin condemned the theories of Marr, the likely direction of the Esperanto movement in the People's Democracies was already determined. The Esperantists had to submit to the requirement of dedicating all their strength to the building of socialism. And in the linguistic field, which concerned them more specifically, this effort had to focus primarily

---

[16] Kurisu Kei provided the author with a translation of this letter.

on the advancement of the Russian language.[17] In this respect nothing had changed with Stalin's initiative against Marr. Esperanto remained out of favor in practice, and not because of the domination of this or that linguistic school but for political considerations, particularly the desire to protect, in addition to the Soviet Esperantists, also those of Eastern Europe, against undogmatic internationalism. However, the authorities could now use Stalin's statements to justify their position. Citing Stalin's words, they attacked the Esperantists for their 'erroneous assumption that the vaulting of language barriers will bring nations together in a spirit of fraternization'.[18] And if there was any doubt still left, it was enough simply to consult the Great Soviet Encyclopedia, which called Esperanto 'a peculiar surrogate of the Romance languages'.

> [...] Such projects [of an artificial language] have a cosmopolitan character and are, therefore, vicious in principle [...]. The utopian character of artificial languages has been especially clear since the publication of J.V. Stalin's works [...], in which the real perspectives of the development of the national languages and of the formation of the future unified language of mankind are indicated [...].[19]

Given this thoroughly hostile official position, we should find consolation in the fact that East European Esperantists were not, as far as we know, sent to labor camps as their Soviet and Baltic-country peers had been. It is true that there were arrests: for example, the Worldwide Esperantist Journalist Association mentioned in its annual report of 1951–52 that members in Eastern Europe had been arrested[20] and that in a factory in the Czech city of Děčín the members of an Esperanto circle were dismissed because they refused to teach Russian instead of

---

[17] Before relations with the Soviet Union were broken off in 1948, the enthusiasm of party functionaries for Russian as the language of socialism also hindered the activities of the Esperantists in Yugoslavia: Zlatnar (1976), p. 19.

[18] In the Czechoslovakian document 'Answer to a Japanese Friend'.

[19] 'Iskusstvennye iazyki' (Artificial languages), *Bol'shaia sovetskaia ėntsiklopediia*, 2nd edn., vol. 18, 1953, pp. 504–5. Quoted from Solzbacher (1957), p. 9. See also the article 'Vsemirnyi iazyk' (Worldwide language), vol. 9, 1951, pp. 306–7.

[20] *Jarlibro de la Universala Esperanto-Asocio 1952. Dua parto*, p. 32.

Esperanto.[21] But for the most part it was enough to apply more subtle methods to inhibit activity for Esperanto. Because meetings had to be announced to the police under a registered number and all printed or duplicated texts had to be provided, the practical ban on the Esperanto movement could be guaranteed by ordinary administrative requirements arbitrarily applied, without the need for the authorities to explain their motives in detail every time. In Hungary, where Esperanto was not explicitly forbidden, the Esperantists, particularly in the provinces, backed off in fear, either believing that there was indeed a general ban, or simply not knowing which Esperanto activities were still tolerated and which were not. [22]

Social ostracism was often almost as feared as direct punishment. Party members who continued to spread the word about Esperanto risked dismissal from the Party—with negative consequences for their professional careers. Thus, in the GDR 'to avoid being considered members of the opposition', former leaders of GLEA or IPE hid their knowledge of Esperanto,[23] and in Hungary the party veteran Borbála Szerémi-Tóth even 'enthusiastically worked to slow down' the Esperanto movement.[24] But there were also party members who freely resigned, complaining that the Party was afraid to provide its members with 'a means for the revolutionary education of thoughtful workers'.[25] A Hungarian Esperantist who was summoned before his party superiors and the political police because of his 'cosmopolitan' activities courageously replied that first they should show him the law forbidding correspondence in Esperanto.[26] Others registered their contempt for some Esperantist leaders who 'hastened

---

[21] Václav Růžička, 'Iom pri nia situacio en Děčín', *La Pacdefendanto*, 1955, 37 (Jan.): 5. The Esperantists declared themselves not competent to teach Russian.

[22] Personal communication from Ervin Fenyvesi, 10 May 1981.

[23] Letter from Ludwig Schödl, himself a former GLEA activist, in *La Pacdefendanto*, 1955, 39 (Mar.): 5 (partially reprinted in *Sennaciulo* 26 [1955], 5: 3). Schödl also mentions the expulsion of party members who recruited for Esperanto.

[24] J. Reininger in *Sennaciulo* 37 (1966): 91.

[25] 'SAT restas por mi la sola organizo subteninda', *Sennaciulo* 28 (1957), 2: 3. The article was written by a resident of the GDR who had attended the founding congress of SAT (1921). He signed as 'A Sincere Socialist Ready for Sacrifice' ('Sincera Oferema Socialisto'—SOS).

[26] Personal communication from Miklós Ábrahám, 20 Sept. 1982. (He continued to correspond in Esperanto in defiance of the authorities.)

to abandon their decades-long Esperantism and immediately became enthusiastic learners and propagandists of the Russian language'.[27] If that was the model offered by a few of the earlier leaders, it is no wonder that often the 'ordinary' Esperantists (of whom only a minority belonged to the Party) preferred 'to abandon even the simplest correspondence'.[28]

---

[27] 'Laborista esperantismo kaj SAT-aneco', *Sennaciulo* 28 (1957), 5: 7. When this article was republished five years later, the editors revealed that the author was the Hungarian Imre Baranyai, known as an Esperanto author under the pseudonym Emba: *Sennaciulo* 33 (1962): 46.

[28] 'Laborista esperantismo kaj SAT-aneco'.

9

Revival of the Movement

Today, students of modern Soviet history agree that perhaps the most important and consequential statement in the long, tedious discussion about linguistics was Stalin's final conclusion (in the letter to Kholopov) that 'Marxism is the enemy of all dogmatism'.[1] Regardless of Stalin's motives (evidently he expressed himself in this way so as to have complete freedom of movement and to find a way out of the constant contradictions between the internationalist tradition of socialism on the one hand and practical politics on the other, the latter giving preference to the national interests of the Soviet state) in retrospect, we should note that the emphasis on anti-dogmatic Marxism not only led Soviet linguistics, paralyzed by the influence of Marr, out of dangerous isolation, but slowly, particularly after Stalin's death, made 'destalinization' possible in other fields. Among those who profited from this development were the Esperantists.

The way in which the Esperanto movement in Eastern Europe, including the Soviet Union, was gradually revived is one of the most interesting chapters in the history of Esperanto. It is a case study in the Esperantist goal-directed, anti-authoritarian conviction and grass-roots wisdom and cleverness.

---

[1] Stalin, *Marxism and Problems of Linguistics*, p. 53.

The starting point for the process of revival in the socialist countries was the courage of a handful of Esperantists who refused to remain silent even during the most unfavorable years. One of these brave figures was Miloslav Vlk, a high school student in České Budějovice, who later, from 1994 to 2010, was cardinal archbishop in Prague. In 1952, in preparation for his final school examination, he wrote a paper entitled 'Esperanto in the mirror of Stalin's language theory' in which he indirectly criticized Stalin's anti-Esperanto position.[2] Even more courageous was the earlier mentioned Rudolf Burda in Czechoslovakia,[3] who insistently described the suppression of the movement in his country as a profound injustice irreconcilable with communist principles (or at least with his idealistic understanding of communism). Burda didn't just protest. His bulletin *La Pacdefendanto*, early on, started naming motives that the authorities preferred to keep hidden. Citing a speech by Klement Gottwald, in which the Russian language was glorified as the 'international language of progress, of the battle for national and social deliverance, the language of the battle for peace', Burda instructed his readers on why 'Esperanto is not desired in our country'.[4] In addition, Burda outlined a fundamental problem of which the hostility to Esperanto was symptomatic. He quoted the following confession from a letter written by the French communist Esperantist William Gilbert:

> It has now been proved that the communist parties accept international relations in their propaganda but in practice have no intention of realizing it. And that, too, is political hypocrisy. In my opinion this matter goes beyond the problem of Esperanto itself.[5]

---

[2] Conversation with Cardinal Vlk, Prague, 20 April 1998. Vlk began learning Esperanto in 1946, using it frequently for correspondence. In May 1952 in a regional conference he rejected the accusations of cosmopolitanism and insufficient patriotism; see *Esperanto-Junularo* (České Budějovice), 1952, 5: 2–3. See also Alain Boudre, *Laveur de vitres et archevêque. Biographie de Mgr Miloslav Vlk (Prague)*. Préface de Vaclav Havel, Paris: Nouvelle Cité, 1994, p. 33.
[3] Burda was a member of SAT from its foundation. As a communist, he spent six years in the Nazi concentration camp Buchenwald.
[4] R. Burda, 'Internacia rusa lingvo', *La Pacdefendanto*, 1953, 22 (Oct.): 2. Burda quotes from *Rudé právo*, 5 October 1953. Gottwald (d. March 1953) was leader of the Czechoslovakian Party and President of the Republic.
[5] 'Eĥo el eksterlando', *La Pacdefendanto*, 1952, 11: 1.

Protests and attempts at analysis were paralleled by efforts to encourage the Esperantists. At first, such encouragement consisted of advice on how to survive. Burda published what was in effect an updated report on the secret activities of communist Esperantists under fascist regimes, where they, for example, 'became chess players or philatelists and used that business card [...] to continue their Esperantist life'.[6] At the same time, Burda also provided the Esperantists with arguments aimed at changing the situation. He showed no hesitation in fighting the dominant position of the Russian language—using as a weapon the words of Stalin himself. In August 1952, six months before Stalin's death, Burda wrote:

> A few misguided Marxist popularizers still assert that Esperanto is a bourgeois, cosmopolitical [*sic*] language that cannot be taught to socialists, who have their own proletarian, socialist language, the language of our geniuses Stalin and Lenin, namely Russian! Stalin, however, said quite clearly that the international language could be neither Russian nor any other national language, because that would mean imposing the language of a stronger nation on the less strong, which would be completely non-Marxist and reactionary.

Quoting Stalin's statement that a language must serve the whole nation and that there is no such thing as a bourgeois or proletarian national language, Burda continued: 'we can readily apply this principle also to [...] Esperanto', which serves people equally in capitalist and in socialist countries.[7] To be sure, Burda could not convince, or barely reach, the authorities, but at a minimum he might avoid the paralyzing resignation endemic among the Esperantists. As for the goal of reviving the movement, progress in that direction depended on external circumstances. And in fact these circumstances evolved, beginning in 1953, to the Esperantists' advantage in Eastern Europe. Stalin died on 5 March 1953. His successors, the new leaders of the Soviet Union, moved, at least formally, to more flexible policies. In June, during a conference in Budapest, the World Peace Council, founded in 1950 as an instrument of Soviet foreign policy, accepted an unusually worded resolution:

---

[6] R. Burda, 'Esperanto en la ilegaleco', *La Pacdefendanto*, 1952, 8 (Aug.): 4.
[7] R. Burda, 'Uzu fiakriston, ĉar aŭtomobilo estas burĝa!', *La Pacdefendanto*, 1952, 8 (Aug.): 1–3.

Each people has the right to decide freely on its way of life and must respect the forms of living freely chosen by other peoples. This permits the needed peaceful coexistence of different systems, and relations among the peoples can develop to the advantage of all.[8]

When at the end of July an armistice was signed ending the Korean War, the World Peace Council called for 'a renewal of international friendship', naming as an important factor in this renewal a major expansion in cultural exchange.[9] Burda and a few of his colleagues soon found a way to utilize the changed political climate to improve the situation of Eastern European Esperantists. At the beginning of September 1953 in the Austrian town of St. Pölten an 'International Meeting of Esperantist Defenders of Peace' took place. The two or three dozen attendees, among them Austrian pacifists and communist Esperantists from France, agreed to found the World Peace Esperantist Movement (MEM). Burda, who was unable to attend, became its first president.

It is interesting that the founding manifesto was inspired less by the language of communists and more by the traditional Esperantist aspirations for the contribution of Esperanto to peace. The call went out: 'Help our much-loved language to be an instrument of true love and world peace!' The way forward for MEM included the sentence: 'We should avoid allowing [the organization] to fall under the discipline of a political party.'[10] The intention was obvious. With the motto 'For world peace through Esperanto' MEM wished to demonstrate the utility of such an application of the language and legitimize the activities of Esperantists in the People's Democracies as worthy of recognition as one form of the general battle for peace proclaimed by the regimes as every citizen's obligation. In articles in *La Pacdefendanto* and MEM's journal *Paco*, Burda tirelessly ordered the Esperantists 'not to allow themselves to be pushed into illegality'. He explained that, because work for peace was in line with resolutions of the World Peace Council 'you can't be harassed for carrying out its decisions'.[11]

---

[8] Cited in Jörg K. Hoensch, *Sowjetische Osteuropa-Politik 1945–1975*, Kronberg: Athenäum, 1977, p. 57.

[9] *Paco*, 1954, 3 (Jan.): 4.

[10] 'Manifesto. Al la esperantistoj pacamantoj de la tuta mondo!', *La Esperantista Laboristo*, n.s., 1953, 41 (Sept./Oct.): 1–2.

[11] Rud. Burda, 'Necesas disvastigi nian movadon!', *Paco*, 1954, 4 (Feb.): 1.

Burda's efforts to instill in the Esperantists a new confidence were not without effect, particularly in Czechoslovakia and Hungary. In fact, the argument of Esperanto's utility in the 'battle for peace' gave some of them a certain freedom of action. But in most of the People's Democracies there was scarcely any progress. Many preferred to wait for permission from above, or feared the consequences of what might be considered action against party discipline. Although Burda called such attitudes timid, regularly insisting that the Esperantists should not wait, but take action for peace (through Esperanto), he realized how great the obstacles were, and also understood their origin.

One of those skeptical about the path taken by MEM displayed his hesitancy in the assertion that 'As long as there is no Esperanto movement in the Soviet Union, as there once was, we will not achieve anything'.[12] Indeed, Burda and his colleagues often found that party authorities disapproved of using Esperanto in the battle for peace on the grounds that Moscow had given no signal in that direction. But his conclusions were different from those of the doubters. Seeing the absence of a model of flowering Esperanto in the Soviet Union as the chief obstacle, he and his colleagues grew convinced of the need to reawaken the long-dead Soviet Esperanto movement.[13]

In the year 1954, this no longer seemed a hopeless dream: the Soviet Union had made it clear that, after an almost 20-year isolation, it was ready to revive its cultural contacts abroad. A significant beginning came in April with its joining of UNESCO, the leading international cultural organization, and in August 1954 an official Soviet institution broke the silence on Esperanto—for the first time in many years. In response to a question from Canada, an official of the All-Union Society for Friendship and Cultural Relations with Foreign Countries denied that the learning of Esperanto was forbidden in the Soviet Union.[14] The official raised no ideological accusations against the Esperantists, but expressed a pragmatic doubt about the qualities of the language and the movement's

---

[12] Cited in A. Balague, 'Malferma letero al esperantista pacamiko X en Polio', *Paco*, 1954, 12 (Oct.): 7.

[13] R. Burda, 'Batalo ĉirkaŭ la laŭroj', *Paco*, 1956, 29/30 (Apr./May): 3.

[14] *News-Facts about the USSR* (Toronto), 1954, 48 (Aug.); cited in *La Revuo Orienta* 36 (1955): 53.

chances of success. His arguments resembled the reasoning of conservative opponents of Esperanto, but they were encouraging in the sense that Esperanto was no longer simply ignored, and the Esperantists were no longer denounced as bourgeois cosmopolitans (an accusation almost impossible to refute).

In December 1954, when the Eighth General Conference of UNESCO took place in Montevideo, the Universal Esperanto Association was approved as an organization in consultative relations with UNESCO. Even more important was the fact that the conference accepted a resolution noting 'the results attained by Esperanto in the field of international intellectual relations and the rapprochement of the peoples of the world' and recognized 'that these results correspond with the aims and ideals of UNESCO'. Surprisingly, in the vote on the resolution the delegations from the Soviet Union and its allies chose to abstain.[15]

The fact that the Soviet Union did not oppose a declaration recognizing Esperanto probably had a deciding influence on later developments. The Esperantists in the People's Democracies now had an argument to use against attempts at sabotage by the authorities.[16] They felt encouraged to intensify what were up to then sporadic contacts with Soviet Esperantists who had survived the persecutions and were now, little by little, becoming aware that an Esperanto movement still existed in the larger world. Much joy accompanied the arrival in Budapest in December 1954 of an Esperanto letter from Evgenii Bokarev, a researcher in the Institute of Linguistics at the Academy of Sciences, who in 1928, as a young linguist, had participated in the search for a Marxist linguistics and the possible place of Esperanto in it.[17] As though in the meantime there had been no other priorities, Bokarev reported that 'Esperanto will play an important role in the process of ultimate realization of a language of the future for all humankind. Thus, the Marxist science of language also has Esperanto among its objects of study.'[18]

---

[15] *EeP*, pp. 772–3.

[16] R. Burda, 'Al niaj popoldemokrataj gek-doj!', *La Pacdefendanto*, 1955, 38 (Feb.): 1.

[17] See vol. 1, chapter 7, pp. 253–4. For a summary of his activities see the obituary article by A.D. Duličenko, 'E.A. Bokarev', in Bokarjova (2010), pp. 134–9.

[18] Bokarev wrote to the Hungarian Pál Balkányi, 27 December 1954; see Paŭlo Balkányi, 'Kun malĝojo pri Bokarev', *La Pacaktivulo*, 1971, 89: 13–14. See also the letter from Bokarev to Balkányi,

Further letters arrived from the Soviet Union, and soon the first Soviet requests for exchanges of letters appeared in *Paco* and *La Pacdefendanto*. The replies from other countries were so great that the requesters could not answer all of them. Although hundreds of issues of *La Pacdefendanto* were sent to the Soviet Union (thanks to which, e.g. Esperantists in Leningrad found out about one another's existence[19]), they were not enough to satisfy the interests of Soviet Esperantists, old and new. And when Bokarev announced in early July 1955 that, on the initiative of influential Soviet linguists,[20] plans were proceeding for a 'Soviet Union Esperanto Association' within the Academy of Sciences and that the Esperantists 'meet with approval and assistance everywhere',[21] the ice seemed to be broken. News circulating at the end of 1955 indicated that the Soviet Esperantists 'await the legalization' of the movement 'in a matter of days'.[22]

Such optimism was not baseless—if we consider the historical background. At the beginning of June 1955 the Soviet leaders Nikita Khrushchev and Nikolai Bulganin, with their Canossa visit to Belgrade, restored peace with Yugoslavia—an action that also seemed to bring greater Soviet respect for the sovereignty of the People's Democracies. In July, at a conference in Geneva, the heads of government of the USA, the Soviet Union, Britain and France agreed to expand cultural relations between East and West. The 'Geneva spirit' inspired UEA's journal to refer to the beginning of a new era also for the world Esperanto movement, heralded, among other things, by the 'happy news' coming from the East.[23] Such news included, in addition to the revival of Esperanto in the Soviet

---

26 June 1955; quoted in R. Burda, 'Batalo ĉirkaŭ la laŭroj', *Paco*, 1956, 29/30 (Apr./May): 2.

[19] 'Leningradanoj interkonatiĝas trans [= tra] Ĉeĥoslovakio', *La Pacdefendanto*, 1956, 50 (Feb.): 3, on Varvara Tsvetkova and Semyon Podkaminer.

[20] Bokarev mentioned the names of Viktor Vinogradov, Viktoriia Iartseva, Lev Zhirkov, Klara Maitinskaia and Boris Serebrennikov. Of those, Zhirkov and Maitinskaia, and perhaps others, were Esperantists.

[21] Letter from Bokarev to a conference of Czechoslovakian Esperantists in Otrokovice, 3 July 1955, in *Paco*, 1955, 21/22: 5–6 (quotation p. 5). Bokarev reported that the decision on the founding of the association was taken during a meeting of the department of literature and languages at the Academy (18 June 1955).

[22] Information from Simon Mkrtchian, Yerevan, in *La Pacdefendanto*, 1955, 48 (Dec.): 5.

[23] Ivo Lapenna, 'Sur la sojlo de nova epoko', *Esperanto* 48 (1955): 273–4.

Union, the reactivation of the Bulgarian Esperantist Association, the founding of an All-State Esperantist Consultative Committee (TKKE) in Czechoslovakia and the return of the Polish association to UEA. Also occurring, at the beginning of August 1955, was the first meeting of Esperantists from West and East since the Cold War began—at the Fifth World Youth Festival in Warsaw. Some 150 Esperantists from 15 countries participated, though none from the Soviet Union.[24]

When Khrushchev, during the 20th Congress of the Communist Party of the Soviet Union in February 1956, revealed the terrible crimes committed during Stalin's reign, his speech further increased the hopes of the formerly persecuted and discriminated Esperantists. On 5 March 1956, a mere ten days after the end of the Congress, the Soviet news agency TASS announced that Esperantist circles were being formed in the Soviet Union.[25] A few days later, on 12 March, Pavel Kiriushin of Minsk thanked Sergei Sarychev in Moscow for his letter, the first letter in Esperanto that he had received since 1936.[26] On 1 July, the Hungarian Ministry of Education officially recognized the Esperanto Council of Hungary, founded in the previous September; thus the persistent efforts of 'bourgeois' Esperantists finally bore fruit.[27] Also early in July, after an eight-year interruption, a Bulgarian Esperanto Congress took place in Sofia. At it, representatives of the Bulgarian, Czechoslovakian, Hungarian and Romanian Esperanto movements called for immediate affiliation of the re-established associations with UEA.[28] A few weeks later, at the 41st World Congress of Esperanto in Copenhagen, delegates appeared from Bulgaria, Czechoslovakia, Hungary, Poland and China.[29]

---

[24] Michel Duc Goninaz, 'Mi estis en Varsovio', *La Juna Vivo*, 1955, 3/4 (Nov./Dec.): 14–15, 18.

[25] J. Tilindris, 'Trairita vojo', *Horizonto de Soveta Litovio*, 1979, 4: 36. This article states that on 3 May 1956 an 'initiating group' was formed in Lithuania consisting of Esperantists from various locations.

[26] A copy of Kiriushin's letter was kindly provided by Lev Vulfovich. Kiriushin (on whom see vol. 1, chapter 5, pp. 187–8) indicated that the Esperantists in Belarus were for the most part Jews and that all were murdered by the Nazis.

[27] Borbála Szerémi-Tóth, who argued for the disbanding of HES, later admitted that the revival of the movement in Hungary was due to the 'bourgeois Esperantists': B. Szerémi, '1918–1958', *Bulteno. Cirkulero de la Hungarlanda Esperanto-Konsilantaro*, 1958, p. 78.

[28] The Bulgarian association joined UEA in 1956, the Hungarian in 1962. That of the Czechoslovaks was delayed until 1970.

[29] Paradoxically, in that same congress the conflict of several years between UEA and its US national association, the Esperanto Association of North America (EANA) came to a head. In the atmo-

Particularly noteworthy was the participation of the Yugoslav delegation in the Bulgarian Congress. Its leader, Ivo Borovečki, delivered a speech in the first working session in which almost every sentence drew applause from the enthusiastic audience because it openly addressed the situation of Esperanto in the Soviet Union and the People's Democracies. Borovečki, behind whom hung a large portrait of Stalin, then clearly enunciated, word by word, the name of the person whom he found guilty of the suppression of Esperanto: 'Iosif Vissarionovich Stalin'—and the applause died away in shocked silence. The denunciation of Stalin's crimes was still too fresh an event for the Bulgarian Esperantists, unprovided with directives from their Party, to dare applaud this unprecedentedly frank utterance of a long hidden truth.[30] In Poland, on the other hand, the Esperantists could hear revealing words about the past from their own association president. At the end of October—the same month in which the country underwent a dangerous political crisis—the 13th Polish Esperanto Congress took place in Warsaw; Andrzej Rajski's opening address welcomed the new party leader Gomułka and accused Hitler, Franco and Stalin, all three, of persecuting Esperanto, declaring: 'Democracy and the development of Esperanto are inseparable.'[31]

A mere six months after the 20th CPSU Congress, 'destalinization' reached Soviet linguistics. *Voprosy iazykoznaniia*, the principal Soviet linguistics journal, in its July–August 1956 issue delivered a major surprise by beginning with criticism of Stalin and ending with praise of Esperanto.[32] The first article, on current problems in Soviet linguistics,[33] assailed the 'sterile discussions' and 'abstract theorizing' of the past and

---

sphere of McCarthyism then prevailing, particularly between 1954 and 1956, EANA launched a campaign against 'communist infiltration of the Esperanto movement', interpreting the revival of Esperanto in Eastern Europe as a clever maneuver by Moscow, and attacking UEA for its favorable reaction to that revival. Ivo Lapenna, the UEA general secretary, was even denounced to foreign security services. In Copenhagen, the UEA Committee confirmed an earlier decision to expel EANA's general secretary, George A. Connor, and began the procedure to expel EANA. EANA left voluntarily before the expulsion could occur. See Lins (2008), pp. 88–93.

[30] Atanasov, *Kelkaj rememoroj*, p. 7; personal communication from Dr Ivo Borovečki, 26 October 1975.
[31] *Bulteno de Asocio de Esperantistoj en Pollando*, 1956, 10/11: 5.
[32] Cf. Solzbacher (1957), p. 5.
[33] 'O nekotorykh aktual'nykh zadachakh sovremennogo sovetskogo iazykoznaniia', *Voprosy iazykoznaniia*, 1956, 4: 3–13.

specifically blamed Stalin for paralyzing independent theoretical work in general linguistics. At the same time the editors distanced themselves from the 'vulgar Marxist concepts' of Marr, who was nonetheless partially defended against Stalin's attacks. Self-criticism for earlier acceptance of Stalin's every utterance as 'untouchable dogma' was accompanied by the confession that Soviet linguists could learn much from their foreign colleagues. The same issue published a report of a session of the Institute of Linguistics of 24 January 1956 dedicated to the present state of the international auxiliary language question.[34] The report largely consisted of a summary of the paper given by Bokarev[35] at that session. It included the following:

> There can be no doubt that attempts to impose by force one of the leading national languages upon all the nations of the world are perfectly hopeless. They have nothing in common with the Marxist-Leninist concept of national development and must be rejected as bound to fail.

To solve the problem of facilitating international communication, said Bokarev, 'the greatest interest' lay in attempts at an artificial language, among which only Esperanto had achieved significant dissemination and practical value.

As the report went on to say, particularly notable in Bokarev's paper was 'the need for theoretical study of Esperanto and its significance as a collective linguistic experiment'.[36] In fact, two issues later, *Voprosy iazykoznaniia* published an article on 'the international auxiliary language as a linguistic problem'.[37] This article provided an overview of the theoretical

---

[34] V.P. Grigor'ev, 'V Institute iazykoznaniia AN SSSR', *Voprosy iazykoznaniia*, 1956, 4: 158–9. English translation: *American Esperanto Magazine* 71 (1957): 6–8 (quotation p. 7).

[35] The text of the paper, 'Sovremennoe sostoianie voprosa o mezhdunarodnom vspomogatel'nom iazyke. Fakty ob esperanto' (Present state of the question of an international auxiliary language. Facts on Esperanto), appeared in Isaev (1976), pp. 12–20; Esperanto translation in Bokarjova (2010), pp. 63–72.

[36] The report also mentions the point of view expressed in the discussion that 'the question of the absolute utility of Esperanto in our era needs to be separated from the general question of an international auxiliary language in the future, when Esperanto—as a product of the Indo-European language group—will have to yield its place to another auxiliary language that considers roots from the Asian languages as well'.

[37] O.S. Akhmanova & E.A. Bokarev, 'Mezhdunarodnyi vspomogatel'nyi iazyk kak lingvisticheskaia problema', *Voprosy iazykoznaniia*, 1956, 6: 65–78. Esperanto translation in Bokarjova (2010),

questions so far arising from research on an international auxiliary language and concluded by expressing regret that Soviet linguists have not given the matter sufficient attention. It was written in a calm, unemotional style, but it did make one observation evidently aimed at discrediting the opponents of Esperanto: it cited disapprovingly the German linguist Gustav Meyer's opinion of 1891 questioning the possibility of an artificial language and supporting the view that 'the large world languages continue to expand their subject territory, with the result that the number of participants in the battle for hegemony will continue to decline'.[38] It was unnecessary to explain to readers how similar this opinion was to the 'zonal' theories formulated by Stalin in 1950.

It seemed only a matter of time before organized activities for Esperanto would again be possible in the Soviet Union. Under Bokarev's chairmanship an 'Initiating Group of Soviet Esperantists' was founded.[39] For a while there was hope of re-establishing SEU, which had never been officially disbanded. But the Party put an emphatic end to this effort.[40] Obtaining permission for an all-Soviet Esperanto Association would prove much more difficult than Bokarev and his colleagues anticipated.

Nor in the People's Democracies did the new beginning go smoothly everywhere. The degree of revival varied considerably from country to country. The Poles were able to gather strength fast enough to organize in 1959—a hundred years after Zamenhof's birth—the 44th World Congress in Warsaw. A little earlier, Polish Radio began daily broadcasts in Esperanto. In January 1957 the Bulgarians launched a monthly Esperanto-language review, *Nuntempa Bulgario*, aimed at publicizing abroad the achievements of socialist construction[41]; the Bulgarian Esperantist Association became one of the strongest national associations

---

pp. 72–94.
[38] Akhmanova and Bokarev cite, among other opinions, that of Meyer, that it is 'a regrettable pursuit of national chauvinism in our times' that 'the smallest little nations' want to publish scientific works only in their mother tongues. Meyer's essay, 'Weltsprache und Weltsprachen', is reprinted in Reinhard Haupenthal (ed.), *Plansprachen. Beiträge zur Interlinguistik*, Darmstadt: Wissenschaftliche Buchgesellschaft, 1976, pp. 27–45 (esp. pp. 40, 43); cf. Bokarjova (2010), p. 74.
[39] Information from Sergei Sarychev, secretary of the Initiating Group, in *Paco*, 1956, (Apr./May): 7.
[40] Nikolaj Danovskij,'Lasta ekflamo de SEU', *Spektro*, 1993, 2: 14–16.
[41] It appeared until 1970 (in 1964–65 under the name *Bulgario*).

in UEA. The Hungarians found their definitive organizational base in 1960 with the establishment of the Hungarian Esperanto Association; in 1961 the journal *Hungara Vivo* began publication, remaining for almost 30 years what was perhaps the most attractive Esperanto-language periodical in Eastern Europe. In North Vietnam, probably not unrelated to the Esperanto revival in the People's Democracies, the 'Vietnamese Esperantist Association for the Defense of Peace' was founded in December 1956 with approval from ministers and well-known intellectuals. The Chinese Esperanto League resumed operations in March 1957; in the same year the propaganda review *El Popola Ĉinio* resumed bimonthly publication.

Disillusionment struck those who had most courageously endured during the difficult years: the Czechoslovakians. At the end of 1956 Burda was forced to cease publication of *La Pacdefendanto*, which at the end had 3000 subscribers in Czechoslovakia.[42] A further disagreeable surprise followed in September 1957, when the Czechoslovak Esperantists learned that the authorities had decided to establish a Czechoslovakian Esperanto Committee (ĈSEK) with Adolf Malík as its chair—precisely the person who in 1952 had carried out the disbandment and who later on various occasions declared that Esperantists should stop Esperanto activities and learn Russian instead. Though Malík's return horrified the Esperantists, they could not prevent his appointment as secretary of ĈSEK in mid-1958. He at once showed himself compliant with the primary wish of the authorities, policing the Esperantists.[43] Although the Esperantists finally succeeded in causing Malík to disappear from the scene,[44] publication of Theodor Kilian's *Cviĉebnice esperanta* (Exercises in Esperanto) was delayed for four years (until 1961) for political and ideological reasons. In February 1959 the Czechoslovakian section of MEM

---

[42] Rudolf Burda, '"La Pacdefendanto" ĉesas aperi', *La Pacdefendanto*, 1956, 58/59 (Nov./Dec.): 3–4.

[43] The authorities explained that they did not aim to enlarge the number of Esperantists, but register and 'educate and instruct on proper conceptualization' the existing Esperantists: Ivo Lapenna, *Hamburgo en retrospektivo*, 2nd edn., Copenhagen: Horizonto, 1977, p. 17. In 1958 Jaroslav Šustr, president of the Prague club and head representative (*ĉefdelegito*) of UEA, was suspected of organizing a protest against the appointment of Malík; he was freed after three months in prison (personal communication from Jaroslav Mařík, 3 August 1991).

[44] 'Esperanto-novajoj el Ĉeĥoslovakio', *Sennaciulo* 30 (1959), 11: 4.

was forced to merge with ĈSEK,⁴⁵ leaving Burda unable to influence the future direction of the movement in Czechoslovakia.⁴⁶ Later, conditions improved, but not until 1969—as a result of negotiations during the short-lived political 'spring' in 1968—the Czech Esperanto Association was founded, shortly before the final fall of Alexander Dubček.⁴⁷

In the German Democratic Republic, the Esperanto movement lagged behind that in Czechoslovakia for many years. This was not for lack of courage on the part of the East German Esperantists. They sent constant letters and petitions to party and government authorities not only emphasizing the contribution of Esperanto to peace but also persistently making the argument that prohibition against forming groups did not accord with the GDR Constitution, which gave all citizens the right to meet 'peacefully and unarmed'. One Esperantist wrote to a public prosecutor with the request 'that the police also respect our Constitution'⁴⁸ and when that official denied that banning Esperanto groups was unconstitutional, turned to the Ministry of Justice with the demand that the public prosecutor be dismissed.⁴⁹

Observing that the authorities avoided addressing the legal issue, preferring to argue that the language was unsuitable or culturally valueless, the Esperantists increased their emphasis on the practical utility of Esperanto in the service of peace. Receiving, in March 1955, the admission that Esperanto itself was not forbidden and that people had the right to take a private interest in it,⁵⁰ they succeeded, a few months later, in obtaining declarations from the Central Committee of the Party that

---

⁴⁵ *Paco* 6 (1959), 64/65 (Mar./Apr.): 7. In March 1959 *Zprávy Československého esperantského výbotu / Informoj de Ĉehoslovaka Esperanto-Komitato* began publication.

⁴⁶ On Burda, who in 1959 also lost the presidency of MEM, the Austrian peace activist Adolf Halbedl mentions 'the ungrateful conduct of those who harvested the seeds he sowed': *Paco* 8 (1961), 86 (Jan.): 3.

⁴⁷ In May 1969 the 'Association of Esperantists in the Slovakian Socialist Republic' was founded. Both organizations joined UEA.

⁴⁸ Letter from W. Ranft, Radebeul, in *La Pacdefendanto*, 1953, 22 (Oct.): 2.

⁴⁹ 'La Esperanto-movado en Meza Germanio' (report by Walter Ranft), *Germana Esperanto-Revuo* 9 (1956): 2.

⁵⁰ Curt Kessler, 'Pri la situacio en la Germana Demokrata Respubliko', *La Pacdefendanto*, 1956, 55 (July): 4. See also the newsletters of Kessler, 1956, reprinted in Rolf Beau, *Esperanto in Leipzig und Umgebung 1945–1991*, Althen, 1999, part 1, pp. 139–47.

they could work with the peace movement and that correspondence in Esperanto in the service of peace would not be hindered.[51] Despite these declarations, in the Dresden and Leipzig districts the first efforts to organize in the framework of the peace movement were closed down.[52] Only after Khrushchev's speech were Stalinist polemics reduced in the GDR: in May 1956 the Central Committee decided that it was all right to learn Esperanto and 'in connection with the peace movement' to correspond abroad. Opponents used pragmatic arguments, for example, asserting the greater value of learning 'living languages'. They took pains to emphasize to the Esperantists that wars have economic causes and do not arise from difference of language.[53]

The fact that the leading Soviet linguistic journal had published a very favorable presentation of Esperanto gave the activists in the GDR new ammunition. One of them reported: 'Now we have begun a real attack against our still hesitant institutions—with chaotic effect.' In truth, while various authorities continued to assert that with the help of Esperanto agents, enemies of the state were able to penetrate and poison the political life of the GDR, others were convinced of Esperanto's suitability and value[54] (or preferred to jump on a train to which Moscow had apparently given the green light). But the opposition had the heavier influence. The Esperantists often received replies from officials that were 'so evasive, tortuous, senseless […] that one felt like an idiot'.[55] In 1958 the Education Ministry explicitly justified the GDR's continued backwardness in this matter. To a complaint pointing out the ability to recruit publicly for Esperanto in other socialist countries, it replied that the special political situation of the GDR required separate rules.[56] As late as 1962, the

---

[51] Two letters from the Central Committee, 15 November 1955 and 18 January 1956, published in Esperanto translation in *Paco* 3 (1956), 29/30 (Apr./May): 15.
[52] Communication from Helmut Moesner, Leipzig, 7 May 1957, in *Bulteno de Esperantista Klubo ĉe Osvětová beseda en Praha 2*, 1957, 47 (May/June): 16.
[53] Papers of the Education Ministry, Bundesarchiv, SAPMO, DR 2/4145 and DR 2/4904.
[54] Curt Kessler, 'La evoluo kaj nuna stato de l' Esperanto-movado en la Germana Demokrata Respubliko', *Paco* 5 (1958), 51/52 (Feb./Mar.): 8.
[55] Letter from GDR, *Sennaciulo* 29 (1958), 2: 4.
[56] *Sennaciulo* 29 (1958), 6: 7.

veteran of the workers' movement Ludwig Schödl noted bitterly that in the GDR 'fanatical opposition to Esperanto' prevailed.[57]

In 1961, interestingly, the decree of 1949 was officially canceled[58] one month after the building of the Berlin Wall, constructed by the GDR as an attempt at stabilization. This allowed Esperantists to work under the supervision of the German Peace Council, but did not remove the ban on organizing or on public recruitment. Finally, that important barrier was removed as well. In February 1965 the 'Cultural League', one of the so-called mass organizations, decided to give the GDR Esperantists an organizational home; within its framework the 'Central Working Circle of the Friends of Esperanto' was founded at the end of March 1965.[59]

---

[57] Ludwig Schödl, 'Esperanto kaj pacpolitiko de Germana Demokrata Respubliko', *Paco* 9 (1962), 108 (Nov.): 5.

[58] *Gesetzblatt der Deutschen Demokratischen Republik*, part 1, no. 64 (15 Sept. 1961), p. 425. The decision was taken on 17 August 1961. On the confusing situation in 1956 and later, see Bendias (2011), pp. 76–80.

[59] As of 1976, the GDR Esperantists were represented in UEA when the 'Central Working Circle' joined the association. In 1981 it changed its name to 'Esperanto Association in the GDR Cultural League' (GDREA).

10

Eastern Europe: Progress and Problems

Before the regime change in 1989–90, all Eastern European countries allied with the Soviet Union, with the exception of Romania, were represented in UEA and therefore organizationally linked with the worldwide Esperanto movement. Because of their high membership numbers they constituted a considerable proportion of the UEA Committee: of 84 members, no less than 26 came from Poland, the GDR, Czechoslovakia, Hungary and Bulgaria. Esperanto associations in Western countries viewed this strength with envy, not least because the Eastern European associations received state subsidies and could afford paid staff.[1]

The decision of the authorities to end what was in effect a ban on the Esperanto movement in Eastern Europe meant not only that the language was tolerated but also that it was accompanied by other advantages, namely, direct recognition and official status. At first it seemed that in return for the right to organize, the Esperantists would have to accept

---

[1] Cf. Detlev Blanke, 'Pri specifaĵoj de la Esperanto-movado en kelkaj eŭropaj socialismaj landoj', *Der Esperantist* 22 (1986): 121–5.

control from above.² In Hungary, Antal Koós, a trade union official who barely knew Esperanto, was named secretary of HEA. In the GDR, the Cultural League was at first primarily interested in making sure 'that matters did not get out of control'³; charged with leading the Esperantists was someone who had no knowledge of the language. But these shortcomings were merely temporary. The Hungarian secretary turned out to be someone who argued first for the interests of the Esperantists, less for those of their higher authority, the trade union association, and in the late 1960s, HEA regained, not least thanks to him, enough freedom of action to free itself of its president—that party veteran who in 1950 proposed a halt to the movement. Likewise in the GDR: there the place of the non-Esperantist was taken by a young activist, Detlev Blanke.

Hungary and the GDR were among the countries where the Esperanto movement prospered. The journal *Hungara Vivo*, founded as a state propaganda periodical, acquired characteristics that made it a kind of inheritor of the tradition of *Literatura Mondo*. The Hungarian Education Ministry allowed the introduction of Esperanto as an elective subject at various levels in schools, and at Eötvös Loránd University in Budapest it became possible to study the field of 'Esperanto—language and literature'. According to its department head, all that was required was respect for the primacy of Russian in foreign language instruction.⁴ In the GDR, linguists devoted attention to Esperanto to a degree that their counterparts in the Federal Republic could only dream of.⁵ Similar reports of success came from Poland, Czechoslovakia and Bulgaria. An abundance of letter-writing requests from Eastern Europe (in quantities that the less numerous Esperantists in the West could not always satisfy) testified to Esperanto's penetration of all social levels and the degree to which people sought contact with the outside world by learning Esperanto. The World

---

² Cf. M. Arco (Marek Wajsblum), 'Sur la marĝeno de libero', *The Worker Esperantist*, 1959, 118 (Jul.): 44, 47–8.

³ Blanke, according to Bendias (2011), p. 69.

⁴ In conversation with the author (23 October 1977), Prof. István Szerdahelyi indicated that there was a secret order of the Party to this effect.

⁵ An imposing achievement was the 400-page work of Detlev Blanke, *Internationale Plansprachen. Eine Einführung* (Berlin: Akademie-Verlag, 1985), which appeared in a prestigious linguistics series. See also Blanke's reminiscences (Blanke 2007a).

Congresses in Sofia (1963), Budapest (1966 and 1983) and Varna (1978) were not only important manifestations of the revived self-confidence of Esperantists in the socialist countries but also a source of inspiration for guests from all over the world.

Clearly, Esperanto was attractive to large numbers of citizens in the Eastern European countries. Recognition of the strength of the movement caused the regimes to cut back on trying to limit Esperanto activity. They understood that permitting and legalizing the Esperanto movement would be more prudent than suppressing it and thereby increasing the potential for discontent. To maintain state favor, the Esperantist leaders on occasion made direct demonstration of their loyalty to the prevailing politics—to a degree that varied with the country. While the journals of the associations in Hungary and Poland normally contented themselves with small doses of politically colored articles, those in Bulgaria, Czechoslovakia and GDR devoted a considerable part of the contents to Esperanto-language interpretation and popularization of party politics. But even in these latter countries the Esperantists could not always hide the gap between the party line and their own thinking.

Occasional official campaigns for ideological purity were not without influence. In Bulgaria the BEA Central Committee warned its members about the dangers associated with the relaxation of world political tensions, pointing out that this generally welcome process also provided Western ideologies with new and more subtle means of influence. In a report to its national congress in 1972, the Central Committee admitted the inadequacy of its ideological work and demanded that 'Esperantists who travel to international events abroad' should be more active and flexible in unmasking lies and calumnies 'about our country'.[6] Sometimes the rhetoric was reminiscent of the language of the Stalinist era, for example, when 'national nihilism, abstract internationalism, rootless cosmopolitanism' were called 'a not uncommon phenomenon in Esperantist ranks'.[7] There were calls for 'channeling, regular organization and

---

[6] *La taskoj de la bulgara esperantista movado en la tutpopola batalo por konstruo de evoluinta socialisma socio. Raporto de CK de Bulgara Esperantista Asocio antaŭ la 38-a Nacia Esperantista Kongreso (urbo Smoljan, 3-an—4-an de julio 1972)*, duplicated typescript, pp. 10, 18.

[7] Nikola Aleksiev, 'Georgi Dimitrov pri la patriotismo kaj la internaciismo', *Bulgara Esperantisto* 41 (1972), 1: 1.

political-ideological redirecting of international correspondence' by the Bulgarian Esperantists, who should correspond not only individually but also collectively, refrain from 'narrow practicalism'[8] and do more than simply 'express their personal thoughts and feelings' in letters abroad.[9]

This was the price that BEA had to pay for the extensive support received from the authorities. With its similar calls for member discipline, ĈEA had to do more than simply repay the favors of the official authorities. ĈEA's Second Congress, set to take place in April 1972, had to be twice delayed because the ideological commitment required of the Czech Esperantists by the post-Dubček regime was still seen as insufficient. The Congress finally took place in 1976 and the Association promised in its program of activities that it 'will uncompromisingly resist and prevent dangerous inclinations to Esperantist "sectarianism"'.[10]

Until the fall of 'real socialism', the ideological aspects of Esperanto often caused headaches among the official representatives of the Eastern European movement. Cosmopolitanism and pacifism, ever since the time of Zamenhof, had played a significant role among the adepts of Esperanto. This idealistic legacy collided with the claim of the party ideologues that they and they alone could provide the right interpretation of internationalism and the battle for peace, and so the members often had to listen to directives from their leaders concerning the anachronistic character of the 'internal idea'. Such educational campaigns showed a tendency to exaggerate Zamenhof's naïveté and to attribute to the Esperantists more mysticism than they possessed. Detlev Blanke, for example, the better to assail any false faith in a mysterious internal force or in Esperanto as a panacea, emphasized the obvious fact that language was a tool and nothing more, picturing the traditional Esperantist idea that the language

---

[8] 'Rezolucio de la 38-a Kongreso de la Bulgara Esperantista Asocio [...]', *Bulgara Esperantisto* 41 (1972), 9: 3–6 (quotations pp. 4–5).

[9] 'Al obstina laboro!', *Bulgara Esperantisto* 43 (1974), 5: 2. Similarly, ĈEA criticized non-member Esperantists for 'anachronistically' defending 'their hobbyist, sectarian standpoint' and making of Esperanto 'a mere object of personal amusement': 'Ĉu "nur" politiko?', *Starto*, 1974, 3/4 (41/42): 1.

[10] *Programo de Ĉeĥa Esperanto-Asocio por la jaroj 1976–1980*, duplicated typescript (8 February 1976), p. 5.

serves as a means to a more peaceful world as a naïve belief that Esperanto in and of itself creates brotherhood among humankind.[11]

Such a line of argument barely concealed the nub of the problem. Complaints about the modernization of the 'internal idea' in the form of 'humanitarian internationalism' showed that the problem lay elsewhere—not in sectarian adoration of the language but in any effort to interpret the ideals linked to Esperanto in a fashion different from the prevailing ideology. This ideology did not allow the Esperantists in socialist countries to feel a primary loyalty to humanistic ideals, to an international way of thinking that transcended the interests of socialism—regardless of whether it related to the 'internal idea', or pacifism, or 'contact among people' and 'improvement in the exchange of information', as the Helsinki Final Act put it (see below, pp. 129–30).

Teachings destined for the most part to protect the movement against the authorities' disfavor had little effect on the Esperantists in Eastern Europe. They could easily reply to the invocation that they should work for peace and thereby prove their lack of sectarianism with the argument, hard to contest, that as Esperantists they certainly did not belong to the instigators of war and therefore needed no special admonition to demonstrate their support for peace. Furthermore, there was a limit to the pressure that could be put on them: their leaders, eager to disseminate Esperanto, depended on the idealism of the members and they themselves were more or less consciously under its influence.[12] We should also keep in mind that the governments, facing a crisis of legitimacy, needed support, and 'the clear messianic quality of the Esperanto movement was a characteristic with which the communist mentality had a certain sympathy'.[13]

Many Esperantists in the socialist countries were prevented from fully profiting from the universality of the Esperanto movement. Such obstacles applied equally to the majority of citizens, not only the Esperantists.

---

[11] Detlev Blanke, 'Pri la"interna ideo" de Esperanto', in Blanke (1986), pp. 182–208.

[12] Except perhaps for a few careerist opportunists. An interesting effort to explore the question of whether party membership and Esperanto were compatible was carried out by the former IPE activist Georges Salan: see his *UEA kaj la neŭtraleco* (Nîmes, 1978). The topic is dealt with in greater detail in my article 'Ruĝ-verda malakordo. Observoj pri komunistaj esperantistoj', in Blanke & Lins (2010), pp. 443–61.

[13] Benczik (1990), p. 92; similarly Bendias (2011), p. 143.

In addition to censorship and the confiscation of Western literature we should mention also currency restrictions which hindered subscription to foreign periodicals, the ordering of books, the payment of membership fees to international organizations and, most acutely, mass tourism. It was not always easy to distinguish between general limits on citizen freedom and specific discrimination against Esperantists. In Czechoslovakia, Esperantists found that what in most parts of the world would be regarded as perfectly understandable, in their country aroused suspicion. In 1973 an Esperantist who entertained Western guests later learned from his employer that the employer was informed by the secret police that the Esperantist had Esperanto contacts abroad. Other Esperantists were also subjected to detailed questioning by the police, who informed their places of work about their international communications.

To these obstacles we can juxtapose the fact that developments were in many ways positive for the Esperanto movement. This was most evident in Hungary and Poland, the most 'liberal' countries. But also in the GDR, when legalization finally came, the Esperantists were able to enjoy through their umbrella institution, the Cultural League, a status that—considering their weakness of numbers—was even privileged. Specifically, this meant the availability of a favorable budget that included Western currency. Almost all Eastern European associations were equipped with large offices. HEA, beginning in 1976, published no less than 138 books, at first to satisfy the thirst for books among Hungarian Esperantists and later also those in the Soviet Union. The Association finally even managed to use official channels, for example by informing the Soviet agency for the import of books that the thoroughly Esperantist novel by Julio Baghy, *La verda koro*, 'describes the heroic battle of the Red Army against the imperialist invaders'.[14]

According to one Hungarian activist, the Esperanto movement in Eastern Europe functioned 'as a specific micro-society, providing an opportunity for a certain kind of spiritual emigration'.[15] A Bulgarian sociologist who in the 1980s carried out interviews primarily in Bulgaria,

---

[14] Vilmos Benczik, *Pri la natureco kaj artefariteco de lingvoj*, Budapest: Trezor, 2016, p. 144.
[15] Benczik (1990), p. 92.

Czechoslovakia and Poland, noted that the Esperantists in those countries did not isolate themselves from their surroundings: family, school, work. If a letter came from abroad (which in itself could be a major event), they gladly showed it to those of their acquaintances who were most interested in human-interest topics.[16] Such contacts with other countries, customarily regarded with suspicion by the regime, finally ceased to be out of the ordinary if the members of Esperanto associations shared them. They possessed a kind of exotic attraction, particularly evident in the GDR, whose citizens, unlike, for example, Poles and Hungarians, were prevented from traveling. Instead, they wrote letters (one young woman acquired 100 contacts in 60 countries) or themselves hosted visitors from abroad. It caused something of a sensation to show a Japanese visitor the sights of Potsdam using Esperanto.

In the 1980s, the Ministry for State Security in the GDR (the 'Stasi') conducted a detailed investigation of suspected members of an Esperanto youth group. Over two years a 200-page file was compiled, without concrete results. The informer for the Stasi was so frustrated that he stopped working for them. At least six informers not only discovered that Esperanto was not dangerous but were infected with its charms and accordingly lost their value to the regime.[17]

In more or less every country in Eastern Europe relative harmony was established between the Esperantists and the regime, which did not at all mind gaining a reputation for 'soft dictatorship' because of its tolerance. As early as 1961, HEA removed from its constitution the statement that it acted 'in the spirit of proletarian internationalism', and in 1980 it declared its aim as stimulating 'the establishment of correspondence and direct personal international relations and friendships'[18]—a formula made possible thanks to the agreement among European countries for security and cooperation that culminated in the Helsinki Final Act

---

[16] Velitchkova (2014), p. 66.
[17] Bendias (2011), pp. 265–7.
[18] Rátkai (1985), pp. 89–90. HEA changed its constitution to facilitate its affiliation with UEA (1962).

(1975).¹⁹ Today we appreciate the historical significance of this process, since, in emphasizing the value of contacts and exchanges independently of ideologies, it helped to 'undermine' the socialism of the Eastern Bloc. To the last, the GDR tried to resist such softening, and its Esperanto movement presented itself to the outside world as orthodox. But even in the GDR there were niches that young Esperantists exploited and enlivened. In interviews carried out after German reunification, remembering their former hopes and desires connected with Esperanto, they proudly mentioned the effects of that engagement: Esperanto removed prejudices and strengthened self-confidence, it 'vaccinated' them against nationalism and was a democratizing element even before 1965.²⁰

In Hungary and Poland the room to maneuver was always greater: as early as 1985–86 the Esperanto associations in those countries introduced democratic elections for their leading posts, well before the great transformation in Eastern Europe in 1989–90. In this way they made pioneering contributions to the democratization of their society.²¹ Ultimately, in almost all countries in the 'Eastern Bloc' there were hardly any obstacles to learning the language or publicizing it, although a few political and ideological factors negatively affected the position of Esperanto right up to the end. References to the fact that 'among a few elderly Marxist functionaries' there was still skepticism about Esperanto²² served as reminders of the influence of the Stalinist legacy.

In this connection, it is characteristic that silence was generally maintained about the history of persecutions and that, when Westerners broke that silence, the reaction was extremely sensitive. In 1968 UEA's journal published an article on 'Persecutions against the International Language', evoking a furious attack from the SEU veteran Podkaminer ('a crude and contemptible screed fashioned out of distorted facts, rumors, unashamed

---

[19] Esperanto translation: *Fina Akto de la Konferenco pri Sekureco kaj Kunlaboro en Eŭropo* (Bratislava: Ĉeĥoslovaka Packomitato, 1976).
[20] Bendias (2011), p. 169.
[21] Rátkai (1990), pp. 86–90 (esp. p. 87).
[22] Detlev Blanke, 'Informado kaj argumentado', *Der Esperantist* 16 (1980): 105.

inventions and open calumnies').²³ And when in 1973 it became known that the forthcoming study *Esperanto en perspektivo* would contain a detailed chapter on the history of persecutions, the Esperanto associations in the socialist countries protested to UEA 'against the self-serving publication' of that chapter: the authorities and the Esperantists in those countries would consider it 'an antisocialist maneuver' that 'could only hinder our future activities'.²⁴

The protest, which in fact had no result, was a sign of a persistent taboo. In the Moscow Esperanto club a lecture on the Nazi persecution of Esperanto could not take place for fear that it would provoke comparison between the actions of Hitler and Stalin.²⁵ Even in 1988, UEA was unable to publish the first edition of the present volume in its own name but instead used as surrogate the West German publisher Bleicher. Only China began openly to explain how and why Esperanto had undergone disfavor. The cessation of the activities of the Chinese Esperanto League at the beginning of the 1950s was attributed to the need at the time to follow the model of the Soviet Union, and, on the Cultural Revolution, it was alleged that 'the ultra-leftist flow of thought' almost entirely suppressed the Esperanto movement, allowing the use of the language only for outside propaganda (Fig. 10.1).²⁶

In Eastern Europe under the rule of 'real socialism', on the contrary, at most there were passing mentions of the 'stagnation' of Esperanto

---

[23] S. Podkaminer, 'Kaj ankoraŭfoje pri "neŭtralismo"', *Paco* 15 (1968), 178/179: 39. According to Podkaminer, the article is 'a direct defense of authentic imperialism and aggression'.

[24] Ulrich Lins, 'Ni sentabuigu la historion de la Movado', *Esperanto* 68 (1975): 186–7 (quotation p. 186).

[25] Kharkovsky (http://miresperanto.com).

[26] Hou Zhiping, 'La Esperanto-movado en Ĉinio', *El Popola Ĉinio*, 1982, 4: 19–20. Recruitment for Esperanto and personal contacts abroad grew dangerous in China as of 1966. Several Esperantists were imprisoned. The poet Armand Su (1936–1990), for example, who often published texts in foreign Esperanto periodicals, was arrested in April 1968 and condemned to 20 years imprisonment; he was freed only in 1979. See his remembrances: '23 jaroj per kaj por Esperanto', *El Popola Ĉinio*, 1979, 10: 27–9; 11: 40–3. Similar experiences: Hu Guozhu, 'Punlaboro pro Esperanto', *La Gazeto* 25 (2010), 150: 26–7. On the unremitting underground activity of Chinese Esperantists during the Cultural Revolution, see Ikso (Xu Daorong), 'Post la "kvarpersona bando"', *Esperanto* 72 (1979): 23–4; Shi Chengtai, 'Legenda hieraŭo', *La Gazeto* 14 (1999), 85: 13–15.

Fig. 10.1 The Chinese poet Armand Su endured years of suffering during the cultural revolution because of his foreign contacts

during the 'period of the personality cult'[27] or of 'the unfortunate errors of Stalin'.[28]

This historical reticence was paralleled by a latent uncertainty and unease about the political and ideological implications of work for Esperanto. We have already given a few examples: warnings about sectarianism and admonitions for 'social engagement' were aimed at convincing the authorities of the civic loyalty of the Esperantists, and efforts to prescribe the content of correspondence grew out of awareness that the party jealously protected its monopoly on information. The argumentation for Esperanto was not infrequently accompanied by a defensive tone. Early in October 1972, the then president of MEM, Nikola Aleksiev, felt the

---

[27] Reprinting an article on the founding of the Association of Soviet Esperantists in the UEA journal, *Esperantisto Slovaka* (1979: 33) omitted a sentence about the 'Stalinist pogrom' against SEU (thereby rendering the following sentence meaningless). In 1976 the British IPE veteran William Keable called for breaking the silence, insisting that Stalin's Esperantist victims 'should not be shamefully forgotten as if they were nameless dogs killed in a street accident': Bill Keable, 'Marxism-Leninism requires *all* the facts', *Communist Party Esperanto Group, Bulletin*, 1976, 8 (Apr.): 1–5 (quotation p. 5). Keable seems to have been the first communist Esperantist to make any mention of the persecution of Esperantists in the Soviet Union. He published a short article on the subject in *Comment*, an internal periodical of the British Communist Party, 18 November 1972.

[28] Ervin Fenyvesi, 'Revuo de revuoj', *Hungara Vivo* 23 (1983), 1: 23. At the founding of the association in GDR, according to Bendias (2011), p. 66, silence on the persecutions was a *sine qua non*.

10 Eastern Europe: Progress and Problems

need to publicly distance himself from 'incorrect concepts and "theories"' spreading through the Esperanto movement. In Moscow he used a conference of representatives of societies for friendship with the Soviet Union as a forum to criticize certain aspects of the campaign against 'linguistic imperialism'. What worried him was the fact that the users of this increasingly popular slogan in the Western Esperanto movement made no distinction between the dominance of the languages of the great imperialist states on the one hand and the position of Russian and the Soviet Union on the other—that they did not understand 'that the Russian language has equal rights with all languages of the nations of the socialist community' and that the peoples of the Soviet Union freely chose it as 'a means for international understanding without any loss for the national languages and cultures of all other nations'.[29] Aleksiev's initiative was not unique. Similarly, in 1975 the general secretary of MEM, William Gilbert, declared that it was unacceptable to wage an isolated campaign against 'linguistic imperialism' while neglecting the battle against the 'social, economic, and military blunders' of imperialism, compared with which 'the language problem is entirely accessory'.[30]

Remarkable in these statements from two important communist Esperantists is the fact that both linked Esperanto to linguistic and political problems of greater significance and that their attention was directed at the Soviet Union.

---

[29] N. Aleksiev, 'Pri unu aspekto de la interŝtataj rilatoj en la socialisma komuneco de nacioj', *Paco*, 1974, Soviet edition, pp. 24–5.

[30] William Gilbert, 'Esperanto kontraŭ naciaj lingvoj?', *Paco*, 1979, GDR edition, p. 27. Earlier, Gilbert had a different opinion, seeing no difference between the dominance of English and French in Western Europe and that of Russian in the Soviet Union: *La Pacdefendanto*, 1952, 11: 2.

11

The Soviet Union: Between Hope and Doubt

The Soviet revival of Esperanto brought new opportunities for action that the Esperantists seized enthusiastically, although their hopes for the immediate establishment of an association were not fulfilled. At the beginning of August 1957, as part of the Sixth World Youth Festival in Moscow, a meeting of 250 Esperantists from 26 countries took place—the first such international Esperanto event ever organized in the Soviet capital (Fig. 11.1).[1]

Shortly before the meeting, the first Esperanto book to be published in the Soviet Union in 20 years appeared: a modest textbook[2] in 95,000 copies, which sold out immediately. At the end of 1959 the Moscow International Esperanto Club was founded in the Central House of Medical Workers,[3] and elsewhere the Esperantists similarly organized themselves under the

---

[1] See the reports of participants: *Esperanto* 50 (1957): 172; 51 (1958): 12–13; *Germana Esperanto-Revuo* 10 (1957): 125. While the West German Esperantists who participated in the festival encountered suspicion from their own authorities because of their visit to Moscow, in Moscow they had to overcome efforts by bureaucrats to prevent a meeting between foreigners and Moscow Esperantists who were not festival attendees.

[2] N.D. Andreev, *Mezhdunarodnyi vspomogatel'nyi iazyk èsperanto. Kratkaia grammatika i slovar'-minimum*, Leningrad, 1957.

[3] A. Ĥarkovskij, 'La Moskva Internacia…', *Bulgara Esperantisto* 44 (1975), 3/4: 23–4.

Fig. 11.1 During the world youth festival in Moscow in 1957, Soviet Esperantists were able to meet with foreigners for the first time. Standing, L to R: 2 Liudmila Bokareva, 4 Nikolai Rytkov, 5 Nguyen Van Kinh (Vietnamese Ambassador)

auspices of trade union clubs and cultural centers.[4] Summer camps, held annually as of 1959 in the Baltic republics, and later elsewhere, helped to strengthen contacts among formerly isolated activists.

The other side of the coin, however, was the fact that in 1959, a hundred years after Zamenhof's birth, not a single Soviet Esperantist could attend the World Congress of Esperanto in Warsaw. The journal *Armena Esperantisto* appeared only once in 1958. When textbooks in Esperanto were published, they appeared in ridiculously small numbers and did not

---

[4] In August 1959 it was decided that Esperanto circles could receive financial support from the budgets of local branches of the Trade Unions and Komsomol: S. Sariĉev, 'La movado en USSR progresas', *Nuntempa Bulgario* 4 (1960), 1: 42.

begin to satisfy the interest.⁵ The youth group 'Fajrero' (Spark), organized after the Festival, vainly sought official recognition. 'There were no refusals—also no replies.'⁶ According to Boris Kolker, a censorship ban on mentioning Esperanto in a favorable context remained in place until 1969.⁷ In the early 1960s, an alleged 'cosmopolitan' maxim was removed from a Moscow university exhibition on Esperanto, namely, a quotation from Zamenhof: 'I see in every human being simply a human being' (*Mi vidas en ĉiu homo nur homon*).⁸

In 1963, after more than a quarter-century, an official delegation of Soviet Esperantists was again able to travel abroad. The occasion was the 48th World Congress of Esperanto in Sofia. The visit was arranged only after the Central Committee of the Bulgarian Communist Party had warned the Soviet Party that the country's lack of representation in such a large international event would create an unfavorable impression.⁹ In the same year the ban on publications in Esperanto was lifted,¹⁰ allowing the publication of a series of brochures—modestly printed propaganda booklets entitled *Por la paco*, but also translations from Russian literature. A more impressive achievement was the 536-page Russian-Esperanto Dictionary compiled by Bokarev and published in 1966 in 50,000 copies by the publisher Soviet Encyclopedia.¹¹

In 1962 a 'Commission for the International Relations of Soviet Esperantists' was founded as part of the 'Union of Soviet Societies of Friendship and Cultural Relations with Foreign Countries' (Russian abbreviation: SSOD) with Bokarev as president. But the Commission was not a national association of Soviet Esperantists; it had neither the mandate nor the right to disseminate Esperanto in the Soviet Union, nor

---

⁵ The textbook by I.V. Sergeev, *Osnovy èsperanto* (Moscow: Institut mezhdunarodnykh otnoshenii 1961), appeared in 50,000 copies, others in still smaller numbers.
⁶ Svetlana Smetanina, 'Lia lasta vojaĝo' [obituary on Vladimir Korchagin], *REGo*, 2012, 1 (68): 17–19 (quotation p. 18).
⁷ Boris Kolker, 'Mia vivo en Esperanto-lando', *REGo*, 2014, 83: 5–19 (esp. p. 11).
⁸ Samodaj (2010), p. 53. The quotation is from the *Deklaracio pri Homaranismo* (1913).
⁹ Samodaj (2010), p. 54. From then on, Soviet Esperantists, even if in small numbers, attended World Congresses in the west. Over a hundred attended the congress in Varna, Bulgaria (1978).
¹⁰ *Hungara Esperantisto* 4 (1964), 11: 6.
¹¹ It was followed in 1974, in 40,000 copies, by Bokarev's Esperanto-Russian Dictionary, which the author finished shortly before he died.

coordinate the work of local Esperanto clubs. This vacuum was gradually filled by the efforts of young activists, who had already created the tradition of camps in forests and mountainous regions. A kind of organization emerged in 1965: the 'Address List of Young Soviet Esperantists', whose bulletin *Juna Esperantisto* was typewritten on tissue paper. This initiative led in 1966 to the formation of the Soviet Esperantist Youth Movement (SEJM). Originally a loose linkage of Esperanto Groups scattered across the Soviet Union, it gradually attained the structure of a national organization. SEJM did what the Commission could not do—recruiting, teaching, organizing meetings—and published regular periodicals that were for many years unknown outside the Soviet Union (Fig. 11.2).[12]

In parallel with youth activity, scholarly work continued, particularly at the Institute of Linguistics at the Academy of Sciences, where in the mid-1950s Bokarev made his courageous new beginning.[13] The goal of these activities was explained in a 1968 article in *Literaturnaia gazeta*. This article laid out the facts on the massive increase in scientific and technological information in a growing number of languages and concluded that agreement was needed on an international language for science. That role could be assumed not by a national language but only by a planned language.[14] This emphasis on a pressing need, long pointed out by the Esperantists, was neither accidental nor ephemeral: in October 1973 (after the death of Bokarev) the Academy of Sciences officially decided 'to explore the problem of an auxiliary language for

---

[12] D.M. Cibulevskij, *SEJM. Historia skizo*, Moscow: Impeto, 1994, pp. 78–82. Of the periodical *Kurte* (Vilnius), 136 issues appeared between September 1976 and July 1982. Of the 'underground' Esperanto periodicals particularly important were *Amikeco* (1961–67, 1974–84) and *Unuiĝo* (1965–69); they were mostly published in the Baltic states. See the series of articles 'Ekstercenzura Esperanta literaturo', in *Litova Stelo*, 1993, no. 5, to 1994, no. 1; Saulcerīte Neilande, 'Ekstercenzuraj eldonajoj en Latvio', *Latvia Esperantisto*, 1995, 23 (May): 1–2; Cibulevskij (2000), pp. 97–9; personal communication from Jaan Ojalo, 18 January 2001. A description of number 13 of a literary almanac, published in only a few copies, was provided by *Bulgara Esperantisto* 47 (1978), 11: 12–13.

[13] See the overview by A.D. Dulichenko, 'Obzor vazhneishikh interlingvisticheskikh izuchenii v SSSR' (Review of the most important interlinguistic studies in the Soviet Union), *Interlinguistica Tartuensis* 3 (1984): 3–39. A useful bibliography is A.D. Dulichenko, *Sovetskaia interlingvistika. Annotirovannaia bibliografiia za 1946–1982 gg.*, Tartu: Tartuskii Gosudarstvennyi Universitet, 1983.

[14] A. Berg, D. Armand, E. Bokarev, '64 iazyka ... i eshche odin' (64 languages ... and one more), *Literaturnaia gazeta*, 28 August 1968; trans. in Bokarjova (2010), pp. 105–9.

Fig. 11.2 Leaders of the semi-legal 'Soviet Esperantist Youth Movement' in 1971: V. Šilas, M. Bronshtein, A. Vizgirdas, A. Goncharov, B. Kolker, V. Arolovich, A. Mediņš

international communication and its applicability under present conditions'. This decision was fulfilled in May 1974 with the founding of a 'Task force on issues of an international auxiliary language' at the Institute of Linguistics; among the research topics listed was the structure and function of Esperanto.[15]

The chairing of the group was confided to the sociolinguist Magomet Isaev, also Bokarev's successor as president of the Commission for the International Relations of Soviet Esperantists. Isaev, who came from Ossetia, learned Esperanto in 1956–57 under Bokarev's influence, seeing the language as a contribution to the solution of a problem that had long concerned him, namely, how to reconcile the goal of a future

---

[15] Text of the decision (of 18 October 1973) in Detlev Blanke (ed.), *Esperanto. Lingvo, movado, instruado,* Berlin: Kulturbund der DDR, 1977, pp. 128–9.

'ethnicity-free' communist society with the existence of hundreds and thousands of languages.[16]

Isaev explained that the goal of the Task Force was, on the basis of its research, to prepare documents to be submitted to 'the highest political organs'.[17] The intent of the Esperantists, then, was to build a solid, scientifically based argument that would assist in removing the remnants of politically and ideologically motivated opposition and attract official support for organized activity for Esperanto. To understand the significance of these efforts we must consider the background against which the Soviet Esperantists sought to revive their activities after years of severe persecution. To do that, we must look at developments relative to the problem of Soviet nationalities and languages.

When, in his famous speech of 1956, Khrushchev revealed the crimes of Stalin, he named among them Stalin's crude disregard for Lenin's principles concerning the nationalities policy. Khrushchev's revelation of injustices, including the mass deportation of minorities, coupled with the fact that the Party had for the first time published Lenin's notes criticizing Stalin's enthusiasm for annexation and warning against the suppression of non-Russian nationalities,[18] seemed to signal more tolerant policies toward the national cultures of the Soviet Union. Undoubtedly the Esperantists also took joyous note of this reminder of Lenin's dictum that no language should be privileged over others.

However, soon the wheel turned again—toward centralization. In August 1958 the Party's theoretical journal published an article by the historian Bobodzhan Gafurov, who invoked the final goals of communism, namely, the 'commingling' and 'melding' of the nations, implicitly conveying the idea that their 'flowering' was merely temporary.[19] Three years later, in 1961, at the 22nd Congress of the CPSU, the new

---

[16] Mahomet Isaev, 'De vilaĝo al ĉefurbo', *REGo*, 2003, 1 (14): 3–4.
[17] M.I. Isaev, 'Pri bazaj metodologiaj problemoj de interlingvistiko', *Der Esperantist* 11 (1975), 3 (71): 11–15 (quotation p. 15).
[18] 'On the Question of Nationalities or "Autonomisation"' (1922), Lenin, *Collected Works*, vol. 36, 1966, p. 606.
[19] B. Gafurov, 'Uspekhi natsional'noi politiki KPSS i nekotorye voprosy internatsional'nogo vospitaniia' (Successes of the nationalities policy of the CPSU and some problems of international education), *Kommunist*, 1958, 11 (Aug.): 10–24; cf. Gerhard Simon (1991), p. 246.

party program essentially adopted this position. It proclaimed the coming transition to communism and, in line with this transition, directed the peoples of the Soviet Union to join together to prepare for the coming complete unity. The program noted that 'an international culture common to the Soviet nations' was evolving, and it drew particular attention to the growing significance of the Russian language (Khrushchev called it 'a second mother tongue'), which also allowed the Russian people access to world culture.[20]

The program spelt discouragement for the efforts of the non-Russian peoples to strengthen and further develop their cultural identity. The Party regarded such efforts as divisive, in contrast to the struggle for the solidarity of all Soviet citizens working for unity in communism. The new political direction also had unfavorable implications for the Esperantists. In his reorienting article of 1958, Gafurov declared that, in connection with the transition from socialism to communism, 'we cannot *not* be interested' in formation of a unifying language. His meaning was clear: he reiterated the contention that on the way to merger the national languages would first join together in 'zonal languages'. As we know, the concept, proclaimed by Stalin and legitimizing the formation of a Russian 'zonal language', served as theoretical justification for suppression of the Esperanto movement, so it is no wonder that Gafurov expressed his opposition to Esperanto.[21] The Soviet Esperantists, whose leader Bokarev had in 1956 linked this idea with linguistic imperialism, had clearly lost ground.

The party program itself did not touch on the question of a world language. But authoritative theorists on the nationalities problem did. One of them, Kuchkar Khanazarov, also re-popularized Stalin's idea and added disapproving words on Esperanto.[22] A similar position was taken by the philosopher Mikhail Kammari, who proudly named himself 'an ardent opponent of Esperanto', explaining his position as follows:

---

[20] Leonard Schapiro (ed.), *The U.S.S.R. and the Future: An Analysis of the New Program of the CPSU*, New York & London: Praeger, 1963, pp. 82, 302; Gerhard Simon (1991), p. 313.

[21] Gafurov, p. 17; see also *Paco* 6 (1959), 63 (Feb.): 4.

[22] K.Kh. Khanazarov, *Sblizhenie natsii i natsional'nye iazyki v SSSR* (The intermingling of nationalities and national languages in the USSR), Tashkent: Akademia nauk Uzbekskoi SSR, 1963, pp. 224–5.

[...] first because Esperantists promote their language as the future language of a classless society, while the language, created by a single person, a non-Marxist, 75 years ago, cannot satisfy us today. Meanwhile, a battle is developing between the English and Russian languages over the role of the future dominant language of communism. Accordingly, Esperanto will at best find itself in last place in this battle. [...] Secondly, from letters received, it is perfectly evident that a few passionate Esperantists aim to replace the Russian language in the Soviet Union with Esperanto and force the Soviet republics to deal with one another through Esperanto. [...] For us this is an alien ideology of bourgeois internationalism, which we have destroyed but which is again raising its head under the banner of Esperanto. Thus, Esperanto, feeding on the juices of bourgeois nationalism, is for us a dangerous, poisonous creation.[23]

This is a rare example of treatment of Esperanto by a Soviet theorist in connection with the language situation internal to the Soviet Union. It shows that Esperanto—rightly or wrongly—was feared as a weapon in the hands of people who refused to submit to official advocacy of Russian as the common language of all Soviet citizens.

The change in party policy was not without its opponents. There was much discontent among the non-Russian peoples, particularly the Ukrainians, who suspected that the Party, under the guise of internationalism, aimed to speed up assimilation. And this opposition was not without effect. After the fall of Khrushchev in October 1964, there was a discernible weakening of propaganda for the commingling of the Soviet peoples. Voices were raised calling for defense of the pluralism of ethnic groups and languages. In Georgia, for example, the writer Irakli Abashidze pointed out in 1966 that it was the 'renegade' Kautsky who once foresaw the merger of peoples and languages in one nation and one language, yet the almost 50-year Soviet experience with cultural development negated that prognosis entirely.[24] Encouraging the aspirations of non-Russians

---

[23] Minutes of 14 May 1964; see below, p. 143 and note 28. On Kammari's position see also his articles 'Stroitel'stvo kommunizma i razvitie natsional'nykh iazykov' (The building of communism and the development of national languages), *Politicheskoe samoobrazovanie*, 1960, 4: 66–76; 'K voprosu o budushchem vsemirnom iazyke' (On the question of a future world language), *Kommunist Ėstonii*, 1964, July: 66–71.

[24] V. Stanley Vardys, 'Altes und Neues in der sowjetischen Nationalitätenpolitik seit Chruschtschows Sturz', *Osteuropa* 18 (1968): 83.

were demographic trends: the census of 1970 showed that, while the proportion of Russians among all Soviet ethnic groups had declined (from 54.8% to 50.5%), the southern and eastern ethnic groups had undergone a considerable 'baby boom', and less than half of the non-Russian population indicated a good knowledge of the Russian language.[25]

Under the impression of these facts, which cast doubt on the vision of unification, and faced with a more resentful attitude among non-Russians, in the mid-1960s the Party abandoned its intrusive campaigning for Russian as a second mother tongue and instead declared that in the 'dialectical' process of simultaneous melding and flowering of the nations, Russian had assumed the role of 'a medium of exchange [...] between nations'.[26] The Party continued to stress the internationalist unity of the Soviet peoples (as of 1971 the formula used was 'a new historic commonwealth of individuals—the Soviet people'), and the final goal of a melding of the nations did not disappear from the ideology, but, in contrast to the era of Khrushchev, the melding was pushed out to the distant future. In the 1970s the Party followed a middle path in its nationalities policy, on the one hand supporting the process of commingling and on the other avoiding superfluously upsetting the non-Russians by propagandizing imminent merger. Leonid Brezhnev himself said in 1972 that rapprochement was an objective process that should not be artificially speeded up or restrained.[27]

For the Soviet Esperantists it was advantageous that the Party had moderated its formerly sharply 'assimilationist' approach to the problem of nationalities and languages. An important colloquium on Esperanto took place in May 1964 at the Council on Cybernetics,[28] with participation by senior members of the Academy of Sciences and of various institutes

---

[25] Carrère d'Encausse (1979), pp. 48–90, 165–88; Gerhard Simon (1991), p. 322–7.

[26] *Fiftieth Anniversary of the Great October Socialist Revolution. Theses of the Central Committee of the CPSU*. Washington, DC: U.S.S.R. Embassy, 1967, p. 33.

[27] *Pravda*, 22-12-1972, quoted by Kenneth C. Farmer, *Ukrainian Nationalism in the Post-Stalin Era: Myth, Symbols and Ideology in Soviet Nationalities Policy*, The Hague: Nijhoff, 1980, p. 73; see also Gerhard Simon (1991), p. 228 and following.

[28] An Esperanto translation of the minutes (four typed pages) of that meeting (14 May 1964) reached the west (I am grateful to SAT for supplying a copy); excerpts in *Sennaciulo* 36 (1965): 30; another translation appeared in *Litova Stelo* 10 (2000), 2 (132): 20–3. Probably the same meeting is discussed in N. Danovskij, 'Scienco, sciencisto kaj *Esperanto*', *Internacia Jurnalisto* 20 (1981), 2 (May/June): 3.

attached to it.[29] It was organized by Academician Aksel Berg, after whose opening speech those present expressed their views. The position of opponents of Esperanto was taken by the philosopher Kammari, whom we quoted above. Against him, Berg argued that the discussion did not concern the future language of humanity but the current utility of an auxiliary language, particularly for science. Of such practical use of Esperanto Kammari did not express disapproval, but he insisted that the Esperantists wanted more and that they hindered the battle for the common language of a classless society.[30] Kammari even denied that Esperanto had been persecuted, though he later tempered his position when he heard that the Chinese were making extensive use of the language in their anti-Soviet agitation, and he finally joined the unanimous conclusion, which contained eight proposals for the future stimulation of the Soviet Esperanto movement.

A section on interlinguistics was founded in the Institute of Linguistics, and the linguist Viktor Grigoriev was able to publish a long, carefully argued article in 1966 in the journal *Voprosy iazykoznaniia* entitled 'Some questions in interlinguistics'.[31] He labeled as unscientific Gafurov and Kammari's assumption that the future language would be created naturally and spontaneously through gradual merger of national languages and presented his premise that a universal language could be achieved only by conscious creation—'by an artificial international auxiliary language—a kind of "linguistic Sputnik"'.

Grigoriev was mostly interested in delivering arguments against 'the unjustifiable hostility to interlinguistics'. Isaev, another participant in the meeting, used a similar approach. In an article written in collaboration with the Kyrgyz M.S. Dzhunusov (known for his warnings against assimilationist internationalization), the Ossetian Isaev, opposing

---

[29] Present were A.I. Berg, B.A. Serebrennikov, Iu.D. Desheriev, M.D. Kammari, V.N. Iarceva, V.A. Vasiliev, V.P. Grigoriev, A.G. Spirkin, B.A. Uspensky, S.S. Mikhailov, M.I. Isaev, K.M. Gusev, F.L. Zolotarev and N.F. Danovsky. The organizer, Academician Berg, is considered the founding father of cybernetics in Russia. Stalinist ideology condemned the field as an imperialist pseudoscience, but as of around 1959 it was popularized as the science of the future.

[30] Kammari said: '[…] if you give Esperantists a finger-tip, they catch your whole hand'.

[31] V.P. Grigor'ev, 'O nekotorykh voprosakh interlingvistiki', *Voprosy iazykoznaniia* 16 (1966), 1: 37–46; English translation in *Pensiero e linguaggio in operazioni / Thought and Language in Operations* 2 (1971), 5: 17–30.

Khanazarov, the theorist of merger, carefully differentiated between the future human language and the present artificial language used as an auxiliary beside the national languages.[32]

These exchanges took place in the context of a relatively open and vigorous discussion of the relationship between nation and socialism conducted in scholarly books and journals between 1966 and 1970. During this same period, Bokarev's dictionary appeared, and the Lithuanian government decided to permit, with the academic year 1968–69, the elective teaching of Esperanto in middle schools. The Esperantists felt new hope that their movement would progress, if slowly.

One contribution to the discussion was a Russian-language book entitled *How Will the Universal Language Emerge?*, published under the auspices of the Institute of Philosophy of the Academy of Sciences.[33] Its author was Ermar Svadost.[34] Svadost affirmed the possibility of achieving a scientific synthesis of human languages and accented the need to have available, in time for the establishment of a world communist society, as perfect a universal language as possible, which might in due time take over the function of the national languages.

Svadost came to this conclusion after analyzing other theories on the emergence of a universal language. He criticized *both* the theory of Kautsky, Bogdanov, Khanazarov and others that a universal language would emerge from national languages, which he called incompatible with Lenin's principle of equal national rights, *and* the theory of a world confluence of languages, to whose chief representative Nikolai Marr he attributed contradictions and 'remarkable inconsistency'. He also rejected Stalin's concept of the transitional emergence of zonal languages.

---

[32] M.S. Dzhunusov & M.I. Isaev, 'Sotsiologicheskie voprosy razvitiia natsional'nykh iazykov' (Sociological questions on the development of nationality languages), *Izvestiia Akademii Nauk SSSR. Seriia literatury i iazyka* 24 (1965): 433–7; German translation in Girke & Jachnow (1975), pp. 306–14 (esp. pp. 309–10).

[33] Svadost (1968). On Svadost see Patrick Sériot, 'Pentecôte scientifique et linguistique spontanée. Un projet soviétique de langue universelle du communisme', *Études de lettres* (Lausanne), 1988, Oct./Dec.: 21–33.

[34] Svadost dedicated over two decades to his research and had to wait for 13 years for his completed manuscript to appear: 'Nekrologo. Ermar Svadost (1907–1971)', *La Monda Lingvo-Problemo* 4 (1972): 52–4. The research was interrupted by an 'erroneous exile in Siberia' (p. 52).

Svadost argued for conscious language creation, using arguments broadly similar to those of the Esperantists. However, he clearly stated that Esperanto could not serve as the core of a future world language because it was an 'individual' creation and flowed 'without limitations'. He took a negative view of the pious pacifist Zamenhof and liberal bourgeois influence in the Esperanto movement. Interestingly, Svadost reproached the Esperantists for not attributing to Esperanto the goal of becoming a worldwide language *in place of* the national languages; the more modest claim of disseminating a mere international auxiliary language, he said, could not fit within the framework of the Marxist-Leninist idea of the confluence of national languages.

Svadost's book, then, disapproved of Marr and Stalin but at the same time criticized the customary prejudices against an artificial language. Among Esperantists it had to have evoked mixed feelings, given its clear, largely ideologically motivated disapproval of Esperanto. In rebuttal, the Esperantists highlighted, not unskillfully, his reproach that their goals were too limited and that they did not wish to banish national languages. They lamented the prospect of 'a very unhappy future for humanity' if all peoples and cultures were cut from the same cloth.[35] Arguing that the question of a universal language was of little importance in the present, they stressed the urgent need of an auxiliary language.[36] Svadost had criticized the Esperantist principle that first the language should be disseminated and used and only afterward made perfect, but the Esperantists replied that his insistence on the reverse order, namely, 'maximum perfection' first, amounted to procrastination, which in the meantime would favor the linguistic imperialism of the major national languages.[37]

Svadost's book was only one contribution by a not particularly influential theorist. We should mention that Bokarev, one of the editors of the book, used the foreword to express reservations particularly about the author's linguistic treatment of Esperanto.[38]

---

[35] D.L. Armand, 'Disputo pri libro far E.P. Svadost "Kiel aperos universala lingvo?"', *Scienca Revuo* 28 (1977): 149–54 (quotation p. 153).
[36] According to Svadost's foreword, this was also Bokarev's position.
[37] Stojan Ĝuĝev, 'Interlingvistika utopiismo', in Violin Oljanov (ed.), *Interlingvistiko, esperantologio*, Sofia: Bulgara Esperantista Asocio, 1985, pp. 19–43 (quotation p. 21).
[38] The other editor was Kammari.

11 The Soviet Union: Between Hope and Doubt   147

On the question of a future language there were many other opinions, though seldom as detailed as those in Svadost's book. Perhaps the most influential were the opinions of those who asserted that some national language would become universal.[39] Their positions were essentially assimilationist and more or less clearly agreed with theorists of the nationalities problem who considered the merger of smaller peoples with the major socialist nations a necessary accompaniment of economic development.[40] The theorist Mikhail Kulichenko, for example, stressed that rapprochement would inevitably lead to merger and that those who, unable to imagine such merger in the distant future, turned against rapprochement of the nations in the present, or reduced internationalism to the flowering of nations, were wrong.[41] Another group inclined to the view that the future language of humankind could be an artificial language, enriched by national languages.[42] Like Svadost, they expressed a strong preference for such a solution. Still others anticipated both possibilities: that of an artificial language and that of the coexistence of three or four highly developed national languages, without expressing a clear preference.[43]

While all these theorists agreed on the goal of linguistic unity, Valentin Avrorin took the opposite position. He expressed doubt about the value of speculating on the formation of a unified language or prognosticating over a matter far in the future. Avrorin tried to discredit the dominant acceptance of the disappearance of small languages, attributing it to Kautsky. In his view, the vitality of these languages defied notions of the gradual unification of cultural content under the conditions of socialism: if languages so obstinately resisted processes of concentration, the emergence of a unified language was hardly conceivable.[44] It was, however,

---

[39] This grouping is based on Baziev & Isaev (1973), pp. 215 and following; partial Esperanto translation in Blanke, *Esperanto. Lingvo, movado, instruado*, pp. 1–12. See also Isayev (1977), pp. 383 and following; Duličenko (2003), pp. 112–6.

[40] A.G. Agaev, in *Sotsializm i natsii*, Moscow: Mysl', 1975; German translation: *Sozialismus und Nationen*, Berlin: Dietz, 1976, p. 240.

[41] M.I. Kulichenko, in *Sozialismus und Nationen*, p. 77–9, 82.

[42] V.G. Kostomarov, *Programma KPSS o russkom iazyke*, Moscow, 1963; cf. Baziev & Isaev, p. 217.

[43] Among them S.T. Kaltakhchian, Iu.D. Desheriev and I.F. Protchenko; cf. Baziev & Isaev, p. 218.

[44] Cf. Baziev & Isaev, p. 219; Jonathan Pool, 'Soviet language planning: Goals, results, options', in Jeremy R. Azrael (ed.), *Soviet Nationality Policies and Practices*, New York: Praeger, 1978, pp. 223–49 (esp. p. 243).

reserved for Aleksandr Iakovlev, an eminent member of the Central Committee, to criticize (at the end of 1972) all nationalism, including Russian nationalism; as a reward, he was 'exiled' for ten years as ambassador to Canada.[45]

If one were to attempt to define the position of the Soviet Esperantists, there would be little doubt that they inclined to the opinion of the minority of theorists who favored maximum freedom of development for the existing Soviet languages. What mattered to them was that topics like rapprochement and merger, assimilation of nations and competition of major languages should not so dominate the discussion that they would be put in the embarrassing position of explaining whether and how Esperanto accorded with preparations for linguistic merger. Taking the position that within the Soviet Union the language problem was solved and that there was no need to be concerned with a universal language, they stressed the present, strictly limiting Esperanto to the current need for international communication. 'Our principle must be "both—and", not "either—or"', wrote Isaev, explaining that by this he meant the parallel existence of numerous national languages, of interethnic languages, of the world languages (Russian, English, French, Spanish, Arabic, Chinese) and of the 'international auxiliary language'.[46] In this way Esperanto was presented as an auxiliary language useful *in the present* and it did not collide with the position (and future claims) of Russian as the 'inter-national' language of the Soviet Union nor as a competitor with the 'major languages' on a worldwide scale.

The fact that the Party hesitated between its desire for centralization and its care to avoid provoking widespread discontent among the non-Russian peoples allowed the Esperantists to make their voice heard. In 1976 it proved possible to publish a collection of scholarly contributions on the typology and development of Esperanto and other planned languages.[47] This book also revealed that the principal goal that the Soviet Esperantists attached to their advocacy of Esperanto was to contribute to

---

[45] Brown (2009), p. 413.

[46] Isaev, 'Pri bazaj metodologiaj problemoj', p. 13; cf. VOKO, 'Kia dulingveco?', *Monato* 8 (1987), 1: 21.

[47] Isaev (1976). The collection was prepared by the interlinguistics section of the 'Scientific Council on the Complex Problem "Regularities in the Development of National Languages in Relation to the Development of Socialist Nations"', founded in 1969. The book was dedicated to the memory of Bokarev.

the solution of the strongly felt problem of multilingualism in various contexts, particularly science. Their arguments were essentially pragmatic and in fact were little different from those used by Esperantists in the West. An additional similarity related to recruitment for Esperanto, where progress, as in the West, was slow. On the other hand, the Esperanto movement did not tie its reason for existence to the question of whether the public displayed broad understanding of a rational solution to the language problem. On the contrary, it developed its own dynamic and authentic strength from the pleasure its members derived from using the language and the desire of individuals to communicate easily across frontiers. However distant this may be from the realization of the original goal of convincing the world about the advantages of Esperanto as a second language for all, the fact is that in many countries Esperanto continues to live simply because its speakers find it useful for travel, international congresses and correspondence.

However, it was precisely these opportunities, particularly the use of Esperanto abroad, that the Soviet Esperantists largely lacked. Other than correspondence, they used the language almost entirely among themselves—within the Soviet Union, where Russian was used as the means of communication 'between peoples'—in a country, then, in which, strictly speaking, there was no need for an 'international' auxiliary language.

The Esperantists' care to emphasize primarily the usefulness of Espcranto for facilitating scientific exchanges and as far as possible to put aside the controversial Soviet nationalities problem therefore contrasted with established practice, namely, the fact that thousands of Soviet Esperantists were using the language among themselves and, instead of considering it as a conveyor of scientific information, linking it to a long tradition of idealistic sentiments. Thus, Isaev's scheme, which anticipated clear boundaries between the spheres of usage of various language types, was not observable in actual Esperantist practice. And the interlinguistic theorists themselves were not entirely successful in observing these boundaries because they could not deny their interest in the future linguistic situation. In an interview with a Hungarian journalist, Isaev observed that no national language, including Russian, could become a universal language, nor was it a possibility that all languages could 'naturally' meld into one—thus suggesting that the claims of Esperanto were not limited to the present.[48] Grigoriev even directly insisted that the 'candidacy' of Esperanto should be examined when socialist society felt the need for a unifying international means of communication. He did not hesitate to recommend Esperanto as a weapon against the 'linguistic imperialism' of the Anglo-Saxons and French, thereby entering terrain that the Bulgarian activist had already diagnosed as too perilous.[49]

Efforts to protect the Esperantists against ideological accusations by accenting the need for a 'rational solution' to the problem of international communication could therefore not prevent the involvement of Esperanto in the extremely delicate field of relations among the peoples of the Soviet Union. Nor could they free themselves from the idealistic tradition that was a source of solidarity for the Esperantists (and could be used in the current political campaigns for peace and friendship). Even more: the Soviet Esperanto movement, reborn after a forced silence, continued from time to time to collide directly with the political and security concerns of the authorities. For unknown reasons an Esperantist camp due to take place in Vilnius in 1973 was forbidden. Esperanto publications from the West were often confiscated, for example, the book *La kaŝita vivo de Zamenhof* (The Hidden Life of Zamenhof), which, among other things, described the quibbles of Tsarist censorship[50]—but also the newsletter of the Austrian communist Esperantists. Sometimes the old fear that Esperanto was serving as a channel for espionage re-emerged. In early 1981 the weekly newspaper *Nedelia* ran a long article accusing the editor of *Heroldo de Esperanto* of arranging a meeting between Soviet Esperantists and Russian émigrés for the purpose of anti-Soviet activity.[51] The article ended with the observation that 'To work with Soviet Esperantists one must not only know Esperanto but also know

---

[48] András Sugár, 'Ĉe komenco de nova, rapida progreso. Interparolo kun la prezidanto de la sovetaj esperantistoj en Moskvo', *Hungara Vivo* 15 (1975), 4: 14.

[49] V.P. Grigor'ev, 'Iskusstvennye vspomogatel'nye mezhdunarodnye iazyki kak interlingvisticheskaia problema' (Artificial international auxiliary languages as an interlinguistic problem), in Isaev (1976), pp. 35–54 (quotation p. 53).

[50] The Soviet censors were evidently bothered by the treatment of Zamenhof's relationship to Zionism.

[51] V. Barsov & L. Sergeev, 'Za kulisami diversii. Operatsiia suprugi' (Behind the curtains of sabotage. Operation husband and wife), *Nedelia*, 1981, 4: 10; 5: 18. See the denial by Ada Fighiera: *Le Travailleur Espérantiste*, 1982, 74 (Oct.): 1.

the character of Soviet Esperantists who have always been, are now, and always will be patriots.' This sounds like praise but could certainly be interpreted as a veiled warning. Ardent opponents of Esperanto could be found not only in official circles. Such an opponent was, for example, the fanatical anti-Zionist Valerii Emelianov, who in the Russian-language book *Detsionizatsiia* (De-zionization) linked Esperanto ideologically with Zionism, Freemasonry and Trotsky.[52]

The position of Esperanto in the Soviet Union during the reign of Leonid Brezhnev remained contradictory. The number of Esperantists was calculated at more than 10,000, of whom 3000 were considered 'activists'. Esperanto clubs operated in 110 towns and villages. Particularly notable was the work of SEJM and its more than 2500 members in 44 cities.[53] This youth organization cultivated its unofficial status: SEJM kept its distance from the Commission in Moscow, which it considered a mere appendage directed abroad and an obstruction to the movement within the Soviet Union. Like the Commission, SEJM did not include the dissemination of Esperanto among its aims, although in fact it steadily pursued that goal. It did so for tactical reasons, because it knew that the authorities disliked direct recruitment for Esperanto. For similar reasons, in organizing events, 'the words *peace, international friendship* etc. were always included in the titles [...] However, that was just for external appearances'.[54] In fact, the young participants 'behaved like tourists, played sports, sang and danced, even drank a little'. 'It was beautiful, that life!' one camping enthusiast, Mikhail Bronshtein, remembered almost three decades later.[55] Around the campfire Esperanto songs continued

---

[52] The book was published by a Palestinian publishing house in Paris in 1979. Extracts in Samodaj (2010), pp. 179–88. See also Vadim Rossman, *Russian Intellectual Antisemitism in the Post-Communist Era*, Lincoln & London: University of Nebraska Press, 2002, p. 192, note 102.

[53] Statistics from Semjon Podkaminer, 'La sovetaj esperantistoj', *Bulgara Esperantisto* 48 (1979), 2: 12. According to a different source, in the former USSR 'more than 13,700 Esperantists were active': Anatolij Sunarkin, 'Historio kaj nuntempo', *REGo*, 2009, 1 (50): 20–5 (quotation p. 24).

[54] Laurynas Skūpas, 'Ankaŭ tio jam estas historio', *Litova Stelo* 11 (2001), 2: 18–21 (quotation p. 20). See the lively description of one such camp in Latvia, with emphasis on its non-serious character: Volodja Ebelj, 'XV-a Junulara Tutsovetia', *Bulgara Esperantisto* 42 (1973), 9: 12–13. Another remembrance is: Vytautas Šilas, 'Aspiranto kaj Esperanto', *Ondo de Esperanto*, 2013, 4/5: 18–19.

[55] Bronŝtejn (2006), pp. 6, 150–1.

into the morning, and there was even a performance of an Esperanto version of the rock opera *Jesus Christ Superstar*.

Two erstwhile leaders of SEJM, Anatolii Goncharov and Boris Kolker, in an interview, described the movement as alternative, informal, nonconforming (*nekonsenta*). They declined the epithet 'dissident' since the majority of SEJM members, knowing almost nothing about the darker aspects of Soviet history, were not positioned in protest against the ruling regime.[56] In SEJM, Kolker explained, there was practically no political discussion: 'Although we were aware of problems in the relationship of officials to Esperanto, we were patriotically loyal to the country.'[57] Bronshtein, however, who grew famous for his protest songs, considered SEJM 'essentially a dissident movement'. It was, he said, 'to an absurd degree' contradictory, undermining the state monopoly on contacts with other countries and yet regularly informing the authorities about its 'socially useful activities'.[58] The young Esperantists both enthusiastically amused themselves and defiantly declared that they used their language for the good of the state. SEJM avoided all provocation and practiced the customary forms of loyalty, but basically it deviated:

> They offended even against the sacred possession of the powerful – information, because they regularly received news from abroad, and often disseminated news at home, that did not square with official statements. They wanted passionately to travel abroad and to speak with foreigners without translators! In a phrase, they tended to serve as a parallel educational force [...].[59]

Goncharov returned to the subject of the Esperanto camps: 'We created a second identity of the kind that students of national languages would never create because of the difficulty of those languages and the impossibility of freely possessing any such language.'[60] As for the habits of learning generated by the youthful use of Esperanto, for example, in the SEJM camps, Aleksandr Melnikov remembers the following:

---

[56] Künzli (2008). Reactions and completions: *REGo*, 2009, 1 (50): 13–27.
[57] Boris Kolker in Künzli (2008), p. 8.
[58] Bronŝtejn (2006), p. 6.
[59] Bronŝtejn (2006), p. 151.
[60] Anatolo Gonĉarov, 'La Esperanta Civito jam okazis...en Sovetio', *Literaturá Foiro* 39 (2008), 235: 269–74 (quotation p. 271). See also Gonĉarov, *Esperanto-identeco: citajoj kaj komentoj*, supplement to *La KancerKliniko*, 2010, no. 136.

Thanks to Esperanto, I found out about things unmentioned in our country. I even got my first reading material on sex from the Esperanto-language *ABZ de amo*. And I secretly received Orwell's forbidden *Animal Farm* (of course in our beloved language) [...]. Esperanto did not make me an active dissident, but it taught me a lot about the world beyond the filters of the regime.[61]

Because of its quasi-illegality, SEJM constantly found itself on the edge of prohibition. A functionary of the regime named a camp in 1980 'a Zionist plot',[62] and probably it was not unknown to the authorities that many campers, through their participation, demonstrated a latent resistance to the confluence of ethnic groups in the Soviet Union. Early on, a party functionary tried to discourage Bronshtein, declaring that Esperanto had no future and that 'its dissemination lessens the significance of Russian, our common state language'.[63] This fear was not without cause, because the popularity of Esperanto in the Baltic republics and also among Ukrainians was motivated in large part by the chance it gave to use Esperanto as an alternative to Russian. One Ukrainian saw the camps as a model of true internationalism based on equal rights—as opposed to the official 'huge fuss about "the yet-to-be-seen friendship of the peoples"' for which Russian served as the unifier.[64]

Why the activities of SEJM were never halted remains a mystery. It probably helped that there was a strong sense of common loyalty among the young Soviet Esperantists and there were no cases of damaging denunciation. If they filed reports with the KGB, they '"greased" the eyes of the authorities' by giving only positive impressions of the SEJM activists or the camps.[65] The young Esperantists also regarded the Jewish aspects of Esperanto as taboo.[66] They not only had no support from the authorities

---

[61] Aleksandro S. Melnikov, 'Ek al VE(L)K? Esperanto—kion ĝi al mi donis kaj kion ĝi prenis?' *Esperanto* 100 (2007): 76–8 (quotation p. 77).
[62] Bronŝtejn (2006), p. 156.
[63] Bronŝtejn (2006), p. 182.
[64] Letter from Orest Samijlenko, *Sennaciulo* 57 (1986): 115. According to Vytautas Šilas, one of the motives for learning Esperanto in Lithuania, in addition to the desire for contacts abroad, was the wish to lessen the importance of Russian: interview 27 July 2005.
[65] Anatolo Gonĉarov, 'SEJM indas vervon de dika romano', *Scienco kaj Kulturo*, 1998, 5 (19): 17–19 (quotation p. 17).
[66] Künzli (2008), p. 20; Viktor Aroloviĉ, 'Ĝustigoj kaj duboj', *REGo*, 2009, 1 (50): 27.

but they also had to resist efforts to demoralize them. Rafael Saakov, an SSOD functionary, cynically told Kolker in 1982:

> You are weak. Among you there are no important people: party leaders, ministers, generals, who support you. Perhaps one way out would be for Esperantists to go to war in Afghanistan and become heroes.[67]

In parallel with the Academy's support for interlinguistic research, SEJM created facts on the ground that were favorable for Esperanto. Under these circumstances it seemed preferable to enlarge the official framework of the Esperanto movement, thus neutralizing the tension between the essentially powerless Commission and the lively but unofficial grassroots youth movement. Many individual Esperantists addressed letters to the Party Central Committee. Isaev advised the Committee that, rather than treating so many active and inquiring young people as dissidents, they would be better off supporting them. A few months later he learned that Iurii Andropov, the KGB chief, had reacted positively.[68] In March 1978 the Central Committee decided in favor of creating an Association of Soviet Esperantists (ASE).[69] The abovementioned SSOD, in whose framework the Commission operated, was charged with establishing the new association, along with the trade unions and the Komsomol, in whose local clubs, cultural centers and committees Esperantist circles operated.

In March 1979 the association's founding conference took place in Moscow. It seemed the fulfillment of a dream (Fig. 11.3). ASE took the place of the Commission but remained linked to the Union. At the same time SEJM, with over 1000 members, was dissolved. Its leaders joined the association board, thus becoming colleagues of Isaev, who continued as president, and a relatively large number of non-Esperantist board members. In his report to the founding conference, Isaev denied that Esperanto

---

[67] Boris Kolker, '35 jaroj en Esperantujo', *Cerbe kaj Kore* (Moscow), 1992, 9 (21): 1–5 (quotation p. 2).

[68] Mahomet Isaev, 'De vilaĝo al ĉefurbo', *REGo*, 2003, 2 (15): 7–10 (esp. p. 8).

[69] See the Esperanto translation of extracts from the March 1978 minutes of the Central Committee, in Samodaj (2010), pp. 137–41.

Fig. 11.3 At the founding conference of the Association of Soviet Esperantists (March 1979): Aleksandr Korolevich, Vladimir Samodai, Boris Kolker, Magomet Isaev, Dmitrii Perevalov

was harassed.[70] He stressed the connection of the Esperanto movement with science and paid homage to the Esperanto scholars Drezen[71] and Bokarev. The theoretical and practical activities of Soviet interlinguists should be based, he said, on the principle that 'we are establishing the "artificial" auxiliary language in opposition to neither interethnic languages, nor so-called world languages, and particularly not national languages'. 'It is not a matter of substituting one for another', he added. Addressing Esperanto more directly, Isaev declared that Esperantists

---

[70] 'Pri la stato kaj pliefikigo de laboro de sovetiaj esperantistoj kaj plibonigo de iliaj internaciaj ligoj' (report by Isaev), *Moscow News*, 1979, supplement to no. 16 (2848), 22 April, pp. 15–16. An official report of the conference attributed to 'western propaganda' the assertion that 'Soviet citizens were not allowed to correspond with other countries': Aleksandr Harkovskij, 'Mi aplaŭdas al kreiĝo de esperantista asocio ... ', *Moscow News*, 1979, supplement to no. 16 (2848), pp. 11–12.

[71] On Drezen's interlinguistic theories see A.D. Dulichenko, 'Kontseptsiia mezhdunarodnogo i vseobshchego jazyka Ė.K. Drezena' (E.K. Drezen's concept of the international and world language), *Interlinguistica Tartuensis* 2 (1983): 89–121.

often 'exaggerate the importance of the language to social development', adding a warning similar to those already met in the GDR and Bulgaria:

> It is worth emphasizing yet again that the language Esperanto, like any other language, is a tool, a tool for communication. In itself it carries no ideational (in the social sense of that word) burden. It can be used equally for good and bad. Up to now, most Soviet Esperantists and interlinguists have relied on this fundamental Marxist-Leninist definition of language. In their future activities the Esperantists should keep it constantly in mind, to avoid damaging mistakes.[72]

Isaev promised that ASE, differently from the Commission, would concern itself not only with the international contacts of the Soviet Esperantists but also with activity at home. But in the first instance this meant the ideological education of the Soviet Esperantists. The internal periodical *Amikeco* addressed this issue directly:

> People often consider Esperantists as strange – individuals who use the language only to collect foreign stamps or picture postcards, to amuse themselves by speaking with a neighbor in a foreign language (there aren't too many foreigners around!), or who adoringly pursue foreign tourists. It is no secret that thanks to this impression many responsible higher-ups regard the ideological basis and social role of Esperantists as distinctly doubtful.[73]

The author of these words attended the founding meeting, coming away with the impression that the Esperantists 'should not see ASE's main task as spreading Esperanto but as raising the quality of the movement'. Indeed, the ASE leaders soon sent the local clubs a letter requiring that they 'Not worry about increasing the number of Esperantists but worry about increasing their linguistic and ideological quality'.[74] In exactly the same way, a trade union official advised: 'In organizing work with Esperantists, special attention must be paid to the qualitative, not quantitative, make-up of the Esperanto movement, and to order-

---

[72] Isaev, 'Pri la stato kaj pliefikigo'. p. 16.
[73] L. Laanest, 'Antaŭprintempo 1979', *Amikeco*, 1979, 32: 1.
[74] 'Pri la nuna stato de la Esperanto-movado en U.S.S.R.', *Horizonto* 6 (1981): 30.

ing its activity and raising the level of political knowledge in Esperanto organizations.'[75]

ASE's first years showed no significant progress in the Soviet Esperanto movement. An unnamed Soviet Esperantist in early 1981 spoke of 'betrayed expectations', blaming ASE for 'even hindering the people who want to do something'.[76] People nostalgically remarked that the 'officious ASE' was totally different from the 'wild SEJM'.[77] A major problem was the lack of learning materials; an Esperanto textbook for Russian speakers, announced for 1978, finally appeared in 1984—in a print run of only 30,000 copies.[78] ASE's newsletter, whose content was largely in Russian, was published in only a few hundred copies. Publication of the long-promised second volume of articles by the interlinguistics section was delayed.[79] Only in the Baltic countries did the publication of a few attractive books in Esperanto continue. Against everyone's expectations, ASE cancelled its promise to join UEA, to protest a review of the memoirs of a Gulag survivor that appeared in UEA's journal.[80]

Attention was still needed to the connection with the Soviet nationalities problem: the notion of a 'Soviet people' was included in the new constitution (1977), and propaganda for the bilingualism of all Soviet citizens was increasing. Because the percentage of Russians in the population had declined and the non-Russians were demonstrating increasing ethnic self-confidence, the Party increased its pressure to disseminate knowledge of Russian and thereby strengthen the internal coherence of

---

[75] P.T. Pimenov, 'V sekretariate VTsSPS', *Informatsionnyi biulleten'* (ASE), 1980, 2/3 (3/4): 12.

[76] 'Pri la nuna stato', pp. 28, 30. Not surprisingly, Soviet Esperantists bitterly protested against the lack of priority given to the dissemination of Esperanto. For details of opposition to the ASE leaders see Cibulevskij (2000), pp. 202–18.

[77] Viktor Aroloviĉ, 'Esperantistaj kolektivoj en REU', *REGo*, 2012, 2 (69): 17–22 (quotation p. 17).

[78] Z.V. Semenova & M.I. Isaev, *Uchebnik iazyka èsperanto*, Moscow: Nauka, 1984. On a quasi-pirated edition of the textbook see Boris Kolker, www.liberafolio.org/2005/aperis/cenzurlibro/.

[79] Oddly, a new book by Isaev (*Iazyk èsperanto*, Moskvo: Nauka, 1981) appeared in a series on languages of Asia and Africa.

[80] The remembrances of Karlo Štajner, *7000 tagoj en Siberio*, trans. Krešimir Barković, Paris: S.A.T., 1983; review: U. Lins, *Esperanto* 77 (1984): 73. On ASE's reaction see Sergei Kuznetsov's afterword to the Moscow edition of *La danĝera lingvo* (1990), pp. 544–5; Cibulevskij (2000) pp. 103–5; Boris Kolker, 'NIA Vilnjuso kaj ILIA Jerusalemo', *Sennacieca Revuo*, 2004, 132: 31–3; Samodaj (2010), pp. 145–6; Boris Kolker, 'La aventuro esti membro de UEA en Sovetunio', *Esperanto* 101 (2008): 126–7.

the country. Although there were limits to Russification, since its opponents could always refer to Lenin's words opposing the privileging of a single language and using it as a weapon, there was no ignoring the trend to relegate the non-Russian languages to the private sphere—to stop using them, for example, as conveyors of science and technology—and thus to reduce them to a secondary position behind Russian. From 1982 on, there was more frequent discussion of confluence. When Andropov succeeded Brezhnev at the end of 1982, he reminded people about the goal of melding the nations and warned against attempts to obstruct the process leading to it.[81]

Whenever the prospect of confluence arose, it worked to the Esperantists' disadvantage. And, in addition to this, other political and ideological causes for suspicion emerged. A constant obstacle to the spread of Esperanto was lack of confidence among the Soviet authorities in direct, and therefore hard to supervise, contacts with other countries. Despite the official propaganda about peace and friendship among the peoples, the Party stuck firmly to the principle that cultivation of international relations was too important to leave in the unsupervised hands of citizens. The Party's view was that foreign contacts were the domain of specially trained and tested people—people 'competent' to the task and charged by the state. The thought that not only a privileged few but thousands of ordinary Soviet citizens might relate with foreign countries was barely imaginable. The Esperantists remained suspected because, needing no interpreters, they could rapidly put their Esperanto to use—this language whose 'danger' lay in the fact that it was much easier to learn than English or French.[82]

The situation of the Soviet movement—the uncertainties and restrictions on a background of official lack of confidence—remained the same until Mikhail Gorbachev took office in 1985. Among the many problems

---

[81] Walker Connor, *The National Question in Marxist-Leninist Theory and Strategy*, Princeton: Princeton University Press, 1984, p. 407.

[82] This was the observation of a secretary of the Central Committee of the CPSU, quoted by Aleksandr Khar'kovskii, "'... i byl na vsei zemle odin iazyk'" ('... and the whole earth was of one language'), *Novyi amerikanets* (New York), 1982, 113: 21.

he inherited, Gorbachev understandably did not give primary attention to questions of language and nation. Notably, given the compromised position of the goals of convergence and merger, he called for a return to the 'equality' once proclaimed by Lenin. Now multiculturalism and tolerance were advocated. However, the leading position of the Russian language was preserved, and in the non-Russian republics the officially required bilingualism did not imply that Russians should learn the language of the principal ethnic group in the republic where they lived, for example, Kazakh or Uzbek.

In any event, the hope and self-confidence generated by Gorbachev's policies energized the non-Russian peoples—and also the Esperantists. The first signs of change came in 1988. They related to the history of the Soviet movement. In February the magazine *Ogonyok* published a letter from a veteran who recalled learning Esperanto in the Red Army in 1922–23; in April a newspaper in Odessa published a plea for the 'rehabilitation' of persecuted Esperantists[83]; and in August *Komsomolskaia pravda*[84] reported that Zhdanov Street in Kazan had been returned to its earlier name, Esperanto Street.

Early in 1989 ASE finally joined UEA as the Soviet national association; in the same year, it took the name of the prewar SEU. By the end of the year, a non-communist government had been formed in Poland, the wall in the GDR was down, political changes had occurred in Hungary, Czechoslovakia and Bulgaria and a revolution in Romania. In the spring of 1990, Estonia, Latvia and Lithuania declared independence. In the Soviet Union, censorship disappeared and for a while gave a strong boost to the movement. In Moscow a second Esperanto-language edition of the present volume, *La danĝera lingvo*, was published,[85] and—too late for

---

[83] Evgenii Goluvovskii, 'Reabilitatsiia ėsperanto' (Rehabilitation of Esperanto), *Vecherniaia Odessa*, 23 April 1988; trans. in Samodaj (1999), pp. 23–6, on Aleksei Vershinin, erstwhile member of the SEU Central Committee.

[84] 20 August 1988. Ironically, the street was recently (June 2015) renamed 'Nazarbayev Street'.

[85] In 1999 a Russian translation appeared: *Opasnyi iazyk. Kniga o presledovaniiakh ėsperanto*, trans. Viktor Arolovich, Lev Vul'fovich and Liudmila Novikova (Moscow: Impėto & Prava cheloveka).

it—the archives of the secret police were partially opened.[86] Publishing companies were founded with good and varied offerings; textbooks and periodicals appeared; Russian Esperantists from the start made active use of the Internet. But, as of 1990, economic upheaval had its negative effect—not only in the Soviet Union but in all 'liberated' countries, even those with an Esperanto movement considerably more developed than the Soviet one. The biggest decline was in Bulgaria, where 40 paid workers had to be laid off and membership of the youth section shrank from 6000 to 300. The movement in the GDR disappeared along with the state; only a few members joined the (All-)German Esperanto Association. In the former communist bloc, fewer and fewer people learned Esperanto, since the need for a means of communication in the vastly increased field of international contacts was filled by the promise of the English language.

Efforts to re-establish SEU and recover its cruelly interrupted tradition did not last long because in 1991 the Soviet Union and its huge multi-ethnic realm ceased to exist. SEU became the Russian Esperantist Union. It was too weak to be heard in the ideological vacuum left by the demise of the Soviet Union and filled by nationalism. In the post-Soviet Russian Federation it was no longer necessary to avoid or bypass the question of Russian as the official language: Russian was incontestably not only the *lingua franca* but also the state language (Fig. 11.4).

---

[86] Nikolai Stepanov, whose studies we have mentioned several times, was able to use extensive material on Esperantist victims from these archives. Since then, a Russian-language study has appeared, based on the papers of the Regional Committee of SEU in Kirov: Oleg Krasnikov, *Istoriia Soiuza Ėsperantistov Sovetskikh Respublik (SĖSR) / Historio de Sovetrespublikara Esperantista Unio*, in *Ėsperanto-dvizhenie: fragmenty istorii / Esperanto-movado: fragmentoj de la historio*, Moscow: Impėto, 2008, pp. 7–114.

11 The Soviet Union: Between Hope and Doubt

Fig. 11.4 The sculptor Nikolai Blazhkov made this bust of Zamenhof at the end of the 1950s. Because the Soviet authorities did not support him and refused permission to send it to the 44th World Congress of Esperanto (Warsaw, 1959), it remained in the courtyard of his home in the center of Odessa. Only after the fall of the Soviet Union did it become a tourist destination

Part III

Conclusion

12

Dangerous Language or Language of Hope?

History is not lacking in examples of the suppression of particular languages, even efforts to stamp out languages by force. Ethnic minorities and colonized peoples, particularly, have suffered such prohibitions on the use of their languages in schools and public life. Generally it is fear that motivates these prohibitions—fear on the part of the dominant power that such unwelcome languages will foster political or social deviation, perhaps the complete division of the state.

The branding of Esperanto as a 'dangerous language' and the persecution of its followers is, however, different from other cases of linguistic discrimination. The Esperanto speech community is scattered across the world, and will remain so; it has never had the backing of a state or a supranational body; it has only slowly created the seeds of its own culture, and—if measured by the number of organized members—it has never come close to the character of a mass movement. Furthermore the desire to cross national boundaries, the chief driver of the international spread of Esperanto, has not in itself been sufficient to weaken significantly the bonds of Esperantists to their respective nations.

Yet Esperanto has been forced to face hostility almost from the time of its birth. Although Zamenhof tried to hide one of his primary motives in creating the language, namely, resistance to the persecution of the Jews, it was precisely the Jews who felt themselves particularly addressed by his message. First in Russia, and later in other countries, it was, above all, the powerless who were attracted to Zamenhof's message of protest against linguistic, ethnic and religious discrimination. Zamenhof was even more careful to hide his larger goal, more important to him even than Esperanto: the idea of Homaranismo; he tried to draw a clear boundary between this larger goal and the Esperanto movement. But, quite early on, he could not prevent the suspicion that he was aiming for more than the dissemination of a practical means of communication. Thus, it is hardly surprising that the Russian authorities, already uneasy about diversity of languages, and engaged in 'a persecution fury'[1] against non-Russian ethnicities and their languages, feared the Esperantists' links with Tolstoy, and soon alliances with other revolutionaries. In the same way, the nationalist press in Germany, even before the First World War, accused the young Esperanto movement of harboring anti-German, internationalist elements.

Such fears and warnings had little basis in reality. Zamenhof himself, despite his missionary zeal, kept a prudent distance from radicals of all persuasions. And most Esperantists carefully avoided getting drawn into political movements; their main desire was to use the language as a means of communication and to strengthen their emerging language community.

But Esperanto was also attacked even without links to pacifism and socialism. Many Esperantists argued that Esperanto was simply a language; the Declaration of Boulogne-sur-Mer (1905) determined that anyone could use the language as he or she pleased. The movement for the dissemination of Esperanto declared its strict neutrality.

Yet its opponents refused to accept Esperanto's neutrality. For them, Esperanto was symptomatic of a supranational mode of thought. The Esperantists, aiming for official recognition, tried to avoid everything that might provoke opposition or suspicion in the eyes of the authorities; much effort went into hiding links with Jews. Enemies were unimpressed

---

[1] Jan Baudouin de Courtenay, 'Einfluss der Sprache auf Weltanschauung und Stimmung', *Prace filologiczne* 14 (1929): 185–256 (quotation p. 195). See also the quotation from Baudouin de Courtenay in the earlier volume, chapter 1, p. 31.

by this insistence on neutrality and independence—also because it was impossible to ignore the fact that the pioneers of Esperanto and most of those who followed them demonstrated an enthusiastic bias toward ideals of peace and human brotherhood and accordingly were hardly neutral in their use of the language. Many Esperantists in fact demonstrated in practice, albeit modestly, what liberal and socialist theories of a new world order, many of them Jewish, imagined as a utopian ideal: hope for a united humanity.

Currently, historians are beginning to recognize that Esperanto is worthy of attention as an indicator of the strength of cosmopolitanism in the years before the First World War, in the so-called *Belle Époque*. At the same time, nationalism hindered the spread of Esperanto. In France, traditional faith in the civilizing properties of the French language set limits to Esperantist ambitions; likewise in Germany the language policies of the rulers were increasingly influenced by emphasis on competition. After the war, with the discrediting of power politics, new opportunities for Esperanto presented themselves, particularly at the League of Nations. But new barriers arose. The Geneva debates and, more drastically, the persecution of worker Esperantists in the 1920s, showed how seriously the people in power took the potential of Esperanto. Disapproving diplomats in Geneva and authorities in dictatorial states warned against the 'denationizing' and 'revolutionary' aims of the Esperantists, nor were they silent in suggesting that these included the thirst of peasants for education. Basically they were opposed to interpersonal trans-border contacts outside the control of elitist intellectuals and security-conscious governments.

On the other hand, the 1920s confirmed that the Esperantists, convinced of the unprovocative nature of their activities, were completely unprepared to defend themselves against attacks motivated by politics and ideology. From today's vantage point, the treatment of Esperanto at the League of Nations is instructive in explaining why the language has never become 'official' internationally, even in conditions free of oppression. Despite the sympathy that it encountered among non-European member states, the decisive weight lay with the French and British governments striving to protect or expand the situation of their languages in the world. The French position was much influenced by the conclusion that

Esperanto was—depending on the point of view—a threat or a promise that the future would be more international than it would be French.[2]

Under the Third Reich Esperanto became an object of systematic destruction. The Nazis constituted an enemy of unprecedented danger. Adolf Hitler and his party skillfully exploited traditional prejudices against the artificiality of the language and its popularity with leftists but, at the same time, emphasized that essentially all Esperantists were enemies of the state, using their language to serve Jewish international goals. Even non-political users were refused the right to spread Esperanto. The persecutions under Hitler demonstrated the existence of enemies who not only fought against the political 'misuse' of Esperanto but condemned the very idea, even abstract talk of peace, or of friendship among the peoples.

What this meant, namely, a new *kind* of persecution, was noted by Joseph Roth, independently of Esperanto, less than two months after Hitler became chancellor. Speaking of the first weeks of Nazi terror, he asserted: 'Here they don't just oppose Jews. [...] Here they oppose European civilization, humanity [...].'[3] The Nazi regime destroyed the illusion, common among the Esperantists, that it was possible to survive by distinguishing between publicity for the language in the present and its beginning inspiration, its 'Jewish origin'. It is a remarkable coincidence that the decree for the disbanding of the German movement was signed by Heydrich's deputy, Werner Best, who in 1926 declared himself the enemy of everything internationalist, explicitly denying that there existed something called 'humankind' that united us all.[4]

For the Esperantists this was an alarming lesson. They discovered the impossibility, even the dangers, of absolute neutrality—namely, neutrality between ideas favorable to Esperanto and ideologies—principally

---

[2] Panchasi (2009), p. 159.

[3] Letter to Stefan Zweig, 22 March 1933, in Joseph Roth, *Briefe 1911–1939*, ed. Hermann Kesten, Cologne & Berlin: Kiepenheuer & Witsch, 1970, p. 257. Earlier, Hannah Arendt pointed out that National Socialism, more than any other movement in history, denied the idea of general humanity: Gabriel Motzkin, 'Hannah Arendt: Von ethnischer Minderheit zu universeller Humanität', in Gary Smith (ed.), *Hannah Arendt Revisited: 'Eichmann in Jerusalem' und die Folgen*, Frankfurt a.M.: Suhrkamp, 2000, p. 177–201 (esp. p. 192); cf. Hannah Arendt, *Eichmann in Jerusalem: A Report on the Banality of Evil*, New York: Viking Press, 1964, p. 268.

[4] Herbert, Ulrich, *Best. Biographische Studien über Radikalismus, Weltanschauung und Vernunft 1903–1989*, Munich: C.H. Beck, 2016, p. 107.

Nazism—that threatened all humanity. The old understanding of neutrality was now inappropriate because it ignored what was in fact the tradition of the Esperanto movement. Many of those who understood the destructive goals of the Nazis accordingly abandoned their abstention from political action to join the anti-fascist ranks.

At precisely the same time a development took place that was incomprehensible to all contemporary observers and affected 'progressive' Esperantists particularly painfully. In the Soviet Union, during the Great Purge, the Esperanto movement perished in almost the same years as the Nazis tried to exterminate Esperanto in Germany. The extent of the persecutions in the Soviet Union exceeded that of the Nazis. Behind them was a regime whose ruling ideology actually seemed in harmony with the idea of Esperanto. The Soviet Esperantists early abandoned their old-style utopianism, mocked the use of Esperanto as a mere hobby, yet enthusiastically endorsed the value of the language for the internationalist education of Soviet citizens. They sought to demonstrate Esperanto's utility for the realization of communism.

As in other countries, there were obstacles. The communist movement had traditionally regarded the Esperantists with skepticism. Under Stalin's rule, Esperanto was unfavorably mentioned in connection with discussion of the nationalities problem, but for some time the conversation seemed to remain within the realm of rational exchange. The Esperantists, loyal to the regime, had no sense that they were failing to observe the political trends. The prevailing ideology seemed a useful basis for their activity and they energetically attached themselves to it, although, increasingly, actual policy seemed to diverge from ideology. The situation became more and more confusing.

Despite every effort to adapt, the Esperantists in the Soviet Union were arrested in 1937–38 as 'spies'—an accusation even more absurd than the Nazi attacks on the 'language of Jews and communists', but comprehensible if one sees its roots in the authorities' profound suspicion of the Soviet Esperantists' direct and extensive letter-writing contact with other countries. Fatally, the Esperantists overlooked the Party's insistence that it, and it alone, had a monopoly on knowledge. Their correspondence allowed comparisons between everyday life in the Soviet Union and living conditions abroad. Such openness caused disillusionment and conveyed information that was all the more 'dangerous' because it came close to the facts; these truths could not be simply branded as products of the propaganda of class enemies. The Soviet Esperantists finally understood that spreading facts was a crime, but by then it was already too late. As for the claim that Esperanto was a tool for easy communication—a claim that elements in the League of Nations refused with the assertion that the masses do not need direct communication, and which the Nazis attacked as an expression of 'Jewish illusions about the brotherhood of peoples'—in the Soviet Union this claim came to a violent end, with unimaginable suffering for the victims. The official doctrine of 'friendship among the peoples' could not disguise the fact that the Soviet rulers were most afraid of unsupervised contacts and exchanges. Given that reality, it is only logical that they ceased to tolerate the Esperanto movement and that all Soviet citizens who had contact abroad were suspected as foreign agents.

We cannot escape comparison between the persecutions under Hitler and those under Stalin. The Nazis, as we have seen, persecuted the Esperanto movement for explicit ideological reasons: the victims were clearly defined. In the Soviet Union there was no such clarity. There the Esperantists were suppressed because of their contacts abroad and the regime's fear of spies—though also in some sense for ideology, namely, the persistent linkage of Esperantists with the goal of world revolution. The persecutions caught the individual Soviet Esperantists completely by surprise; no longer did the link with revolutionary internationalism help them. While the Nazis largely silenced the movement through ideological pressure, making only limited use of the remedy of arrest and imprisonment, the Soviet authorities achieved their goal by terror, by creating hysteria and panic. Caught up in the zeal for unmasking class enemies and enemies of the people, a few Esperantists developed a fervor that finally proved suicidal. They themselves involuntarily contributed to the wave of arrests.

The Stalinists never admitted that specific ethnic groups or 'socially alien elements' were singled out for persecution. They gave no explanations and preferred unsystematic destruction. There was really no necessity for theory to justify the oppression; the customary accusations were enough—petty bourgeois beliefs, Trotskyism, fascism—and they could strike practically anyone. Before the Second World War, no declarations were directed specifically against the Esperantists. That did not save them, because the regime in its hypocrisy and arbitrariness did not feel the need to identify its specific victims: anyone could be persecuted at any time.[5] The Esperantists were in any case suspected because of their foreign contacts. Likewise, Jews as such were not the object of accusations. Several ideological declarations in the Stalin era came close to the anti-human rhetoric of the Nazis, evident in the early Marxist dislike of 'naïve cosmopolitanism' or the complaint of Romain Rolland that the socialist press neglected topics of general human interest. But it would be an exaggeration to find the roots of Stalinist suppression of Esperanto here. As a warning signal we could perhaps identify only the accusation raised in the linguistic debate of 1932 that the 'high-minded goals of Dr Zamenhof [...] concerning the brotherhood of peoples and worldwide harmony were, [...] like all petty-bourgeois illusions, aids to imperialism'.

Finally, after the Second World War, Stalin understood that it was no longer possible or useful to hide the contradictions between official ideology and the actual situation, and so xenophobia was raised to the level of state ideology.[6] This perverse logic justified attacks against Jews. Because anti-Semitism could not be reconciled with official ideology, the campaign against Zionism and cosmopolitanism was particularly convenient as a way of disguising anti-Jewish attacks and it was easy to include Esperantists in that class of enemies as well. At the same time this campaign demonstrated that Soviet communism explicitly betrayed itself by rejecting its own founding ideology and recognizing the failure of its utopia.[7]

There is general agreement that the sheer quantity of victims of Nazism and Stalinism prevent meaningful analysis of the two merely by compar-

---

[5] Cf. Arendt (1951), p. 6.

[6] Jörg Baberowski & Anselm Doering-Manteuffel, 'The quest for order and the pursuit of terror: National Socialist Germany and the Stalinist Soviet Union as multiethnic empires', in Michael Geyer & Sheila Fitzpatrick (ed.), *Beyond Totalitarianism: Stalinism and Nazism Compared*, Cambridge: Cambridge University Press, 2009, pp. 180–230 (esp. p. 224).

[7] See the observation, which mentions Esperanto in this context, in Marci Shore, 'On cosmopolitanism, the avant-garde, and a lost innocence of Central Europe', in Michael D. Gordin and others (ed.), *Utopia/Dystopia: Conditions of Historical Possibility*, Princeton: Princeton University Press, 2010, pp. 176–202 (esp. p. 202, note 105).

ing the numbers who were murdered or simply perished. Most historians conclude that both ideologies were guilty of cruelties and terror on a level unprecedented in human history. Although they fought one another, we might call them 'sibling enemies'.[8] Looking only at the Esperantists, we have to conclude that under Stalin they were murdered in larger numbers than under Hitler, even if we cannot assess the degree to which the factor of Esperantism played a role in the general pursuit of spies and the ever-expanding categories of 'enemies of the people'. By comparison, in Nazi Germany fewer people were murdered merely or primarily because of their knowledge and use of Esperanto. But we should not forget that the Nazi persecutors, who closely observed the Esperanto movement and aimed to liquidate it throughout Europe, worked hand-in-glove with Adolf Eichmann and the architects of the Holocaust.

Further proof of the ideological focus of the Nazis was the fact that immediately after the occupation of Poland the SS leaders sought out and arrested leading Esperantists, including members of the Zamenhof family, and that in June 1940, shortly after the beginning of the systematic mass murder of Jews, they prepared an internal study on the 'dangers of Esperantism'.

In comparing the two perpetrators of these persecutions, we find one commonality: both believed in conspiracy theories and fanatically cultivated them. Hitler early attacked Esperanto as a tool for achieving Jewish world rule; Stalin had no similar formula, but toward the end of his life he imitated the Nazis, using the idea of a world conspiracy of Jews to justify his battle against cosmopolitans.

After the Second World War, the Esperantists hastened to re-group and resume their activities. However, the aftereffects of the shock of persecution endured. For a long time, many people, also because of the principle of neutrality, preferred to remain silent. In Germany the first description and analysis of Nazi persecutions appeared over 20 years after the end of the war.[9] Because of the circumstances in the Soviet Union,

---

[8] Jörg Baberowski, 'Verwandte Feinde? Nationalsozialismus, Stalinismus und die Totalitarismustheorie', in Jürgen Danyel and others (ed.), *50 Klassiker der Zeitgeschichte*, Göttingen: Vandenhoeck & Ruprecht, 2007, pp. 52–65.

[9] Ulrich Lins, 'Esperanto dum la Tria Regno', *Germana Esperanto-Revuo*, 1966–67, reprinted in Blanke (1986), pp. 84–122. See also Humphrey Tonkin, 'Chaos in Esperanto-Land: Echoes of the Holocaust', *LPLP* 35 (2011): 161–71.

it took many years before anyone had the courage to break the silence and openly address the tragic fate of Esperantists under Stalin. In fact, in the Soviet Union, to whose disintegration young Esperantists also made a contribution, if small, through their alternative internationalism, the taboo was broken only shortly before Gorbachev took office. We should mention that, among communist Esperantists in other countries who for long held on to a kind of double loyalty,[10] a few were in the vanguard of those who uncovered the contradictions of communism. They too helped destroy the Soviet myth. We might mention particularly the Japanese Kurisu Kei, who learned Esperanto precisely because he was a communist and later—'paradoxically, through Esperanto'—freed himself of communist dogma.[11] Kurisu lived long enough to see the failure of that ideology.

In his work on cosmopolitanism, the German sociologist Ulrich Beck attributes to it two contradictory tendencies. He describes cosmopolitanism as, first, an old, 'unexhausted tradition' and treasure house, and, secondly, he points out that it has suffered through a hell on earth, namely, death in the Holocaust and the Gulag. Beck does not reference the Esperantists whose persecution is chronicled in this book, but in the context of our conclusion it is worth quoting Beck's observation that in many countries cosmopolitans are regarded the same as enemies 'who can or even must be [...] destroyed': 'The Nazis said "Jew" and meant "cosmopolitan"; the Stalinists said "cosmopolitan" and meant "Jew".'[12] This was also the experience of the Esperantists.[13] The persecutions directed against them teach us about a little-known treasure-house, about Esperanto. Expressing modern cosmopolitanism from its start, Esperanto has aimed at representing desires to which politicians are disinclined to give a voice.

---

[10] This is discussed in greater detail in Lins (2010), pp. 443–61.

[11] Lins (2010), p. 457; Kurisu (2010), p. 114.

[12] Beck (2006), pp. 2–3; see also Robert Fine & Robin Cohen, 'Four cosmopolitanism moments', in Stephen Vertovec & Robin Cohen (ed.), *Conceiving Cosmopolitanism: Theory, Context and Practice*, Oxford: Oxford University Press, 2002, pp. 137–62 (esp. p. 146).

[13] Arthur Koestler, as early as 1944, concluded that the Soviet regime aimed to eliminate all cosmopolitan elements: Koestler (1983), p. 187. To prove his argument he quotes from a Lithuanian NKVD document of November 1940, which also mentions Esperantists.

As readers of this book will recall, the urge to respond to people's longing for direct communication runs like a red line through many declarations by authoritative representatives of the Esperanto movement—from that 'blessed' day over a hundred years ago when Zamenhof uttered his heartfelt understanding that 'within the hospitable walls of Boulogne-sur-mer, we are not witnessing a meeting of French with English, Russians with Poles, but of *human beings* with *human beings*'.[14] It was a sign of clear thinking when Hector Hodler pointed out in 1919 that 'this League [of Nations] will be capable of life only when it unites not only governments through legal means but also peoples in a spirit of mutual understanding'.[15] And in 1960, Ivo Lapenna, for many years president of UEA, expressed what in international politics lay long neglected: '[…] little has been or is being done for mutual understanding at the lowest but most important level, the level of ordinary people. […] The talk has always been, and always is, about the coexistence of states, and much less, if at all, about the friendly, peaceful common life of the peoples, of ordinary individuals.'[16] Because of their belief in this simple truth and their—sometimes naïve—efforts to act on it, the speakers of Esperanto have suffered mockery, persecution and murder.

There were various degrees of persecution, and the enemies of Esperanto were different in themselves, but a common characteristic of the anti-Esperanto battle was that it was directed not at a language project (aiming for general acceptance) but at an already developed language that uniquely symbolized the struggle for equality of communication among people regardless of race, language and religion. And that battle was aimed at more than a language. The fate of the Esperanto movement serves as a kind of barometer measuring the degree of recognition accorded by the world to grass-roots internationalism, the spontaneous search for contacts abroad, the effort to educate oneself, outside prescribed national or ideological forms—in sum, the urge to communicate free of prejudice.

---

[14] Orig II 1557. Translation in Korzhenkov (2010), p. 42.
[15] Jakob (1928), p. 88.
[16] Ivo Lapenna, *Elektitaj paroladoj kaj prelegoj*, 2nd edn., Rotterdam: Universala Esperanto-Asocio, 2009, p. 66.

Esperantists are no longer oppressed today. The legitimacy of supranational organizations is little questioned; no government dares to express dislike for goals such as peace and understanding among peoples. But the language still has only a relatively small following worldwide. Esperantists enjoy unprecedented freedom and opportunities for action, which, thanks to modern technology, they can use almost without limits. They are also a lot clearer on the political implications of their goals, despite the origin of these goals in non-political moral protest. Paradoxically, however, the advocates of this means of equal world communication still remain somewhat deviant outsiders.

So what remains of Esperanto? As we contemplate its present state and, at the same time, observe the globalization of the English language, we inevitably ask ourselves what remains of the old dreams—what can and should be preserved. There is wide agreement that ideologies have been ultimately compromised, that utopias have collapsed; old beliefs in the realizability of grandiose ideas are tempered by greater sobriety. That Esperanto has survived the ideologies of hate gives only limited consolation. Yet nationalism, always the most powerful antagonist of Esperanto, is growing stronger in many parts of the world, lending new significance to the idea of uniting people outside their national ties, on the basis of equal rights and beyond ideologies. Esperanto remains a powerful symbol and an instrument of this unification. Part of its power comes from the very knowledge that the language was branded as a 'dangerous language' and that people were persecuted for speaking it. In using the language internationally, in preference to other, national, languages, these victims of persecution can be said to have drawn close to the vision that inspired the 'anti-nationalist' Zamenhof. That vision remains a powerful inspiration today, both to Esperantists and also to others who believe in the universality of the human spirit.

Bibliography

Abol'skaia, Mariia, comp. (1999) *Sub la signo de Liro kaj Verda Stelo. Memorlibro pri aktoro Nikolaj Rytjkov*, Moscow: Impeto.

Arendt, Hannah (1951) *The Origins of Totalitarianism*, New York: Harcourt, Brace & Co.

Baziev, A.T., & M.I. Isaev (1973) *Iazyk i natsiia* (Language and Nation), Moscow: Nauka.

Beck, Ulrich (2010) *The Cosmopolitan Vision*, trans. Ciaran Cronin, Cambridge: Polity Press.

Benczik, Vilmos (1990) 'Esperanto kaj molaj diktaturoj', *Hungara Vivo* 30: 91–3. Reprinted in Benczik, *Pri la natureco kaj artefariteco de lingvoj*, Budapest: Trezor, 2016, pp. 162–7.

Bendias, Torsten (2011) *Die Esperanto-Jugend in der DDR. Zur Praxis und Lebenswelt sozialer Strömungen im Staatssozialismus*, Berlin: Lit.

Blanke, Detlev, ed. (1986) *Socipolitikaj aspektoj de la Esperanto-movado*, 2nd edn., Budapest: Hungara Esperanto-Asocio.

Blanke, Detlev (2007a) *Esperanto kaj socialismo? Pri la movado sur la 'alia flanko'*, 2nd edn., New York: Mondial.

Blanke, Detlev (2007b) 'Agi por Esperanto – sukcese kaj tragike. Intervjuo kun Grigorij Demidjuk pri lia aktivado en kaj por SEU', *La Gazeto* 23, 133: 15–31.

Blanke, Detlev & Ulrich Lins, ed. (2010) *La arto labori kune. Festlibro por Humphrey Tonkin*, Rotterdam: Universala Esperanto-Asocio.
Bokarjova, Antonina (2010) *Sciencisto, esperantisto, patro: Eŭgeno Bokarjov*, Moscow: Impeto.
Borsboom, E. (1976) *Vivo de Lanti*, Paris: SAT.
Bronŝtejn, Mikaelo (2006) *Legendoj pri SEJM*, 3rd edn., Moscow: Impeto.
Brown, Archie (2009) *The Rise and Fall of Communism*, New York: HarperCollins.
Carrère d'Encausse, Hélène (1979) *Decline of an Empire: The Soviet Socialist Republics in Revolt*, New York: Newsweek Books.
Cibulevskij, Dmitrij M. (2000) *ASE (Asocio de Sovetiaj Esperantistoj). Historiaj notoj*, Kharkiv: DMIC.
Cibulevskij, Dmitrij M. (2001) *Kurta historio de E-movado en Ĥarkiv*, 2nd edn., Kharkiv: DMIC.
Conquest, Robert (2008) *The Great Terror: A Reassessment*, Oxford & New York: Oxford University Press.
Drezen, Ernest (1991) *Historio de la mondolingvo. Tri jarcentoj da serĉado*, Leipzig: EKRELO, 1931 (reprint Osaka: Pirato, 1967); 4th edn., ed. S. Kuznecov, Moscow: Progreso.
Duličenko, Aleksandr D. (2003) 'Le marxisme et les projets de langue universelle du communisme', in Patrick Sériot (ed.) *Le discourse sur la langue en URSS à l'époque stalinienne (épistémologie, philosophie, idéologie)*, Cahiers de l'ILSL (Lausanne) 14, pp. 101–120.
Fayet, Jean-François (2008) 'Eine internationale Sprache für die Weltrevolution? Die Komintern und die Esperanto-Frage', *Jahrbuch für Historische Kommunismusforschung*, pp. 9–23.
Girke, Wolfgang, & Helmut Jachnow, ed. (1975) *Sprache und Gesellschaft in der Sowjetunion*, Munich: Fink.
Goodman, Elliot R., 'World state and world language', in Joshua A. Fishman (ed.) *Readings in the Sociology of Language*, The Hague & Paris: Mouton, 1970, pp. 717–36.
Isaev, M.I., ed. (1976) *Problemy interlingvistiki. Tipologiia i èvoliutsiia mezhdunarodnykh iskusstvennykh iazykov* (Problems of Interlinguistics: Typology and Development of International Artificial Languages), Moscow: Nauka.
Isayev, M.I. (1977) *National Languages in the USSR: Problems and Solutions*, Moscow: Progress.
Jakob, Hans, comp. (1928) *Hector Hodler. Lia vivo kaj lia verko*, Geneva: Universala Esperanto-Asocio.
Jansen, Marc, & Nikita Petrov (2002) *Stalin's Loyal Executioner: People's Commissar Nikolai Ezhov*, Stanford: Hoover Institution Press.

Kamarýt, Stanislav (1983) *Historio de la Esperanto-movado en Ĉeĥoslovakio. Iom da historio kaj iom da rememoroj*, Prague: Ĉeĥa Esperanto-Asocio.

Koestler, Arthur (1983) *The Yogi and the Commissar*, London: Hutchinson.

Korzhenkov, Aleksander (2010) *Zamenhof: The Life, Works and Ideas of the Author of Esperanto*, trans. Ian M. Richmond, ed. Humphrey Tonkin, New York: Mondial.

Kucera, Jindrich (1954) 'Soviet nationality policy: The linguistic controversy', *Problems of Communism* 3, 2: 24–9.

Künzli, Andreas (2008) '"Kio ne estas malpermesita, tio estas permesita". Sovetia Esperanto-movado en kvazaŭsekreta misio. Rememora-anekdota intervjuo-konversacio kun Boris Kolker kaj Anatolo Goncarov', *Spegulo*, 3: 134–58; also in *REGo* 6, 49: 1–24, and http://e-novosti.info/forumo/viewtopic.php?t=5124.

Kurisu Kei (2010) *Kajto de Esperanto*, Huhehot: Esp-Asocio de Interna Mongolio.

Kuznecov, S.N. (1991) 'Drezen, lia verko, lia epoko', in Drezen (1991), pp. 3–40.

Lanti, E. (1940) *Leteroj de E. Lanti*, Paris: Sennacieca Asocio Tutmonda (new edition Laroque Timbaut, France, 1987).

Lanti, E. & M. Ivon (1935) *Ĉu socialismo konstruiĝas en Sovetio?*, Paris: Esperanto (reprint Laroque Timbaut, France, 1982).

Laurat, Lucien (1951) *Staline, la linguistique et l'impérialisme russe*, Paris: Les Iles d'or.

Lins, Ulrich (2008) *Utila Estas Aliĝo. Tra la unua jarcento de UEA*, Rotterdam: Universala Esperanto-Asocio.

Lins, Ulrich (2010) 'Ruĝ-verda malakordo. Observoj pri komunistaj esperantistoj', in Blanke & Lins (2010), pp. 443–61.

Martin, Terry (2001) *The Affirmative Action Empire: Nations and Nationalism in the Soviet Union, 1923–1939*, Ithaca & London: Cornell University Press.

Moret, Sébastien (2005) 'Marr, Staline et les espérantistes', *Cahiers de l'ILSL*, 20: 199–214.

Moret, Sébastien (2007) 'Ĉu Esperanto aŭ fremdaj lingvoj? Diskutadoj en Sovetlando 1920–1930', in Detlev Blanke (ed.) *Lingvaj kaj historiaj analizoj. Aktoj de la 28-a Esperantologia Konferenco en la 90-a Universala Kongreso de Esperanto, Vilno 2005*, Rotterdam: Universala Esperanto-Asocio, pp. 47–59.

Moret, Sébastien (2010) 'From technicians to classics: On the rationalization of the Russian language in the USSR (1917–1953)', *Russian Linguistics* 34: 173–86.

Panchasi, Roxanne (2009) *Future Tense: The Culture of Anticipation in France Between the Wars*, New York: Cornell University Press.
Pollock, Ethan (2009) *Stalin and the Soviet Science Wars*, Princeton & Oxford: Princeton University Press.
Rapley, Ian (2016), 'A language for Asia? Transnational encounters in the Japanese Esperanto movement, 1906–28', in Pedro Iacobelli and others (ed.) *Transnational Japan as History: Empire, Migration, and Social Movements*, Basingstoke: Palgrave Macmillan, pp. 167–86.
Rátkai, Árpád (1985) 'Deklaritaj celoj de la hungaria Esperanto-movado', in Czesław Biedulski (ed.) *Strategiaj demandoj de la Esperanto-komunumo*, Warsaw: Pola Esperanto-Asocio, pp. 84–92.
Rátkai, Árpád (1990) 'Longa marŝo de la movado en Orienta Eŭropo', *Hungara Vivo* 30: 86–90.
Samodaj, Vladimir (1999) *Ne nur legendoj, ne nur pri SEJM. Homoj kaj epizodoj*, Moscow: Impeto.
Samodaj, Vladimir (2010) *Esperanto kaj vivo*, Moscow: Impeto.
Sidorov, Anatolo (2005) 'Grigorij Demidjuk – motoro de la sovetia esperantista movado de la 1920-30-aj jaroj', *REGo* 1, 26: 2–7.
Simon, Gerhard (1991) *Nationalism and Policy Toward the Nationalities in the Soviet Union*, trans. Karen Foster & Oswald Foster, Boulder: Westview Press.
Slezkine, Yuri (1996), 'N.Ia. Marr and the national origins of Soviet ethnogenetics', *Slavic Review* 55: 826–62.
Slezkine, Yuri (2004) *The Jewish Century*, Princeton & Oxford: Princeton University Press.
Smith, Michael G. (1998) *Language and Power in the Creation of the USSR, 1917–1953*, Berlin & New York: Mouton de Gruyter.
Solzbacher, William (1957–58) 'Esperanto in the ups and downs of Moscow linguistics and politics', *American Esperanto Magazine* 71: 5–10, 43–46, 74–78; 72: 83–85.
Spiridoviĉ, E.F. (1932) 'La "vera devizo por batalo" en la marks-leninisma lingvoscienco', *La Nova Etapo* 1: 157–60.
Springer, George P. (1956) *Early Soviet Theories in Communication*, Cambridge, MA: MIT.
Stepanov, Nikolaj (1990a) 'Ĉu SAT estis sidejo de germana sekreta polico?', *Sennaciulo* 61: 18–19, 23.
Stepanov, Nikolaj (1990b) 'Esperantistaj viktimoj de stalinismo', *Sennaciulo* 61: 76–8.

Stepanov, Nikolaj (1990c) *La vivo kaj morto de Vladimir Varankin (1902–1938)*, Budapest: Fenikso.

Stepanov, Nikolaj (1992) 'Tri renkontiĝoj kun N.K.V.D.', *Sennaciulo* 63: 53–5.

Stepanov, Nikolaj (1994) 'Viktor Belogorcev. Tragika sorto de laboristo-esperantisto', *Sennacieca Revuo* 122: 20–4.

Svadost, Èrmar (1968) *Kak vozniknet vseobshchii iazyk?* (How will a universal language emerge?), Moscow: Nauka.

Ungar, Krys (1994) 'La vivo kaj pereo de Eŭgeno Miĥalski', in Eŭgeno Miĥalski, *Plena poemaro 1917–1937*, ed. William Auld, Antwerp: Flandra Esperanto-Ligo, pp. 9–27.

Velitchkova, Ana (2014) *Esperanto, Civility, and the Politics of Fellowship: A Cosmopolitan Movement from the Eastern European Periphery*, Ph.D. dissertation, University of Notre Dame, Indiana.

Vokoun, Franjo, and others, ed. (1976) *Honore al ili. Memorlibro pri falintaj esperantistoj 1941–1945*, Zagreb: Kroatia Esperanto-Ligo.

Zlatnar, Peter (1976) 'Ideoj kaj agoj de esperantistoj en Jugoslavio', in Vokoun (1976), pp. 9–21.

Chronology

1859	15 December. Birth of Lazar Zamenhof in Białystok
1878	17 December. Project of a 'lingwe uniwersala' readied
1881	13 March. Tsar Alexander II murdered. Anti-Jewish pogroms follow
1887	26 July. The 'Unua Libro' (First Book) published in Warsaw
1889	September. First issue of *La Esperantisto* (Nuremberg)
1892	April. Officialization of the Club 'Espero' in Saint Petersburg
1895	April. The Russian censor forbids entry of the periodical *La Esperantisto*
	December. The periodical *Lingvo Internacia* begins publication in Uppsala
1898	January. Louis de Beaufront founds the Society for the Dissemination of Esperanto
	13 January. Letter of Émile Zola on the Dreyfus Affair
1901	February. Zamenhof's Russian-language booklet on Hillelism
1905	Bourgeois-democratic revolution in Russia
	April. *Ruslanda Esperantisto* begins publication

	5–13 August. First World Congress of Esperanto in Boulogne-sur-Mer
1906	19 May. German Esperantist Society founded
	12 June. Japanese Esperantist Association founded
	21 June. Anti-Jewish pogrom in Białystok
	12 July. Dreyfus rehabilitated
	28 August–5 September. Second World Congress of Esperanto in Geneva
1907	June. Chinese anarchists in Paris launch weekly newspaper *La Novaj Tempoj*
	24 October. Committee of the 'Delegates for the Adoption of an International Auxiliary Language' decides 'in principle to adopt Esperanto […] on the condition of certain modifications'
1908	18 January. Zamenhof breaks off relations with the 'Delegates' Committee' (Ido schism)
	28 April. Universal Esperanto Association founded
1911	10 October. Revolution in China
1914/1918	First World War
1917	14 April. Zamenhof dies
	6/7 November. October Revolution in Russia
	15 November. 'Declaration of the Rights of the Peoples of Russia'
1919	March. Third (Communist) International founded
1920	January. League of Nations founded
1921	June. Soviet Esperantist Union founded
	August. Sennacieca Asocio Tutmonda (SAT) founded
1922	April. Stalin becomes General Secretary
	3 June. Circular of Minister Léon Bérard against teaching Esperanto in French schools
	28 June. Report of the Secretariat of the League of Nations on 'Esperanto as an international auxiliary language'
	30 October. Benito Mussolini becomes prime minister of Italy
1924	21 January. Lenin dies
	17 June–8 July. Fifth Comintern Congress; appeal for international workers' correspondence

1926	5–10 August. Sixth SAT Congress, Leningrad
1927	2–19 December. 15th Congress of Communist Party of the Soviet Union (CPSU); Trotsky expelled
1928	First Five-Year Plan in the Soviet Union
1929	October. World economic crisis explodes
1930	April. Schism in the German workers' Esperanto movement
	May. Soviet authorities block transfer of membership payments to SAT
	30 May. Speech of Mykola Skrypnyk against non-nationalism
	13 July–14 August. 16th Congress of CPSU; Stalin addresses future universal language
1931	August. Communist opponents of SAT found the 'International Unification Committee to reorganize the proletarian Esperanto movement'
1932	August. Proletarian Esperantist International founded
1933	30 January. Adolf Hitler becomes Chancellor of Germany
	29 July–5 August. 25th World Congress of Esperanto, Cologne
1935	17 May. Teaching of Esperanto in German schools banned
	25 July–21 August. Seventh Comintern Congress; call for an anti-fascist popular front
	15 September. Anti-Jewish Nuremberg 'race laws' enacted
1936	18 February. Decree of Martin Bormann
	20 June. Decree of Heinrich Himmler; German Esperanto Association dissolved
	18 July. Spanish Civil War breaks out
	August. Schism in the neutral Esperanto movement
	September. Esperanto societies closed in Portugal
	5 December. New Soviet Union constitution
1937	March. The Great Purge begins in the Soviet Union; Soviet Esperanto movement liquidated
	7 July. Outbreak of Japanese war against China
1938	12–13 March. Germany annexes Austria
	13 March. Russian language made compulsory in all Soviet schools
	20 April. International Esperanto Museum in Vienna closed

1939/1945 Second World War
1939 28 September. German troops occupy Warsaw; members of the Zamenhof family arrested
1940 8 June. Internal report of Heydrich on Esperanto
August. Japanese Esperanto Institute leaves the International Esperanto League
1941 13/14 June. Mass deportations from Baltic countries
22 June. Germany invades the Soviet Union
1942 30 January. Secret Berlin conference on the 'final solution to the Jewish question'
1945 8 May. Germany surrenders
1947 17 January. Lanti commits suicide in Mexico
28 April. Neutral Esperanto movement reunites
1948 14 May. State of Israel proclaimed
23 June. West Berlin blockaded
28 June. Yugoslavia expelled from Cominform
10 December. Universal Declaration of Human Rights
1949 12 January. Esperanto groups banned in the Soviet Zone of Germany
2 October. Broadcasts in Esperanto by Radio Budapest discontinued
15 October. Hungarian minister László Rajk executed
1950 6 April. Hungarian Esperanto Society disbanded
20 June. Stalin's article in *Pravda*, 'Marxism and Problems of Linguistics'
1951 March. Chinese Esperanto League founded
1952 6 September. Esperanto Association in the Czechoslovakian Republic dissolved
3 December. Rudolf Slánský executed
1953 5 March. Stalin dies
27 July. Armistice in Korea
September. World Peace Esperantist Movement (MEM) founded

1954	10 December. Resolution of UNESCO in Montevideo favourable to Esperanto
1955	Revival of Esperanto movement in Poland, Bulgaria, Czechoslovakia, Hungary; revival in the Soviet Union
1956	14–25 February. 20th CPSU Congress; Krushchev reveals Stalin's crimes
	October–November. Hungarian uprising
1959	1–8 August. 44th World Congress of Esperanto, Warsaw
1962	Commission for the International Relations of Soviet Esperantists founded
1965	31 March. Central Working Circle of Friends of Esperanto founded in GDR
1969	29 March. Czech Esperanto Association founded
1972	15 March. Portuguese Esperanto Association re-founded
1979	14 March. Association of Soviet Esperantists founded
1987	Centennial of Esperanto; 72nd World Congress of Esperanto, Warsaw
1991	21 December. Soviet Union dissolved

Author Index[1]

A

Abashidze, I.V., 142
Ábrahám, Miklós, 105n26
Adam, Eugène. *See* Lanti
Aldworth, Thomas, 60, 61
Aleksiev, Nikola, 72n3, 132, 133n29
Amouroux, Jean, 7n18
Andropov, Iu.V., 154, 158
Arendt, Hannah, 168n3, 171n5
Arolovich, V.S., 139
Avrorin, V.A., 147

B

Baghy, Gyula, 128
Balkányi, Pál, 93n19, 100n10, 112n18
Barbusse, Henri, 25
Barks, Horace, 48n35
Bastien, Louis, 7, 7n18, 26
Batta, József, 9
Batta, Margit, 10n26
Baudouin de Courtenay, Jan, 166n1
Bazhenov, Vladimir, 48
Beck, Ulrich, 173
Belogortsev, V.S., 11
Berg, A.I., 138n14, 144n29
Bergiers, Léon, 50n40
Beriia, L.P., 5n7
Best, Werner, 168
Blanke, Detlev, 124, 126
Blazhkov, N.V., 161
Blinov, E.V., 58
Bogdanov, A.A., 145
Bokarev, E.A., 112, 113, 116, 117, 137–9, 141, 145–6, 148n47, 155
Bonesper, Ralph, 62
Borovečki, Ivo, 115
Brezhnev, L.I., 143, 151, 158

---

[1] Note: Page number followed by n denote footnotes

Bronshtein, M.Ts., 139, 151–3
Brun, S., 44n18
Bukharin, N.I., 9, 14n41, 23n17, 32
Bulganin, N.A., 113
Burda, Rudolf, 80, 81, 83, 102, 108–11, 112n16, 118, 119n46

Carminová, E., 101
Charkviani, K.N., 90, 98
Chavenon, F.A., 51, 52
Chikobava, A.S., 90, 93
Connor, George A., 115n29, 158n81

Danovsky, N.F., 144n29
Demidiuk, G.P., 9, 10, 15
Desheriev, Iu.D., 144n29, 147n43
Deshkin, G.F., 5, 6
Diatlov, V.P., 43, 49n38
Dietze, Walter, 76n20
Dimitrov, Georgi, 72n1, 77, 125n7
Dresen, Helmi, 19
Drezen, E.K., 5–9, 11, 11n29, 12, 15, 23, 24n19, 49, 55, 63–8, 155
Dubček, Alexander, 119
Dušanskis, Michaelis, 19
Dzhunusov, M.S., 144, 145n32

Eichmann, Adolf, 168n3, 172
Ekström, Erik, 5
Emelianov, V.N., 151
Eriukhin, A.P., 15n47

Evans, E.A., 62
Ezhov, N.I., 21, 27, 34

Fayet, Jean-François, 24n19, 25, 26, 51n45
Fenyvesi, Ervin, 100n9, 105n22, 132n28
Fučík, Julius, 81

Gafurov, B.G., 140, 141n21, 144
Gavrilov, P.B., 9, 13
Giedra, Balys, 20
Gilbert, William, 62n21, 108, 133
Gishpling, Mikhail, 74
Glazunov, V.A., 15n47
Gomułka, Władysław, 74, 115
Goncharov, A.E., 139, 152
Gorbachev, M.S., 11n29, 158, 159, 173
Gorky, Maksim, 59
Gottwald, Klement, 108
Grigoriev, V.P., 144, 150
Grigorov, Asen, 4n6, 72
Guiheneuf, Robert, 45n24
Gurov, Evgenii, 9
Gusev, K.M., 15n47
Guzevičius, Aleksandras, 19

Halbedl, Adolf, 119n46
Heydrich, Reinhard, 168
Higginbottom, Eleanor, 5n10

Author Index

Hitler, Adolf, 17n1, 76, 102, 115, 131, 168, 170, 172
Hodler, Hector, 174

Iakovlev, A.N., 88
Iakovlev, N.T., 148
Iartseva, V.N., 113n20
Indra, Tālivaldis, 20
Intsertov, N.Ia., 9, 11, 21, 23, 27
Isaev, M.I., 116n35, 139, 140, 144, 145n32, 147n39, 148n46, 149, 154–6, 157n78, 157n79

Jeanneret, Henri, 50, 50n40
Jevsejeva, Ludmila, 20, 20n12, 22

Kaltakhchian, S.T., 147n43
Kamenev, L.B., 26n27
Kammari, M.D., 141, 142n23, 144, 146n38
Kapper, Rein, 20
Kautsky, Karl, 88, 91, 142, 145, 147
Keable, William, 132n27
Khanazarov, K.Kh., 141, 145
Kharkovsky, A.S., 15, 42n10, 131n25
Khokhlov, N.I., 15
Kholopov, A., 90, 107
Khrushchev, N.S., 113, 114, 120, 140–3
Kiriushin, P.M., 114
Kirov, S.M., 27, 160n86
Klimovsky, A.L., 62

Koestler, Arthur, 57n9, 173n13
Köhncke, Friedrich, 10n28, 16n53
Kökény, Lajos, 87
Kokushkin, Iakob, 94
Kolchinsky, V.M., 11, 26, 65
Kolker, B.G., 137, 139, 152, 154n67, 155, 157n78, 157n80
Koós, Antal, 124
Kopelev, L.Z., 27, 27n30, 28n32, 98n2
Kosushkin, F.F., 48n33
Kriukov, Maksim, 4, 68
Krupskaia, N.K., 23n17
Kulichenko, M.I., 147
Kurisu Kei, 4n6, 10n28, 16n53, 21, 21n15, 46, 62, 101, 103n16, 173
Kuzmych, V.S., 11
Kuznetsov, S.N., 26, 157n80

Lakov, Atanas, 88, 94n20, 95n24
Lanti, Eugène, 4, 9, 33n19, 40n5, 43–5, 46n29, 48–51, 53, 58n10
Lapenna, Ivo, 4, 77, 113n23, 115n29, 118n43, 174n16
Lapovenko, Aleksandr, 49n38
Laurat, Lucien, 62, 63n22, 88n6, 89n9, 89n10
Laval, Raymond, 49n37, 51n46, 58n10
Lenin, V.I., 3, 5, 15n50, 103, 109, 159
Levenzon, L.S., 42
Levinskas, Eduard, 20n12
Logvin, A.P., 4n2, 16
Lomtev, T.P., 88, 89
Lozovsky, A., 24, 24n19
Lunacharsky, A.V., 30

M

Malík, Adolf, 79n33, 80n38, 118
Manuilsky, D.Z., 24, 24n19
Mařík, Jaroslav, 118n43
Marr, N.Ia., 98, 103, 104, 107, 145, 146
Masiliunas, Jonas, 19
Mastepanov, S.D., 15
Mediņš, Aristids, 139
Medvedev, R.A., 21
Melnik, Evgenii, 16
Melnikov, A.S., 152, 153n61
Meyer, Gustav, 117n38
Mikhailov, S.S., 144n29
Mikhalsky, E.I., 4, 15n46, 67
Minke, J.W., 45n24, 49n37
Mironov, I., 13
Mkrtchian, Simon, 113n22
Muravkin, Herbert, 12, 13n37, 24n19, 25, 25n21, 26

N

Nagy, Imre, 78
Nekrasov, N.V., 9, 11, 11n31, 28n32, 65
Nguyen Van Kinh, 136
Nikiforova, Nina, 74
Nikolsky, R.B., 9, 28n32, 66

O

Obruchev, S.V., 15n45
Ockey, Edward, 61n18
Ojalo, Jaan, 138n12
Orwell, George, 153

P

Perevalov, D.A., 155
Persson, Pelle, 59n13

Podkaminer, S.N., 10n28, 113n19, 130, 131n23, 151n53
Polivanov, E.D., 11n32
Poška, Antanas, 20n12, 22
Potseluevsky, A.P., 30n6
Protchenko, I.F., 147n43
Pushkin, A.S., 90

R

Rajk, László, 78
Rajski, Andrzej, 115
Rákosi, Mátyás, 78
Ranft, Walter, 119n48, 119n49
Respe, A. (= Schwenk, August), 24n20
Reznichuk, I.G., 60
Robicsek, Ferenc, 10, 13
Rolland, Romain, 171
Roth, Joseph, 168
Ruus, Neeme, 19
Rykov, A.I., 9, 32
Rytkov, N.N., 5, 11–15, 21, 58, 136

S

Saakov, R.R., 154
Sakharov, A.A., 15n45
Sakowicz, Roman, 8n22
Salan, Georges, 127n12
Samoilenko, A.T., 28n32
Sarychev, S.V., 114, 117n39
Sazonova, E.K., 11, 11n30
Schödl, Ludwig, 105n23, 121
Seppik, Henrik, 20n12, 21
Serebrennikov, B.A., 113n20, 144n29
Serov, I.A., 19
Sevak, Gurgen, 30n5
Shaw, George Bernard, 45
Shchegolev, N.G., 43n13
Shcherbakov, A.S., 54, 55

Shinkarenko, N.A., 5n11
Shumilov, P.N., 26, 26n26
Sidorov, Andrei, 15n49, 59n13
Šilas, Vytautas, 19n5, 20n12, 139, 151n54, 153n64
Skrypnyk, M.O., 32, 33
Slánský, Rudolf, 80
Snezhko, D.S., 12
Sokolov, B.I., 62n21, 82n47
Solzhenitsyn, A.I., 16n50, 17n1, 17n2
Spiridovich, E.F., 32, 33
Spirkin, A.G., 144n29
Stakhanov, A.G., 57
Stalin, I.V., 3, 17, 18, 25–7, 29, 32, 34, 44, 52, 85–95, 103, 107n1, 109, 115–17, 131, 132, 140, 141, 143n27, 146, 170–3
Stepanov, N.P., 12n36, 33n18, 160n86
Streblow, Gustav, 75n13, 76n17
Su, Armand, 131n26, 132
Šustr, Jaroslav, 118n43
Sutkovoi, V.G., 4n2
Svadost, E.P., 145–7
Szerdahelyi, István, 124n4
Szerémi-Tóth, Borbála, 100n10, 105, 114n27

Tito, Josip Broz, 76
Titov, G.S., 16
Titov, S.P., 16
Tolstoy, L.N., 20n12, 166
Trotsky, L.D., 14n41, 26, 27n29, 32, 52, 151, 170
Tsvetkova, V.P., 113n19
Tukhachevsky, M.N., 9

Ulianova, M.I., 23n17
Usmanov, Sh.Kh., 68
Uspensky, B.A., 144n29

Varankin, V.V., 11, 11n32, 25n21, 66
Vares-Barbarus, J.J., 19
Vasiliev, V.A., 144n29
Vershinin, A.I., 159n83
Vinogradov, V.V., 92n16, 113n20
Vizgirdas, Algimantas, 139
Vlk, Miloslav, 108, 108n2
Vulfovich, L.B., 5n11, 114n26

Wagner, Hermann, 45n24
Warnke, Hans, 77n21
Webb, Beatrice, 46
Weissberg-Cybulski, Alexander, 18
Wüster, Eugen, 6–8
Wutte, Jean, 46n29

Zamenhof, L.L., 14n41, 47n31, 83, 117, 126, 136, 137, 146, 150, 150n50, 161, 165, 166, 171, 172, 174, 175
Zápotocký, Antonín, 102, 103
Zhdanov, A.A., 97, 159
Zhirkov, L.I., 31n7, 113n20
Zilberfarb, I.I., 15
Zinoviev, G.E., 26n27, 27
Zolotarev, F.L., 144n29

Subject Index[1]

A

anarchism, 4
anti-Semitism, 98, 171

B

Baltic countries, 19–21, 157
Boulogne-sur-Mer, 166, 174
British government, 61, 167
brotherhood of peoples, 127, 167, 170, 171
Bulgaria, Esperanto movement in, 71–3, 77–80, 82, 94, 100, 101, 114, 115, 117, 123–6, 128, 160

C

censorship, 48, 62, 128, 137, 150, 159
chauvinism, 29, 117n39
China, 82, 100, 114, 118, 131, 131n26
Comintern, 24n19, 26
communism, 15, 29, 34, 35, 50n43, 86, 88, 94, 108, 140–2, 169, 171, 173
Communist International. *See* Comintern
conspiracy theory, 172
correspondence in Esperanto, 37–43, 46, 48–51, 53–6, 58–64, 105, 106, 120, 124
cosmopolitanism, 80, 82, 88, 97–9, 101, 102, 108n2, 125, 126, 132, 149, 167, 169, 171, 173
Czechoslovakia, 56, 57, 71, 73n5, 73n7, 74, 79–83, 100, 101, 103, 108, 111, 114, 118, 119, 123–5, 128, 129, 159

---

[1] Note: Page number followed by n denote footnotes

E

English language, 61, 88, 91, 92, 101, 133n30, 142, 148, 158, 160, 175
Esperantization, 33

F

fascism, 45, 52, 71, 73, 79, 109
Festival, World Youth, 114, 135, 136
foreigners, 16, 40, 41, 48, 54, 60, 62, 63, 135n1, 136, 152, 156
freemasons, 151
French language, 33, 47, 133n30, 148, 158, 167

G

German Democratic Republic, 76, 82, 83, 99, 105, 119–21, 123–5, 128–30, 156, 159, 160
German language, 89, 91
Gestapo, 10
globalization, 175
Great Purge, 9, 17, 18, 28, 30, 34, 35, 169

H

Helsinki Final Act, 127, 129
historiography, 48, 107, 130, 131, 159, 172
Homaranismo, 166
Hungary, Esperanto movement in, 105, 114, 123

I

Iazykfront, 8, 87, 88n5

Ido, 8, 94
imperialism, 43, 76, 78, 80, 88, 92, 97, 99, 133, 141, 146, 150, 171
internal idea of Esperanto, 169
International Esperanto League (IEL), 4, 73
internationalism, 3, 26n26, 33, 34, 37, 38, 63, 92, 99, 104, 107, 125–7, 129, 142, 147, 153, 166, 168–70, 173, 174

J

Japan, 46, 83, 101
Jews and Judaism, 98, 169

K

Komsomol, 24, 25, 27, 136n4, 154, 159

L

language planning, 30
language policy, 30, 31, 33, 35, 88, 167
Latin, 30, 31, 33, 34, 88
Latinization, 30, 31
League of Nations, 167, 170, 174
letter-writing. *See* correspondence
Lithuania, 18–22, 114n25, 145, 153n64, 159, 173n13

M

Marxism and linguistics, 86, 107, 146
multilingualism, 149

nationalism, 3, 30, 130, 140, 142, 148, 160, 167, 175
nationalities problem, 29, 34n21, 57, 94, 140–3, 147, 149, 153, 157, 159, 165, 166, 169
National Socialism, 71, 75, 131, 168–73
Nazi. *See* National Socialism
neutrality, 7, 73, 166, 168, 169, 172
NKVD, 11, 12n36, 18, 18n2, 19, 21, 27, 28n32, 60, 173n13

Odessa, 4n2, 159, 161

pacifism, 78, 126, 127, 166
Palestine, 73n7
petty-bourgeois, 40, 171
Poland, 71, 73n5, 73n7, 74, 83, 100n11, 114, 115, 117, 123–5, 128–30, 159, 172
Proletarian Esperantist International (IPE), 3, 10, 12, 23, 25, 26, 46, 105, 127n12, 132n27

Romania, 73, 73n7, 74, 77, 82, 114, 123, 159
Russian language, 30–4, 76, 82, 86, 88–92, 94, 95, 103, 104, 106, 108, 109, 118, 124, 133, 141–3, 145, 151, 153, 157–60
Russification, 32, 33, 89, 158

secret police, 5n7, 9, 13, 15, 18n2, 28, 128, 160
Sennacieca Asocio Tutmonda (SAT), 3, 4, 8, 9, 23, 27, 41–4, 49, 50, 55, 74, 79, 80, 105n25, 108n3
Sennaciulo (periodical), 43, 60, 61,
socialism, 3, 29, 33, 34, 38, 40, 41, 45, 47, 63, 81, 88, 91, 92, 94, 101, 103, 104n17, 107, 126, 127, 130, 131, 141, 145, 147, 166
Soviet Esperantist Union (SEU), 15, 21, 23–8, 31, 35, 37, 40–3, 46–51, 54, 55, 62, 64, 117, 130, 159, 160
Soviet patriotism, 33, 34, 89, 90, 98n1
Stalinism, 48, 50, 74, 171, 173

teaching of Esperanto, 6, 77, 145
terminology, 6, 7
Trotskyism, 4, 26–8, 52, 170
Tsarist regime, 45

Ukraine, 24, 32, 33, 142, 153
Ukrainian language, 31, 33
UNESCO, 111, 112
United States of America, 74, 76, 82, 99, 113
Universal Esperanto Association (UEA), 4, 7, 26, 73, 79, 80, 113, 114, 115n29, 118, 123, 130, 131, 157, 159, 174

W

Warsaw, 11n31, 83, 114, 115, 117, 136, 161
workers' movement, 43, 121
World Congress of Esperanto, 16, 114, 136, 137, 161
world language, 34, 38, 88, 91–4, 98, 99, 104, 141, 142n23, 146, 147, 155
World Peace Esperantist Movement (MEM), 110, 111, 118, 132, 133
world revolution, 38, 91, 170
World War II, 71–9, 171, 172

Y

Yiddish, 98
Yugoslavia, 71, 73, 74, 77, 97, 98, 104n17

Z

Zionism, 150n50, 151, 171

GPSR Compliance
The European Union's (EU) General Product Safety Regulation (GPSR) is a set of rules that requires consumer products to be safe and our obligations to ensure this.

If you have any concerns about our products, you can contact us on

ProductSafety@springernature.com

In case Publisher is established outside the EU, the EU authorized representative is:

Springer Nature Customer Service Center GmbH
Europaplatz 3
69115 Heidelberg, Germany

www.ingramcontent.com/pod-product-compliance
Lightning Source LLC
LaVergne TN
LVHW012100070526
838200LV00074BA/3833